RENEWALS 458-4574

WITHDRAWN
UTSA LIBRARIES

THE GLOBAL TOURISM SYSTEM

New Directions in Tourism Analysis

Series Editors: Kevin Meethan, University of Plymouth
                  Dimitri Ioannides, Southwest Missouri State University

Although tourism is becoming increasingly popular as both a taught subject and an area for empirical investigation, the theoretical underpinnings of many approaches have tended to be eclectic and somewhat underdeveloped. However, recent developments indicate that the field of tourism studies is beginning to develop in a more theoretically informed manner, but this has not yet been matched by current publications.

The aim of this series is to fill this gap with high quality monographs or edited collections that seek to develop tourism analysis at both theoretical and substantive levels using approaches which are broadly derived from allied social science disciplines such as Sociology, Social Anthropology, Human and Social Geography, and Cultural Studies. As tourism studies covers a wide range of activities and sub fields, certain areas such as Hospitality Management and Business, which are already well provided for, would be excluded. The series will therefore fill a gap in the current overall pattern of publication.

Suggested themes to be covered by the series, either singly or in combination, include – consumption; cultural change; development; gender; globalisation; political economy; social theory; sustainability.

Also in the series

Performing Tourist Places
Jørgen Ole Bærenholdt, Michael Haldrup, Jonas Larsen and John Urry
ISBN 0 7546 3838 3

The Challenge of Tourism Carrying Capacity Assessment
Edited by Harry Coccossis and Alexandra Mexa
ISBN 0 7546 3569 4

New Directions in Rural Tourism
Edited by Derek Hall, Lesley Roberts and Morag Mitchell
ISBN 0 7546 3633 X

The Global Tourism System
Governance, Development and Lessons from South Africa

SCARLETT CORNELISSEN
University of Stellenbosch, South Africa

ASHGATE

© Scarlett Cornelissen 2005

All rights reserved. No part of this publication may be reproduced, stored in a retrieval system, or transmitted in any form or by any means, electronic, mechanical, photocopying, recording or otherwise without the prior permission of the publisher.

Scarlett Cornelissen has asserted her right under the Copyright, Designs and Patents Act, 1988, to be identified as the author of this work.

Published by
Ashgate Publishing Limited
Gower House
Croft Road
Aldershot
Hants GU11 3HR
England

Ashgate Publishing Company
Suite 420
101 Cherry Street
Burlington, VT 05401-4405
USA

Ashgate website: http://www.ashgate.com

British Library Cataloguing in Publication Data
Cornelissen, Scarlett
  The global tourism system : governance, development and lessons from South Africa. - (New directions in tourism analysis)
  1. Tourism - South Africa 2. Tourism - Economic aspects - South Africa 3. Tourism 4. Tourism - Economic aspects
  I. Title
  338.4'791'0968

Library of Congress Cataloging-in-Publication Data
Cornelissen, Scarlett.
  The global tourism system : governance, development and lessons from South Africa / by Scarlett Cornelissen.
    p. cm. -- (New directions in tourism analysis)
  Includes bibliographical references and index.
  ISBN 0-7546-4250-X
  1. Tourism--Political aspects. 2. Globalization--Political aspects. 3. Tourism--Government policy--South Africa--Case studies. 4. Tourism--Industrial capacity--South Africa--Case studies. 5. Developing countries--Economic conditions--Case studies. I. Title. II. Series.

G155.A1C716 2005
338.4'791--dc22

2005021162

ISBN 0 7546 4250 X

Printed and bound in Great Britain by MPG Books Ltd, Bodmin, Cornwall.

Contents

List of Figures		*vi*
List of Tables		*vii*
Preface		*viii*
Acknowledgements		*ix*
List of Abbreviations		*x*
1	Introduction: The Global Tourism System	1
2	Globalisation, Tourism and Development	14
3	South Africa's Tourist Sector: Patterns, Parameters and Paradoxes	42
4	The Dynamics of the Global Tourism Production System	76
5	The Political Economy of Destination Marketing: Producing and Imaging 'Place' and 'People'	99
6	The Global Governance of Tourism	116
7	New Global Niches: Tourism, Sport and Mega-Events	137
8	Conclusion: Tourism Development in the Contemporary Era	163
Bibliography		*175*
Index		*191*

List of Figures

Figure 1.1	The global tourism production system	7
Figure 3.1	Political geography of South Africa	45
Figure 3.2	Foreign tourist arrivals in South Africa, 1993-2002	57
Figure 3.3	Percentage change in international arrivals, 1993-2002	62
Figure 3.4	Spatial distribution of tourist accommodation in the Western Cape, 2001	68
Figure 3.5	Major tourism investments in the Western Cape	68
Figure 4.1	The structure of the South African tour operator sector	85
Figure 4.2	Commercial interaction in the global tourism production system	89
Figure 5.1	Main South African destinations sold by overseas tour operators	107
Figure 6.1	International and domestic regulatory bodies in the South African system	120

List of Tables

Table 3.1	World tourism patterns	49
Table 3.2	South Africa's ten main international tourist attractions	56
Table 3.3	Breakdown of South Africa's tourist markets, 1993-2002	57
Table 3.4	Trends in SA's main overseas markets, selected years: Number of arrivals by origin and share of total overseas arrivals	58
Table 3.5	Main market segments in South African overseas tourism	60
Table 3.6	Profile of German and British tourists to South Africa	61
Table 3.7	Gross economic impact of tourism in South Africa	64
Table 4.1	International air traffic to and from Johannesburg and Cape Town International Airports	87
Table 4.2	Car rental franchises dominant in the market for international tourists to South Africa	87
Table 4.3	Major hotel chains operating in South Africa	88
Table 5.1	Tourist representations of South Africa	109
Table 6.1	Flight frequencies on the SA-UK route, 2001	128
Table 6.2	Flight frequencies on the SA-Germany route, 2001	129

Preface

International tourism has become one of the largest sectors in the world and is seen as an important economic driver. In the era of globalisation, moreover, global tourism has seen rapid expansion. Yet such expansion brings differential gains and costs for different countries. Developing countries stand to benefit immensely from the economic, production and technological diffusion inherent in global tourism.

However, the composite dimensions of tourism – comprised as it is of various crosscutting systems of global trade, finance, transport, consumption, marketing and production – mean that a wide array of actors are involved – at the global, local and intermediate levels – in determining tourism outcomes.

This book is an analysis of the three structures of global tourism – production, consumption and governance. It uses case study analysis of South Africa, a country that has reaped the rewards of global tourism growth, but has also been subject to the precariousness of this sector. The book is an exploration of how global tourism as an interrelated system of trade, exchange, production and governance play out in developing and developed countries, and what its benefits and disadvantages are.

The book is focused on expanding the theoretical development of tourism through the use of in-depth empirical investigations. Tourism scholars will find value in the book's analysis of the nature and dynamics of the global tourism system and the politico-economic relationships that shape this system.

Acknowledgements

This book is the culmination of a lengthy period of research on tourism development in South Africa. Many people have played a role in shaping my ideas on the global tourism economy and South Africa's location in it. I would like to thank Ivan Turok of the Department of Urban Studies at the University of Glasgow whose at times not-so-gentle prodding first sparked an interest in the topic and whose guidance played a major part in the eventual outcome of the book.

In collaborating with various groups of people new ideas and arguments were formed, while lengthy discussions with close friends and colleagues had major effects on the direction of the research. In this regard I would like to single out Steffen Horstmeier, Janis van der Westhuizen, Karen Smith, Timothy Shaw, Jane Parpart, Philip Nel and Wolfgang Thomas who all had a great intellectual influence. A generous grant from the Association of Commonwealth Universities under a research exchange scheme enabled the study in the first instance. Lastly, I would like to thank Mervyn, Sarah, Amber, Damianne, Brian and Steffen for their unrelenting support.

Chapter 5 first appeared as research article in *Review of International Political Economy*, while Chapter 7 is a substantially revised and extended version of an article that was published in *Tourism Hospitality Development Planning* (2004, vol. 1, issue 1). Copyright permission has been granted by the publishers, Taylor and Francis (www.tandf.co.uk), to reprint these articles here.

List of Abbreviations

ACSA	Airports Company of South Africa
ASEAN	Association of Southeast Asian Nations
AU	African Union (formerly Organisation of African Unity)
BA	British Airways
BEE	Black Economic Empowerment
CBNRM	Community-based Natural Resource Management
COSATU	Congress of South African Trade Unions
DEAT	Department of Environmental Affairs and Tourism
DEAAT	Western Cape Department of Economic Affairs, Agriculture and Tourism
EU	European Union
FIT	Free Independent Travellers
IATA	International Air Transport Association
ICAO	International Civil Aviation Organisation
GATS	General Agreement on Trade in Services
GDP	Gross Domestic Product
GEAR	Growth, Employment and Redistribution Programme
MDC	Movement for Democratic Change
MICE	Meetings, Incentives, Conferences and Exhibitions
Nedlac	National Economic Development and Labour Council
NAM	Non-Aligned Movement
NGOs	Non-Governmental Organisations
RDP	Reconstruction and Development Programme
RETOSA	Regional Tourism Organisation of Southern Africa
SA	South Africa
SAA	South African Airways
SACP	South African Communist Party
SADC	Southern African Development Community
SANParks	South African National Parks
SARS	Severe Acute Respiratory Syndrome
SATOUR	South African National Tourism Organisation
SA Tourism	South African Tourism
SETA	Sector Education and Training Authority
SMM	Small, Medium and Micro (operators)
SSA	Statistics South Africa
TBNRM	Transboundary Natural Resource Management
TGCSA	Tourism Grading Council of South Africa

TSA	Tourism Satellite Account
Theta	Tourism, Hospitality and Sport Education and Training Authority
UNCTAD	United Nations Conference on Trade and Development
UK	United Kingdom
US(A)	United States (of America)
USAID	United States Agency for International Development
VFR	Visiting Friends and Relatives
WTO	World Tourism Organisation
WTTC	World Travel and Tourism Council
ZANU-PF	Zimbabwe African National Union-Progressive Front
9/11	Attacks on World Trade Center and United States Pentagon on 11 September 2001

Chapter 1

Introduction: The Global Tourism System

Introduction

This book focuses on the political economy of the global tourism system in the era of globalisation, and its impacts in developing contexts. It uses case study analysis of South Africa, a country that has emerged as an increasingly popular international destination since the end of apartheid, but whose sector had been greatly shaped and often constricted by outside factors, to assess how tourism as a global system of trade, production, exchange and governance play out in developing countries and what its benefits and disadvantages are for them.

It is a truism that tourism has become one of the world's major economic sectors. The scale of international tourism, the swift pace of growth it has seen over the past two decades and the economic benefits this sector is thought to carry has meant that tourism development has come to occupy the development policy agendas of most governments in the world. Yet it can be a very volatile sector, sensitive to disturbances caused by factors such as political instability, global economic shocks or even negative media portrayals, and as much as a country's sector can expand briskly, it can also promptly suffer significant setbacks.

This volatility is perhaps best illustrated by two recent, global incidents. The first is the dramatic impact that the September 11th attacks on the United States in 2001 had wrought on international tourism. Not only did world tourist arrivals decline for the first time in more than a decade, but the tourist sectors of major international destinations in North America, South Asia and the Caribbean contracted by large volumes. Given the nature of the September 11th attacks the airline industry, one of the main components of the global tourism system, was particularly negatively affected and some of the world's largest airlines were either forced to close down or to restructure.

Second, at the end of 2004 the South and Southeast Asian regions, whose sectors have already been battered by the stultifying SARS virus, experienced the catastrophic effects of the tsunami disaster. Perhaps most damaging for countries such as Thailand, and to a lesser extent, the Maldives and Seychelles was that the disaster had affected some of their prime international tourist locales. For these countries, where tourism is a vital element of their national economies, rebuilding not only means reconstructing infrastructure, but more importantly, restoring global confidence in them as tourist destinations. As such the effects of the disaster are likely to be particularly prolonged.

In contrast, other tourist areas may experience an expansion in their sectors, as tourists substitute one destination for another. In South Africa, for example, 9/11 brought brief growth benefits, as travellers simply redirected from the Americas. Like many other countries the South African government is placing a high policy premium on extending the country's sector and using tourism as a pathway to development. Indeed, following the end of apartheid tourism has seen dramatic growth and the government has developed a number of initiatives, policies and projects to fully exploit the country's emergence as a destination of international significance. Its prospects for successful tourism development are greatly influenced by a range of internal aspects (e.g. the nature of the tourism offer and how it fares against other competitor destinations) and external factors (such as the 'positive' consequences of 9/11). The country's experience in attempting to develop a competitive sector, to use tourism as a means toward development and the obstacles it faces in the context of global conditions and structures is one commonly shared by many developing and developed countries.

Tourism growth has gained a particular momentum with globalisation and is of great economic significance. Yet the two events cited above starkly illustrate how intricate the global tourism system is. First, factors exogenous to the system can have severe and often detrimental impacts and events in one part of the world can shape the tourist sectors of many other countries. Second, the global tourism system is an interwoven compound: it consists of a multiplicity of actors involved in the production and consumption of tourism; it is made up of several different structures of governance, trade, finance, transport and marketing; and it is shaped by numerous forces, agents and factors.

It is an analysis of how these different structures, actors and forces interrelate and how this constrains and/or fosters tourism growth that constitutes the focus of this book. There are three main components to the book. The first examines the political economy of international tourism. It explores the building blocks of the global tourism system, consisting as it does of complex arrangements of production and consumption. The closeness of the producer-consumer interface is one of the most distinctive aspects of tourism, yet it can pose significant challenges for aspects such as production, destination marketing and tourism planning. Globalisation has brought significant changes to both the culture of consumption and the relationship between producers and consumers. It has also reshaped predominant modes of production and affected the nature of producer interaction.

The second component of the book focuses on governance of and within the global tourism system. The different producer spheres and economic sectors that make up tourism have particular means of organisation and self-regulation. Tourism is an elaborate economic activity that as a system of production is formed by series of competitive and collaborative interactions among different producers. Mechanisms such as subcontracting, the provision of trade commissions and marketing cooperation help to order relations. Overarching tourism-specific institutions of regulation also fulfil the function of maintaining stability in what is otherwise a fractious system. Often, however, governance regimes can act as constrictions on tourism growth. This particularly pertains to the global aviation regime that, structured through bilateral agreements among states, can constitute institutional barriers to expansion. In the era of globalisation, furthermore, economic and trade liberalisation and their concomitant institutions of governance can have major tourism implications. Under the General Agreement on Trade in Services (GATS), global tourism and its various production components will be liberalised. Developing countries tend to be locked into the global tourism system at unequal points of exchange. Provisions such as the GATS can be more disadvantageous to their tourist sectors.

Following from the above, the third major component of the book is an exploration of how tourism production, consumption and governance relate to development. Using the example of South Africa it investigates how changed global consumption patterns, different forms and relations of production and global institutions of regulation can impact on tourism's economic and social benefits. Tourism policy-making is often premised on even patterns of global expansion and stable environments. South Africa, like many countries has invested much in establishing a progressively expanding sector that can contribute to national development. Yet, tourism is shaped by many factors affecting how it functions as a global system of trade, transport and finance and dissemination. This book is a comprehensive study of South African tourism and its linkage to the wider international sector. It examines the nature and extent of global tourism production, consumption and regulation and how these bear upon developmental prospects, specifically in the South. It aims to draw out lessons for other developing countries about the limitations and possibilities for greater linkage to the global tourism system.

The International Political Economy of Tourism

International Political Economy as an Approach

At its most rudimentary, International Political Economy may be defined as the study of the intersection between states, markets, and societies, the interaction among actors predominant in each sphere, and the consequences of such interaction (Gilpin, 1987; Stiles and Akaha, 1991). Strange (1988: 18) defines international political economy as that which involves 'the social, political and economic arrangements affecting the global systems of production, exchange and distribution, and the mix of values reflected therein'.

The study of international political economy has long theoretical antecedents, and stems from the eighteenth century works of Adam Smith and others on the relationship between economic activities and authority, and the role of the nation-state in the market. As it has evolved, three broad theoretical traditions predominate the academic discipline of international political economy. These are liberalism (embodied in the works of Adam Smith, and characterised by its emphasis on the primacy of the market over all other spheres); realism/statism/mercantilism (which holds that economics should be subordinate to, and directed by state interests), and the Marxist, or critical tradition (which, broadly, offers a critique of prevailing economic and political structures) (Gilpin,

1987). The international political economy framework draws attention to the fact that events are the consequences of actions undertaken by a range of actors present at a number of levels, whose (often conflicting) interests intersect to produce certain outcomes.

Global tourism is a highly complex system. It consists of a multitude of actors who interact at crosscutting levels to produce certain outcomes and is built around overlapping structures of trade, finance, production, marketing and consumption. To understand tourism's economic outcome in a given location requires an understanding of the structure of this system, and of the events, forces and agents that shape it. This means *analysing the linkage(s) between the domestic and international sectors, in terms of the prevailing patterns of production, diffusion, consumption and regulation, and the economic and social relations evolving from these*. Given the nature of global tourism, which is made up of a disparate number of producing and consuming bodies stemming from locales across international boundaries, an International Political Economy framework is particularly well suited to analyse the international tourism system and its economic outcome in given locations (Clancy, 1999; Yamamoto and Gill, 2002).

The Nature of Tourism

Tourism refers to the movement of people from one geographical location to another for the purpose of engaging in leisure and/or business acts, and the economic transactions that accompany this. It is essentially a service activity, and involves the flow of capital, finance, goods, knowledge and humans (Britton, 1991). Tourism has both a production and a consumption component. As a form of production, tourism is multisectoral and multifaceted, drawing upon the activities of a wide range of actors from a number of economic sectors (Debbage and Daniels, 1998). As an activity of consumption tourism is distinct in that the consumer has to travel some distance to a destination in order to consume the product. This feature of tourism means it is referred to as an invisible sector (Mathieson and Wall, 1982). It also means that tourism is the nexus between systems of production and systems of consumption. The tourist product is varied. It consists of both tangible (e.g. flights, hotel accommodation) and intangible (e.g. customer satisfaction or perception) elements (S. Smith, 1994). Given its ephemeral nature, the tourist product can be viewed as a highly perishable item (Mathieson and Wall, 1982).

The standard and most widely accepted definition of what constitutes tourism is that utilised by the World Tourism Organisation (WTO, *Basic References on Tourism Statistics*). A tourist is a person who travels to and stays in a place outside his/her usual environment for at least one night and less than one year, and whose primary purpose of travel is not remunerated from within the place visited. Tourism is defined as the set of activities engaged upon by a tourist. Domestic tourism refers to the movement of residents within their national borders, whilst international tourism involves people travelling to another country.

The WTO definition is a demand-side description of tourism, defining the activity from the point of view of the tourist (S. Smith, 1998). In tourism literature there is a sharp division between scholars who promote a demand-side approach to tourism and those who advocate a supply-side approach (e.g. Crick, 1989). According to S. Smith (1989), for example, many researchers commit a methodological error by defining tourism from the perspective of the product and those who consume it, a fallacy, he claims 'equivalent to defining the health care industry by defining a sick person'. Such an approach, he argues, leads to a disparate picture of what is essentially a collection of production activities. To many others (e.g. Ioannides and Debbage, 1998) a supply-side approach – focused on the producer facets of tourism and the firms and institutions responsible for this – should be adopted.

The process of defining tourism is therefore not without contestation. Part of the reason for this may be the definitional inadequacy of the key concepts related to tourist activities – *leisure* and *leisure time*. The conventional treatment of leisure sees it as that state or condition where no work is being carried out, and where there is no (tangible or intangible) product or commodity as outcome. Leisure is seen as the opposite of work or labour, as 'free time' with no economic value. Similarly, tourism as a form of leisure activity, is that action engaged in by people in their 'free time'. The problem posed by such an understanding is that it treats labour, and the value of labour, in a minimal way; it is only true for some parts of some societies some of the time. As noted by Britton (1991) the concept of 'free time' (the condition of an absence of work) disregards the disparity in the value accorded to, for example, men and women's work, and particularly labour in the domestic (household-level) sphere. Furthermore, 'free time' is a culturally-determined, context-specific concept – different societies orient themselves differently to time. A similar epistemological problem is the lack of distinction between a tourist and a traveller. As it has evolved, contemporary standard treatments of tourists see them as present-day reincarnations of the pioneering travellers from former times. While in one sense this is valid, particularly when one considers the psychological dimensions involved in the selling of tourist packages in the advent of cultural tourism[1] (see discussions below), in another it fails to distinguish between the very different economic origins and significances of touring and travelling: a business traveller is something different to a business tourist – the latter is set apart by his/her consumption of explicit tourist goods. How one draws a discrepancy between these has a very important impact on how one gathers information in tourism research.

A parallel and equally vigorous debate in tourism studies is on whether tourism constitutes a single industry. Several researchers argue that tourism should not be seen as a monolithic industry, but rather as a collection of industries that share similar functions and produce similar products (e.g. Tremblay, 1998). Leiper (1990), one of the most vehement proponents of this view, contends that tourist activities do not constitute an industry in the conventional sense since no single or standard product is produced. The outcome is rather an array of products; the fact that these are both tangible and intangible leads Leiper to conclude that tourism is in addition only partially industrialised. Specifically, Leiper argues, a large part of those economic sectors or functions involved in tourism can exist independent of any tourist activities, e.g. restaurants or retail stores whose primary market base comprise of households. This industrial duality precludes any logical typification of a single tourism industry (Leiper, 1990). This book's analysis of global tourism uses the concept of sector, rather than industry.

Historically, scholarly analyses of tourism tended to be centred in the fields of Anthropology and Sociology, where works by authors such as Cohen (1972, 1974, 1979, 1984), MacCannell (1973, 1976), Lanfant (1980), and Urry (1990) provide a rich tradition. It is only over the last three decades that tourism has come to be more seriously treated as a research subject in other social science disciplines, most notably Geography, Politics and Economics (Ioannides and Debbage, 1998), and various sub-branches thereof (e.g. human geography, economic geography, environmental studies, marketing and management studies, development studies).

A broad categorisation may be made of demand-side and supply-side approaches to tourism. A simplified distinction is that the former is occupied with aspects and activities related to the buying and using (i.e. consumption) of tourist goods, while the latter is concerned with the creation (procurement and production) of those goods.

Demand-side studies by definition, are focused on the tourist consumer, and mainly on the behavioural aspects related to travel and tourism. Such studies seek to explain why it is that people (want to) travel, engage in leisure, or recreate, and the choices people make with regard to tourist destinations. These approaches are essentially motivation-based and delineate the psychological and psycho-social factors that cause people to undertake tourist activities – the 'push' and 'pull' factors of tourism (Uysal, 1998; Pearce, 1995). Motivational factors for tourism may be classed into personal characteristics (e.g. individuals' need for self-esteem or social status); changes in the economic capability of persons (i.e. rising disposable incomes); and increased leisure time (Lea, 1988). Supply factors such as easier access to destinations through enhanced and cheaper transport also play a role. Tourism motivation is in addition influenced by tourists' perception and evaluation of the physical, natural or tourist resources in particular destinations, and people's perceptions of the social, economic or political conditions in destinations. Specific marketing factors, and the sorts of images that tourism producers create about destinations, also influence people's decision-making (Uysal, 1998; Hall and Page, 1999).

Demand-side studies also focus on the manifest preferences and tastes of travellers and tourists. These are used to devise models of tourist demand and as bases to predict potential demand (e.g. Archer, 1976; Witt and Witt, 1995). Tourism production, development, marketing and management policies are largely informed by the perceived desires and needs of tourists (e.g. Perez and Sampol, 2000).

Supply-side approaches focus more specifically on the various components of tourism and the producer aspects related to it. Such analyses are usually industry-specific, and look at the firms and institutions responsible for creating tourism products, the various factors and forces that shape the industries, and the resultant impact on the tourism market. Studies that fall under this category generally investigate the structures, trends and changes in the core sectors of tourism, i.e. the airline industry (e.g. Wheatcroft, 1994, 1998; Page, 1999), the hotel sector (e.g. Dunning and McQueen, 1982; Milne and Pohlman, 1998) and the tour operator sector (e.g. Ioannides, 1998; Delaney-Smith, 1987; Sheldon, 1986). Within the realms of physical and economic geography, supply-side studies include research on the spatial features of tourism, such as the location of accommodation establishments or sites of tourist attractions within a given region (e.g. Pearce, 1995; S. Smith, 1983). Another focus of supply-side studies is the human resource or employment aspects of tourism, and more specialised subjects such as labour relations in tourism.

The Components of the Global Tourism System

In a seminal analysis Britton (1991) groups the array of economic activities linked to tourism into the *tourism production system*. It includes:

- those economic activities aimed at producing and selling travel and tourist products;
- the social groups, cultural features and physical components which serve as tourism attractions;
- the ordering institutions and bodies set up to regulate 'commercial behaviour and social externalities associated with such production' (Britton, 1991: 455).

The various components of the global tourism system may be depicted as follows:

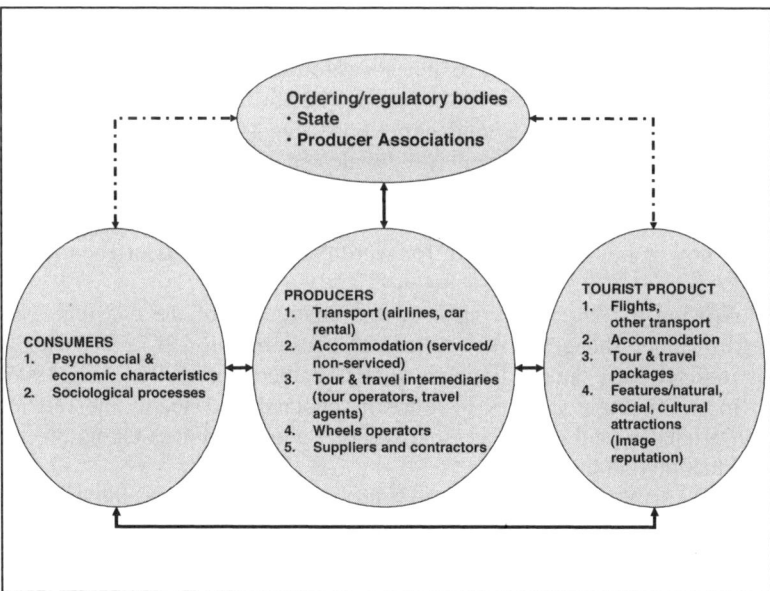

Figure 1.1 The global tourism production system
Source: Author's own design. Based on Britton (1991)

According to Britton, tourism can be conceptualised

> as having its own division of labour between diverse functions (transport, accommodation, travel and tour operators, marketing, ancillary services, attractions), its own markets (the demand for, and supply of, travel and tourist products), and formal regulatory agencies. Beyond these features are commercial practices, industry structures, and organisations which have evolved in response to the interrelated technical requirements of creating tourism products, changes in technology, and conditions shaping competition (including government licensing and controls) (1991: 456).[2]

In all, global tourism entails distinct markets based on the exchange between tourism producers and consumers. On the demand side it consists of societal groupings with certain socio-economic and socio-cultural attributes, desires, needs and wants. On the supply side it consists of producers that interact, innovate and compete. The interrelationship between producers is monitored and ordered by various regulatory bodies that set the parameters for tourism production.

The Producer-Consumer Nexus

One of the peculiarities of tourism and as is illustrated in Figure 1.1, is that as an economic activity, it involves the close interface between production and consumption: tourist products are often produced and consumed at the same time, and producers and consumers often occupy the same physical realms. While this is characteristic of most service activities, tourism is distinguished in the degree to which this interface is part of the eventual product – tourist enjoyment often depends on the extent to which a consumer believes a producer (be it a tour operator, waitress or tour guide) has fulfilled in his/her expectations or has contributed toward a total experience. On the basis of such intangible factors, tourists make assessments of locales or destinations and future travel plans (Urry, 1995; Uysal, 1998). The close proximity between producers and consumers, therefore importantly relate to wider aspects regarding the tourism system – how goods are produced, for whom, and what sorts of economic gains are made.

Following the larger discourse on the emergence of the consumer society, commodification, changes in the culture of consumption and related changes in production (see for example Bauman, 1992; Featherstone, 1991; Urry, 1995) one of the most important debates in tourism scholarship concerns the relationship between producers and consumers and whether consumption is taking precedence over production (Gotham, 2002).

In the main tourism literature and praxis ascribe to the neoclassical economics view on the sovereignty of the consumer.[3] This is particularly reflected in the proliferation of academic writing on the effect of neo-Fordist changes in consumption patterns on the tourism industry (see discussion in Chapter 2) and in tourism promotion, of lifestyle marketing and market segmentation. With regard to the former Ioannides and Debbage (1998: 100) for instance argue:

Under the logic of this post-modern culture of consumption, the constant search for novelty and alternative experiences is emphasised. As a result, in the travel industry, a premium has been increasingly placed on providing the post-modern citizen... with an unending range of novel travel experiences.

These works make the argument that tourist preferences and tastes shape the production and location of tourist goods.

There is an opposite view in tourism literature that holds that tourism producers exert power over consumers. One example is Cheong and Miller's (2000) application of Foucauldian analysis to tourism. They argue that tourism consumers are subject to the influence of (producer) bodies such as government officials, tour guides, hotel or restaurant employees. Such bodies, they contend, 'compel the tourist to function in a certain way' (p.381) by guiding tourists to certain locales and attractions, and through promotional and information material, even determining how tourists (should) see the places they visit.

According to these authors,

Tourists are power-bound and are influenced by (Foucauldian) agents (*tourism producers*) from the time they first seek information and make travel plans until they return home (Cheong and Miller, 2000: 381).

By this analysis, the power of producers specifically lies in the knowledge they hold and selectively filter through to consumers.

The 'consumer over producer' debate is rooted in a wider socio-theoretic analysis of cultural changes in modern society. In tourism studies it provides the analytical framework for understanding how aspects such as development and management policies are informed by the perceived desires and needs of tourists, or how processes of destination marketing involve the moulding of tourists' views (and therefore often travel flows) by producers.

In this book the position is adopted that the nature and consequences of producer-consumer relations vary depending on the type of product element that is involved in the commercial exchange between them. On aspects such as travel components (flights, car rental, excursions) consumers have limited choice. In this case it is tourism producers who steer tourism demand. On aspects such as the content of tour itineraries (the focus of the Chapter 5) demand impulses do affect what is produced and offered by producers.

The Developmental Significance of Tourism

In the present era tourism is widely accepted as an economic sector with large growth potential. Tourism is often associated with the inflow of foreign currency, the generation of income, the creation of employment, an expanded revenue and tax base for governments and a contribution to a country's balance of payments (e.g. Archer, 1977; 1982; Elkan, 1975; Fletcher and Archer, 1991; Lea, 1988; Sinclair and Bote Gómez, 1996). This stands in marked contrast to the earlier part of the twentieth century when scholars and policy-makers' general bias stood against the services sector in favour of production and manufacturing, the latter which were seen to be the only economic activities which produced real, sustained growth. Today, tourism is viewed as an important outward-oriented growth sector (Brohman, 1996). This is indicative of a theoretical repositioning with regard to what is accepted as export or import goods, with a much larger parameter allowing for intangible tourist goods, such as 'tourist enjoyment' being classified as an exportable tourist commodity.

In spite of this, little consensus exists precisely where the developmental potential of tourism lies or how it can be fostered (Shaw and Williams, 1998). Indeed, many authors are quick to point out that tourism's employment creation potential can be significantly lower when compared to other economic sectors (De Kadt, 1979; Hudson and Townsend, 1992). This is because tourist activities can be subject to seasonal fluctuations and high elasticities of demand, causing seasonal or part-time employment in destinations to be a common feature.

Research indicates that three structural factors influence the economic impact of tourism: the strength of backward and forward linkages among industries (Britton, 1991; Sinclair and Tsegaye, 1990); the ownership structures and patterns that characterise the tourism sector; and the spatial features of tourism production and related consumption in a given tourism economy (Britton, 1982; Pearce, 1995). If weak linkages prevail among economic sectors and industries involved in tourism production, the flow-through effect of tourism's impact, particularly from core to ancillary industries (e.g. construction, transport), will be weaker. Similarly, if the ownership of tourism producer and supplier companies does not lie in the tourist destination but in a different country, foreign exchange leakages, rather than earnings may characterise tourism in the destination country (Sinclair, 1998; Brohman, 1996). Finally, if tourism production and consumption occur in spatially concentrated locales in a country, the economic impact of tourism will be limited (Pearce, 1995).

Along with the positive economic effects of tourism, therefore, there are also a number of associated economic costs. Depending on the nature and structure of an economy these factors can have a negative impact. In the case of many developing countries such costs may be high (Mathieson and Wall, 1982). Balance of payments gains may be offset by a high propensity to import goods and services or a high rate of revenue expatriation. Higher inflation or costs could negatively impact on local economies. Further, many smaller countries can develop an overdependence on tourist activities. Bull (1995) for instance shows how in countries such as Antigua and the Bahamas tourism constitutes more than half of the economy, leaving them at risk to the shocks from 'single-sector climatic, political or trade cycles' (Bull, 1995: 131).

While all countries experience both the positive and negative impacts of tourism, developing countries tend to be more vulnerable to the sector's negative externalities. In part this arises from the fact that in the South there tends to a much greater reliance on international tourist activities and the capital created by tourism, and in part this is due to the particular structure of ownership in global tourism, with most of the large tourism multinationals, who often have a commanding influence in the wider system, based in the North. Chapter 2 provides a more complete discussion of the various discourses on tourism and development and how globalisation provides an appropriate framework for understanding the complex interface between global, local and intermediate levels of production, consumption and governance.

The Structure of the Book

The three overarching themes of the book are addressed in various parts and through various analyses of the South African tourism system. Chapter 2 provides an overview of the main theoretical and analytical perspectives regarding tourism and development. It reviews the main discourses that have developed over the past four decades. These range from analyses that focus on unequal power relationships between the global North and South, neo-classical perspectives on tourism's trickle-down effects, and discussions of alternative and sustainable tourism. The chapter details how processes of globalisation have reshaped global forms of production, consumption and governance, and how the producer-consumer nexus has been impacted. This in turn affects the developmental outcomes of tourism.

Chapter 3 provides an overview of South Africa's tourist sector – its historical evolution, market characteristics and broad patterns in policy development. Key challenges faced by the post-apartheid government – both uniquely, resulting from the continued political, economic and social effects of apartheid, but also stemming from South Africa's location in the wider global tourism system – are highlighted.

Chapter 4 focuses on the nature of global tourism production and how this impacts on development. The various components (or producer spheres) of the global tourism system have all varyingly been affected by factors of globalisation. Competition and collaboration among producers are shaped by aspects such as consolidation (or horizontal mergers) and alliance formation. The production process is highly dynamic. Some producers have more leverage in the production process than others. This is based on the size of the producer and relatedly, market access and penetration, although, in the case of airlines and tour operators their position and function provide them with a high degree of influence. South Africa is characteristic of many other developing countries in that its tourism sector is interlocked with that of large international source markets. This can provide international producers a large degree of influence over the South African production process and also determine the dynamics of tourism outcomes.

Chapter 5 explores this latter theme further, by investigating how South Africa is produced, imaged and marketed as an international tourism destination by domestic and international producers. This chapter analyses global tourism as interconnected systems of production and consumption, investigating the nature of interplay between producers and consumers. The image that is predominantly sold by international producers – focused on the natural, rather than the cultural components of the South African tourist product – is a continuation of the image established during the apartheid era. This has a developmental impact, moreover, as tourist imaging affects tourist flows. This negates the attempts of the South African government to develop and promote a more encompassing image, one that is dually aimed at meeting some of the domestic, political and economic objectives of the government, and shore up some of the government's foreign policy endeavours.

Chapter 6 investigates the overall regulatory framework of the tourism system and the institutions, rules and regimes that set the parameters for tourism production and consumption. The roles of various intergovernmental and other institutional bodies and the effect of these on global tourism and the South African sector are examined. The focus falls on two structures of international governance: the aviation regime, and the effect of increased trade liberalisation under the GATS. Tourism governance is an essential element of the global tourism system. Regulatory institutions have a direct impact on tourism production. This is particularly the case with regard to the international aviation regime. In the case of South Africa, for instance, a protective approach to regulating international airline access does have a constricting effect on flight capacity and affects tourism flows. Like many other developing countries, however, South Africa is attempting to contend with a competitive aviation environment and regulation is an important mechanism for this. Liberalisation under the GATS will have major effects – both positive and negative – on the global tourism system. Developing countries are likely to bear a larger cost with respect to the easing of service trade restrictions.

Chapter 7 focuses on the interlinking between two increasingly significant niches in global development – sport and mega-events. As a sector sport tourism has grown tremendously over the past number of years and has become very important. Yet is only recently that the analysis of the economic extent and political and socio-cultural impacts of sport, has developed into a field of study in its own right. The same can be said for mega-events, which may be regarded as one element of the worldwide business that has developed around the hosting and organising of conferences and exhibitions. Today it is relevant to speak of a mega-events industry, one that is global in scope and characterised by the dominance of a few multinational firms that set production and dissemination agendas. Hosting or bidding to host sport hallmark or mega-events such as the Olympic Games or Soccer or Cricket World Cups have started to be included in the development programmes of many countries, both advanced and developing. The aim is to use sport mega-events to profile countries, to draw foreign investments, stimulate infrastructure development and help expand tourism sectors. South Africa is no exception, and has become one of the leading international sport events destinations on the African continent. Chapter 7 examines the political and other dynamics around mega-events and sport tourism development in South Africa. While many advances have been made, particularly in the country's successful hosting of a number of major international events, and in its awarding of the rights to host the 2010 FIFA finals, little progress has been made thus far in the development of a cogent sport tourism or events strategy. If unaddressed, this is likely to have negative consequences for the country's wider sport tourism economy in the longer term.

Chapter 8 summarises the main arguments of the book. It draws together aspects from the case study that are of policy importance to other developing and developed countries, and provides a prognosis for global tourism development.

Notes

[1] It is worth noting here how the image of the explorative, pioneering traveller is a deliberately constructed narrative that emerged out of the interactions of different human groups over different times. It is important to recognise that this narrative has both positive and negative elements, and *a social purpose*.

[2] Britton's concept of a tourism production system is supply-side focused. It highlights the interplay between different producer groups, and some of the factors and forces that both underlie and govern such interaction. The advantage of such an approach is its ability to discern the diverse components that make up tourism. This enables key actors in tourism to be identified and for the flow of goods, ideas, money, and power to be traced.

[3] The orthodox treatment in economics of the relationship between consumers and producers in a market economy attributes primacy to the consumer. In neoclassical economic theory producers compete to produce goods at the lowest possible costs and highest rates of return. Goods are only produced for which there is a demand, defined as the quantity of a good or service that potential buyers are willing and able to buy during a certain period. Demand is determined by the price of the good, the price of related goods, and the income and taste(s) of the actual or potential purchaser. The fact that producers act so as to satisfy the needs and preferences of consumers, impart leverage to consumers in determining the flow of the market (Keat, 1994). This view of the sovereignty of consumers is one that is contested. In one of the stronger counter-views, Herbert Marcuse, in his theory of society postulates that modern capitalist society is characterised by the control of people by producers, who through the use of media and advertising attempt to create and perpetuate mass consumption. According to Marcuse (2001: 83-84), 'What we have in fact is a highly centralized society, systematically managed from above, in all spheres of culture. This management ... works through the control of the huge technical and technological apparatus of production, distribution, and communication; an apparatus which is so huge and so rational that individuals, and even groups of individuals, are powerless against it.' This control of the masses is necessitated by economic and technological advances that ultimately reduce scarcity. In order to counter this, 'the very needs of the individual (even his instinctual needs and satisfactions) are manipulated' (Marcuse, 2001: 85). In a contrasting analysis Abercrombie (1994) contends that in contemporary societies goods are as much consumed by people for their meaning than for satisfying certain needs. Through advertising producers effectively give meaning to goods, what Abercrombie (1994: 51) terms the 'commodification of meaning', thus providing them with a degree of power over consumers. Abercrombie argues however that rather than being dominated by producers, consumers respond to, and give their own signification to what they (choose to) purchase.

Chapter 2

Globalisation, Tourism and Development

Introduction

The relationship between tourism and development is one that has received much scholarly attention, although, as noted in Chapter 1, there is little consensus among researchers precisely what the nature of that relationship is, or how causal ties can be strengthened. Indeed, the past four decades have seen the rise of a plethora of different theoretical and analytical viewpoints on the complex connection between tourism and development. Characteristically, earlier works tended to focus on the economic aspects of tourism and the direct growth impacts of the sector. Over the past two decades, scholars started to emphasise the social, cultural and ecological effects – both positive and negative – of tourism and how the sector should be an instrument of participation and empowerment. Most recently tourism studies have been influenced by the 'cultural turn' in core fields such as Economic Geography, which has affected the specific variables that are emphasised. The centrality of the 'consumer over producer' debate, highlighted in Chapter 1, is reflective of this cultural turn in tourism analyses.

Tourism is an intricate economic, political and social activity that involves different types of actors from different levels and spheres. The emphasis in this book falls on the wide range of role players – consumers, producers, states, regulatory institutions – that shape tourism outcomes, and the overlapping levels – local, global and intermediate – at which they interact. Milne and Ateljevic's (2001: 371-372) characterisation of tourism as 'a transaction process which is at once driven by the global priorities of multi-national corporations, geo-political forces and broader forces of economic change, and the complexities of the local', aptly captures the elaborateness of global tourism. The phenomenon of globalisation – the process whereby a range of economic, political, technological, social and cultural factors and events over the past two decades have intensified interaction between firms, states, markets and people – provides an overarching framework for understanding the complex interface that exists between global and local levels and the different actors that are present at those levels and all impact on tourism.

This chapter provides an analytical frame for viewing the nature of the relationship between tourism and development in the era of globalisation. The first part of the chapter reviews some of the main theoretical discourses on tourism and development. The way that tourism should be understood as a complex system of production, consumption and governance and how forces that can be attributed to globalisation impact on this, is the focus of the remainder of the chapter.

Discourses on Tourism and Development

Traditional Perspectives: Modernisation (Neo-classical) and
Dependency in Tourism

Theoretical perspectives on the link between tourism and development have broadly followed trends in the larger development discourse (Hein, 1997; Ledbury, 1997). As such two main approaches have historically dominated understanding of the relationship between tourism and development – modernisation and dependency (Clancy, 1999; Meethan, 2001; Opperman, 1993).

Modernisation, built on the insights of Rostow (1960) is primarily a neo-classical account of tourism impact. The key assumption of this approach is that development in one economic sector and at one social level can permeate to other sectors and levels: development hence occurs through a process of 'trickle-down'.[1] In a broader sense, the modernisation perspective holds that the underdevelopment of traditional societies is the consequence of internal cultural and social factors, which once removed, clears the path for development. The dependency perspective, in contrast, holds that the source of countries' lack of development is external. According to this perspective there are unequal economic and political relationships between countries in the North and South that lead to the underdevelopment of the latter (e.g. Frank, 1967; Valenzuela and Valenzuela, 1978).[2]

Modernisation and tourism The modernisationist stance was most predominant in tourism analyses in the 1960s, when the beginning of the growth of mass tourism led to optimism about the potentials of tourism. Indeed, a United Nations conference on Tourism and International Trade held in 1963 emphasised the advantages of tourism for countries in the South (Ledbury, 1997). Tourism was seen as an effective path to modernity for developing countries (Meethan, 2001). It was seen as a means through which the social and cultural institutions and practices deemed so necessary by modernisationists for the transformation of traditional to modern societies, could be established (Ledbury, 1997; Khan, 1997). The tourism sector was also thought to present opportune growth poles, which through a process of diffusion and trickle-down could stimulate further growth (Opperman, 1993).

A vast body of literature couched in the modernisationist frame, has developed on the direct and positive economic benefits of international tourism. It is widely held that one of tourism's prime advantages is its ability to generate foreign currency, and to help assuage balance of payments constraints (Beauregard, 1998; Bull, 1995; Lea, 1988; Mathieson and Wall, 1982; Sinclair, 1998). Several authors have noted the importance of tourism as foreign currency earner in some developing countries. For instance, according to Sinclair (1991) tourism receipts have surpassed that of the traditional export commodity, coffee, in Kenya, while in The Gambia tourism is the second largest foreign currency earner (Dieke, 1993). Tourism's potential contribution to the balance of payments has led it to be promoted as an important means to increase the export base of developing countries (Brohman, 1996). Since the 1960s, therefore, tourism has come to be seen as a way in which developing countries could enhance international trade (Sinclair and Tsegaye, 1990; Crick, 1989).

Authors have also stressed the internal growth potential of tourism as a key economic benefit. Archer's work on tourism's multiplier effect (1977, 1982) has indicated that because of the diverse production structure of tourism, it has the ability to generate revenue in multiple ways: money spent by tourists induces spending by residents, businesses and governments in destinations. In this way tourist spending can provide impetus to growth in ancillary economic sectors (e.g. construction, (public) transport, hospitality suppliers and contractors), lead to the improvement of economic and social infrastructure, and to more investments in destination countries (Mathieson and Wall, 1982; Beauregard, 1998). Using this principle, authors have investigated the flow-through effect of tourist expenditure in the Caribbean (Archer, 1977), the Seychelles (Archer and Fletcher, 1996) and Singapore (Heng and Low, 1990), where it was found that tourism makes significant contributions to the countries' economies.

A further advantage of tourism that has been noted is its potential to generate employment in destination countries. Elkan's (1975) study of Kenya and Sinclair and Bote Gómez's (1996) study of Spain for instance showed the tourism sector to be a large employer in these countries. Mathieson and Wall (1982: 73) argue that because tourism involves a range of economic sectors, entry costs are not very high, and it is labour-intensive, it is seen as a vital source of employment for developing countries.

Notwithstanding, tourism's employment creation capacity has been widely questioned. In an analysis of the Turkish tourist sector, Diamond (1977) found that even though there was tourist expansion in this country, it was capital, rather than labour-intensive. He argues that tourism is not a very efficient means of employment creation in developing country contexts. Others have argued that because tourist activities can be subject to seasonal fluctuations and high elasticities of demand in source markets (De Kadt, 1979; Haywood, 1998), this can produce seasonal or part-time employment in destinations (Sinclair, 1998). Tourism's ability to provide a source of stable employment has therefore been disputed (e.g. Hall and Page, 1999; De Kadt, 1979). In a similar vein, Sinclair and Tsegaye (1990) have found that in numerous developing and medium-income countries in the Caribbean, Asia, Africa and the Middle East, tourist income as reflected in receipts, varied greatly due to varying demand levels. They concluded that tourism is a relatively unstable source of export earnings.

Following this, several authors (e.g. Brohman, 1996; Crick, 1989; Lea, 1988; Mathieson and Wall, 1982) have cautioned that along with the economic benefits that tourism can bring, there are also a number of associated economic costs. This can include higher inflation, higher property costs and income leakage. Given some of the disadvantages associated with international tourism, a number of scholars have argued that developing countries, in an effort to use tourism as pathway to development, should seek to build out their domestic tourist bases instead. For instance, Ghimire (2001) and Sindiga (1996) note that domestic and regional tourism (among developing countries) can be important counterbalances to seasonal and other fluctuations in international demand and may provide more stable bases. Ghimire (2001: 5) contends:

> national and regional tourism (could) represent 'self-reliance' and become an economic dynamo for (developing countries) (as in theory it should be less sensitive to international political instability and economic stagnation, less detrimental to the country's balance of payments, less 'leaky', and able to create substantial income and employment) (Ghimiri, 2001: 5).

Domestic and intra-regional tourism in the South, its economic development impact, and the potentials and problems related to it, is however an under-researched area in tourism (Ghimire, 2001).[3]

In spite of the costs related to tourism, on balance literature on tourism's economic impact stresses that tourism holds significant prospects for fostering development. A key principle that underlies this is that tourism is an effective means for developing countries to bolster trade, generate employment, and through enhanced tourism exports (i.e. increased tourist arrivals) be integrated into the larger international economy (Crick, 1989; Opperman, 1993). Further, tourism is viewed as presenting low-cost opportunities for the populations of developing countries to move from 'traditional', subsistence sectors to 'modern' sectors (Clancy, 1999: 4). As such, much of the literature on tourism's developmental potential is both explicitly and tacitly embedded in the modernisation approach (Brohman, 1996; Ledbury, 1997).

The dependency perspective in tourism During the 1970s and 1980s a strong counter-view developed that was an outright questioning of the developmental virtues of tourism. During this time an increasing number of researchers noted the undesirable social, environmental and economic consequences of tourism in destination countries. De Kadt's (1979) publication, *Tourism – Passport to Development?*, the outcome of another UN-sponsored conference constituted one of the first reviews of the physical impacts that tourism could have, which include environmental degradation and a drain on the physical resources of a destination country. V. Smith (1978) and MacCannell (1973) provided analyses of the social and cultural effects of tourists' interaction with host societies. Hostility, loss of identity, social alienation and conflict could all arise from tourists' apathetic treatment of hosts (e.g. Koch, 1994; Stock, 1997). Others have also noted the negative effect of forms such as sex tourism on both host societies and tourists (Hall, 1994a; Karch and Dann, 1981; Phongpaichit, 1986).

Revisionist theoretical works on tourism and development, influenced by the world-systems analysis of Wallerstein, and the works of dependency theorists such as Frank (1967), became more prominent during this time, and a dependency perspective on the international tourism system developed. Britton (1982) in his analysis of tourism in the South Pacific argued that multinational corporations dominated and controlled tourism in countries such as Fiji, the Cook Islands and

Tonga. This he contended, precluded any economic advantages accruing to the destinations, and led to a condition of dependency.

Based on the examples of the South Pacific, Britton (1989) argues that in order to understand the nature of the tourism industry in a specific developing country, it is necessary to develop an understanding of the international structure of the industry itself, through an analysis of 'particularly the power and dominance of certain activity components and ownership groups' (Britton, 1989: 25).

More specifically, Britton argues that the international tourism industry is a peripheral capitalist economy and characteristically monopolistic. Its main features are the following: tourism production, the creation of tourist products, and ultimately power, are centralised in the core capitalist countries. This is most pertinent in the organisation of the various sectors of the tourism industry, such as hotels, airlines, cruise ships and travel and tour operations. Local élites in the peripheral countries provide services to overseas companies, and are connected to the international tourism industry in this way. However, because ownership of tourism infrastructure mainly lies in core countries, there is a repatriation of revenue from destination countries to the North. The nature of international tourism organisation, itself a function of neo-colonial relationships (Britton, 1989), therefore means that tourism is disembedded from destination countries' economies, and do not carry benefits for the larger populace in these countries. Instead, due to its structure, it 'frequently perpetuates class and regional inequalities, economic problems and social tensions' (Britton, 1982: 332).

The dependency perspective significantly influenced scholarship on tourism in developing countries throughout the 1970s and 1980s. It provides a critique of the structure of international tourism. Central to this is the exploitative nature of international tourism over the economies and resources of developing countries, its domination by North-based multinational companies and the lack of local ownership in developing countries (Lea, 1988). By the beginning of the 1990s, however, following changes in the larger development discourse, both theories of modernisation and dependency fell into academic disfavour as explanatory frameworks for development processes related to tourism (Clancy, 1999).[4]

Alternative, Sustainable and Community Tourism

In recent years the debate on the economic, physical and social impacts of tourism came to be increasingly framed within a discussion of how tourism can most optimally utilise, and contribute to the larger physical and economic environment. The discourses on *alternative tourism* and *sustainable tourism* gained increasing headway among tourism scholars and researchers in the 1990s. This was due to two factors: developments in the debate on *sustainable development* of the 1980s; and an increasing realisation that the vigorous growth international tourism had seen since the end of the Second World War held implications for the natural environment (Stabler, 1997).

'Sustainability' first entered the lexicon of development policy makers twenty-five years ago, when under the aegis of the United Nations, the World Conservation Strategy (WCS) was published in 1980, a document that sought to promulgate measures to attain economic development through the fortuitous utilisation of natural resources, and the preservation of the natural environment (Hall and Lew, 1998). Conservation, according to the WCS, was 'the management of human use of the biosphere so that it may yield the greatest sustainable benefit to present generations while maintaining its potential to meet the needs and aspirations of future generations' (in Hall and Lew, 1998: 2). The WCS represented the first attempt to define and develop solutions to what became increasingly recognised as internationally common environmental problems, in a multilateral forum. It was spurred on by a broad re-questioning of many of the postulates of modernist development theory (Hall and Lew, 1998).

As a follow up to the WCS, the World Commission on Environment and Development (WCED) was established in 1983, a body charged with concretising the principles enshrined in the WCS. In 1987 the WCED released a report entitled *Our Common Future*. This report, commonly known as the Brundtland Report, defined 'sustainable development' as 'development that meets the needs of the present without compromising the ability of future generations to meet their own needs' (WCED, 1987). Sustainable development, in this sense, occurs through the considered utilisation of the natural environment – while economic growth for the sake of it is rejected, economic development is seen as an objective that is desirable and necessary. Economic development however needs to be harnessed, and should not come through an overexploitation of natural resources.

The Brundtland Report, and the ideas contained in there, is widely hailed for popularising the notion of sustainable development, and the impact it has had on development discourse since (Hall and Lew, 1998). By the 1990s sustainable development has become a standard goal of all development frameworks, although, it should be noted, it is by no means an uncontested concept.[5]

Ideas on sustainability in tourism has a longer precedent than the Brundtland Report, but the extent to which the concept of 'sustainable development' has disseminated throughout the world after the release of this report, has had a significant influence on how tourism is viewed.

Alternative tourism Within this context, by the 1980s, the negative effects of tourism experienced by many countries led to a popular questioning of the virtues of mass tourism, and growing calls for the development of a type of tourism that was less hurtful to the natural, cultural and social environments upon which it inevitably impacted. This form of tourism, which may broadly be termed 'alternative tourism' is meant to be the antithesis of mass tourism, and all the negative externalities associated with it, i.e. the large-scale movement of people from one locale to another, a process which, given the size of it, is assumed to place a heavy burden on natural, and often economic resources (Swanson and Barbier, 1992; France, 1997; Stabler, 1997).

Alternative tourism as used by tourism scholars and practitioners is a broadly encompassing term that includes a multitude of activities and tourist forms. It may varyingly refer to nature(-based), ecological, environmentally friendly, green, ethnic, cultural, indigenous, soft tourism, and eco-tourism (Mowforth and Munt, 1998: 100). Its defining feature is that it attempts to be ecologically conscious, and social and culturally-sensitive, by impacting as little as possible on the physical and host environments in destinations. In terms of production, alternative tourism types are further distinguished in their form and nature of organisation: whereas conventional, mass tourism is characteristically large and dependent on the creation of economies of scale, alternative tourism forms usually cater for small tourist groups, and are geographically focused.[6] This feature, according to some authors (e.g. Brohman, 1996; Khan, 1997) enables a larger number of local residents to be involved in tourism production, allowing for a higher degree of local tourism ownership, greater linkages in the local economy, and a greater multiplier effect.

From alternative to sustainable tourism Through the respect for the natural environment, and for the cultures, traditions and values of host destinations, proponents of alternative tourism posit that the negative consequences of tourism can be obviated, while the economic advantages of tourism can at the same time be optimised (Smith and Eadington, 1992). By virtue of this, alternative tourism is commonly propagated as a means to effect sustainable development. Hein (1997) notes that an uncritical equation of alternative tourism with sustainability is simplistic and short-sighted. This is because tourism of any form, even one that seeks to limit tourist numbers at a locale, still makes physical demands on that locale and on the general environment, not least because tourists have to travel to a destination. Given its requirement for appropriate and efficient infrastructure, therefore, tourism poses an inherent threat to the environment.

In spite of these limitations, notions of 'sustainable tourism' have become ever popular. Recent years have seen attempts to develop the principles of sustainable tourism development into an academic field in its own right, with its own attendant epistemology and methodologies. This is reflected in the number of publications on Sustainable Tourism over the past number of years (e.g. Stabler, 1997; Mowforth and Munt, 1998; Hall and Lew, 1998; Hein, 1997; Honey, 1999). One definition for Sustainable Tourism sees it as:

> ...meeting the needs of present tourists and host regions while protecting and enhancing opportunity for the future. Sustainable tourism development is envisaged as leading to management of all resources in such a way that we can fulfil economic, social and aesthetic needs while maintaining cultural integrity, essential ecological processes, biological diversity and life support systems (Cited in Ledbury, 1997: 30).

This definition echoes that put forward in the Brundtland Report. It acknowledges the tourist enterprise as an essential resource in itself, but one that should be applied and channelled in an appropriate fashion. Several international initiatives on sustainable tourism and sustainable tourism development have been undertaken by a number of bodies over the years. In one of the most important, in 1992, environmental management and related facets were the focal point of the United Nations Conference on Environment and Development (popularly known as the Earth Summit) in Brazil. The conclusion of this summit saw the proclamation of the *Rio Declaration on Environment and Development*, and *Agenda 21*, and the establishment of a Commission on Sustainable Development (CSD). Within the context of *Agenda* 21, a document that details the various roles and responsibilities of a number of local, national and international actors towards resource conservation, the CSD has since delineated tourism as an important economic sector that bears specific ecological, social and cultural costs. The promotion of sustainable tourism is hence an objective of the Commission. In a similar vein, travel and tourism producers and international governmental organisations have launched their own initiatives to promote sustainable tourism. The World Travel and Tourism Council and the World Tourism Organisation for instance, are involved in the *Alliance for Sustainable Tourism*, a collection of travel and tourism producers and interest groups that seek to develop a set of producer practices thought to be ethical and furthering sustainable development. To this end the Alliance has devised its own Agenda 21 for Travel and Tourism. Members of the Alliance and signatories of the Agenda are expected to adopt practices and sell tourist products that are ecologically and socially sensitive.

Community tourism In keeping with shifts in development discourse, it has become increasingly popular for tourism researchers to conflate sustainable development in tourism with democracy and participatory approaches. Consequently in recent years a large body of work focused on community-based or community-involving approaches to tourism has developed (e.g. Ashley, 1998; Mitchell and Reid, 2001; Murphy, 1985; Swanson and Barbier, 1992; Thomas, 1995). 'Community tourism' is an important subset of the broader sustainable tourism debate. It is characterised by two elements – its objective to involve host societies in the tourism process, and the selling of a tourist product that is based on the social and cultural traits of a given society. It is therefore best categorised as a form of alternative tourism that has the explicit objective of engaging social groupings in tourism destinations both in the production of tourist goods, and in the interaction with tourists. 'Participation' is the crux of community tourism.

The theoretical premises of community tourism have a long history, originating from the participatory and empowerment development models that emerged as a new paradigm in development discourse in the 1970s. The fundamental proposition is that the active incorporation of communities in tourist destinations in the planning and production of tourism goods will obviate tourism's negative effects by increasing local ownership of tourism goods and production; providing a direct source of income for host communities; and preventing the social and cultural alienation prevalent in particularly mass tourism. All in all, the economic and social spin-offs from community tourism are held to be an effective means of achieving sustainability in tourism. One of the first attempts to devise a systematic analytical framework of community tourism is found in Murphy (1985) who analogises tourism as an economic and social ecosystem, characterised by the interdependency and symbiotic interaction of its various components (host communities, visitors, and production factors). Murphy argues that communities in host destinations form an integral facet of the final tourist product, and are hence an important tourism resource. To maintain stasis in the tourism ecosystem, and moreover to optimise its renewable use value, Murphy contends that local community participation should be an essential feature of tourism planning. In recognition that tourism is equally affected by exogenous factors, he suggests four core analytical dimensions (derived from systems theory), that should inform an analysis of the environment within which tourism planning and development takes place, and which influence local community involvement. These dimensions are the social and spatial features of both the destination and the tourists who go to that destination; the type and form of information flows that occur between the destination and the tourist source markets; and the temporal juncture at which interaction between the host community and the tourists occurs (Murphy, 1985).

In their analysis of community integration in tourism Mitchell and Reid (2001) put forward a framework that represents the processes involved at each different phase of tourism planning and community integration, and the variety of actors and factors relevant to each phase. According to the authors community-based tourism is a gradual but cumulative process that successfully occurs when a given community is incorporated into a tourism project from the conception and initiation of the project right through the planning and implementation of it. The authors identify three stages in this process. The three stages are temporally disconnected, with each following successively upon the other. In the first stage of 'integration', the authors identify a number of variables that need to be present for a host community to be drawn into the planning and carrying out of a tourism project. These are 'community awareness', 'community unity', and a favourable power structure within, and outside of the community. The authors identify a number of external factors that affect this first stage of integration. These include the nature of the tourism supply structure, and the nature of the tourism market. Once a given community has been integrated into a tourism project, the second stage of 'planning' can go ahead. In a community integrated tourism project, it will ideally be a locally affected community who define, guide and direct the course of planning and implementation of a tourism project. Finally, a third stage of 'impact assessment' follows where the community-based tourism project is evaluated in terms of a number of economic, social, cultural and environmental indicators.

In sub-Saharan Africa a substantial proportion of scholarly work on sustainable tourism development has focused on advancing models for community-based tourism (e.g. Ashley, 1998; Koch, 1994; Reid and Sindiga, 1999; Swanson and Barbier, 1992; Thomas, 1995). A notable feature of community tourism in the continent is that it is predominantly focused on nature conservation, and often entails the drawing in of local residents into existing nature-based tourist enterprises (Ashley and Lafranchi, 1997). The shift since the mid-1980s towards less statist, more inclusionary nature and wildlife management practices, often termed 'community-based natural resource management' (CBNRM) or 'community conservation' has been the main driving force behind this. As a concept, CBNRM aims towards a model of nature conservation that draws in the involvement of local communities.

The central tenet of this approach is that the traditional framework for the protection of natural and wildlife resources – principally through state-established and controlled national parks and game reserves – usually is based on the active exclusion of groups who live in close proximity to protected areas and often rely on resources from such areas. Aside from limiting the livelihoods of such groups, breeding hostility towards nature conservation and leading to poaching, traditional state-led (or 'fortress') conservation practices can also often have ecological counter-effects. CBNRM holds that effective nature conservation can only take place if communities living adjacent to protected areas are included in management objectives and programmes and draw some benefit from protection schemes. The aim is for 'sustainable utilisation', rather than mere protection of wildlife resources (Wolmer, 2003: 267) and sharing of ownership. Community involvement can entail a consumptive or non-consumptive component. In the former neighbouring communities can draw upon the fauna and floral resources in protected parks, and may for example harvest, hunt or use plants for medicinal purposes. This ensures that goals and practices of nature conservation such as wildlife control or culling are maintained. In the more common form of community engagement, non-consumptive use of protected areas enables communities to access or live in small, designated parts of parks without the right to exploit wildlife resources. Such communities are however able to utilise resources for economic use, most commonly through involvement in eco-tourism ventures. Communities may for instance run field tours where they share knowledge about indigenous vegetation, or offer home stays to tourists.

Two main models of CBNRM exist, one where communities have consultative status and may advise on wildlife management. In the second, known as contractual or co-management, communities and conservation authorities (which may be state boards or private firms that operate in parks on concession bases) jointly manage conservation areas and share equal deliberation and decision-making powers. In Africa, there are few examples of true contractual models, although CBNRM has been implemented in several countries such as Zambia, Namibia, Malawi and Kenya.

The fact that community involvement in tourism in Africa has mainly centred around projects of nature conservation and ecotourist enterprises, is partly because of the importance nature-based tourism carries in many sub-Saharan African countries. It is also due to the institutional evolution and implementation of the concept in the sub-continent, which for the most part combined a participatory/empowerment developmental approach with the restoration of land rights lost under colonialism (Koch, 1994). This is because the creation of nature conservation and wildlife domains in many regions in sub-Saharan Africa during the colonial era was often accompanied by resident populations' loss of land tenure and rights to utilise natural resources, leading to populations viewing nature conservation sites as competition areas (Vorlaufer, 1997). In recent times it has become increasingly recognised that this colonial legacy and the very boundaries of nature conservation areas pose an impediment to the preservation of natural resources. In an effort to address this, many sub-Saharan African states and development bodies sought to couple land redistribution processes with community-based local development projects.

Ashley (1998) provides examples of the forms that such community-based eco-tourist enterprises on communal land can take. These are:

- individual, privately owned businesses (e.g. lodges or safari parks) where the owner pays a voluntary fee (bed levy) to the local resident community;
- enterprises where independent business groupings/investors and the community jointly run commercial endeavours, and where, depending on the nature of the contractual agreement between the investors and the community, the community either functions as lessee (in the case of accommodation facilities), as secondary partner/equity holder, or as primary owner;
- individual commercial endeavours operated by individual members of the local community. These may include the selling of local crafts and other goods and services to tourists. Such commercial activities Ashley (1998) terms 'informal sector enterprises'.

The most long-standing African example of community involvement in tourism is found in Zimbabwe. The Communal Areas Management Programme for Indigenous Resources – CAMPFIRE – scheme of Zimbabwe has been under implementation since 1984 (Swanson and Barbier, 1992). It consists of a series of projects where rural Zimbabwean communities residing in wildlife areas accrue financial benefits from the wildlife resources, mainly through safari hunting operations (Dzingirai, 2003; Koch, 1994). CAMPFIRE is widely regarded as a flagship case of successful CBNRM. However, some commentators have noted that the programme has intensified conflict between different local rural communities as some benefits are differentially accessed. Dzingirai (2003) for instance illustrates how the CAMPFIRE scheme, originally focused on designated 'producer communities', the Tonga, has not been redesigned to incorporate recent Ndebele migrants into the area. Excluded from sharing in the benefits, Ndebele communities become hostile to the scheme and wildlife conservation more broadly. Disputes that arise between the two local communities feed into wider political conflict between rival groupings at the national level. CAMPFIRE's relative success has also been due to the involvement of large, and in the context of Zimbabwe's political economy, financially powerful non-state and semi-state bodies. Wolmer (2003) notes how while support of the scheme by groups such as the United States Agency for International Development (USAID) and other western donors has been important for the creation and existence of CAMPFIRE, it has also meant that the agendas of such bodies have played a large role in the course of development of the scheme, and models of community conservation more broadly.

As will be discussed in Chapter 3, the post-apartheid government in South Africa has been involved in initiatives with other states in the Southern African region to found transfrontier conservation parks, areas where countries' natural reserves and conservation regions overlap and are jointly managed by neighbouring states. Part of this entails extending certain resource use rights to indigenous communities, or providing concessions to operate eco-tourist ventures within these parks. Unlike CBNRM, the focus of transborder conservation initiatives is regional, extending across two or more countries and involving more than one government. Within South Africa CBNRM has been implemented with varying degrees of success. The two largest and most important cases are the

Richtersveld Park in the northwest of the country[7] and the Makuleke region in the northeast corner of the extensive Kruger National Park. Both are examples of contractual national parks, i.e. conservation areas where on the basis of co-management agreements, communities and the state (in the South African case, in the form of South African National Parks (SANParks)) are jointly involved in specific aspects of the administration of the parks. Richtersveld is a rare example where the local community has full, institutional management rights.[8] The Makuleke region arose out of a 1995 land claim by the Makuleke community who, during the apartheid era was forcibly removed from their ancestral land. Through an agreement with the state, SANParks leases the land from the community, who has management and utilisation rights.

Establishing contractual national parks is one of the key ways in which the post-apartheid South African government seeks to link objectives regarding land redistribution, development and nature conservation. To date, however, tourism development has been one of the more marginal aspects of these parks (see for instance Reid, 2001). In the case of the Makuleke region, its location in one of the remote corners of the Kruger National Park has meant that tourist numbers have been very low, despite the fact that the promotion of eco-tourism initiatives is one of the explicit goals of the co-management agreement. A further problem for the South African government is that the success of the Makuleke land claim has spurred on other communities to stake their right to ancestral land, many of whom seek to utilise such land for agricultural or commercial purposes. This poses severe challenges to the contractual park and CBNRM models in the country.

A few problems beset theoretical analyses of community(-based) tourism. The first is that the very analytic unit – communities – is often a misnomer (Ashley, 1998). Scholars such as Brohman (1996) and Milne (1997) note that supposed community-based tourism projects often have their origin in the efforts of single individuals, or local economic élites. As a consequence a common feature of studies on community tourism is a multiplicity of definitions and concepts, with 'community' varyingly referring to large or small social groupings, or to individuals. In addition, the concept 'community' presupposes processes of group formation and identity homogeneity that seldom coincide with the geographical parameters utilised by researchers. Koch (1994) notes that the very concept 'community' is a problematic one. Similarly, community tourism studies often assume that access to authority institutions is equitably distributed within social groupings, tending to disregard the effect of power differentials in communities (Ledbury, 1997; Reed, 1997). Finally, proponents of community-based tourism are criticised for overemphasising local agency while not taking into account the influence of larger structural factors (Milne, 1997).

The net result is that analytical frameworks very seldom capture the full density of tourist activities and tourist economies. This criticism is particularly relevant to studies on and projects of community tourism in sub-Saharan Africa, which as detailed above, mainly focus on ecotourist projects. Essentially this has meant that to date, community-based tourism in the sub-continent has mainly been equated with sustainable *rural* development. Considerably less attention has been given to sustainable tourism in urban contexts, or how the principles of community tourism can be applied to tourism forms that centre on the urban environment.

Discourse on alternative/sustainable/community tourism has largely directed research on tourism and development in the recent past. However, as noted by Ledbury (1997) scholarship on alternative or sustainable tourism tends to be characterised by conceptual and definitional obfuscation. Second, a large part of this work tends to be descriptive rather than explanatory (Clancy, 1999). To date scholarship has thus consisted of a disparate body of approaches and methodologies that lack coherence. A more fundamental drawback is that because alternative tourist products must of necessity be limited in scale, some authors have questioned whether an economic basis that can sufficiently serve the needs of a large social grouping can be accrued from such tourist forms (Forsyth, 1997; Hein, 1997).

Studies on community tourism do however provide a few heuristic tools that are of value to an analysis of how tourism can carry sustainable benefits. The first lies in the objectives of community tourism, which seek to investigate ownership structures in tourism, and to devise means of entrenching local ownership. The second lies in the delineation of a set of instruments and related measures that can be employed to operationalise concepts such as 'drawing benefits from tourism', 'distribution of benefits', or 'sustainable development' in tourism.

Further, despite the lack of a single approach to sustainability, tourism literature suggests three general criteria for sustainable tourism development. The first relates to the structure of tourism production. In order for destination countries to optimise the economic gains from tourism, it is considered important that local ownership of the tourism supply sector and linkages between tourism and other economic sectors in the destination country, are enhanced (Mathieson and Wall, 1982; Brohman, 1996). This creates increased tourism opportunities for the residents of destination countries. The extent to which they are actively engaged in tourism as producers, the access that these producers have to consumers, and the connections that exist among various related sectors in the destination country at the local level, are taken as indicators of the degree to which tourism production is rooted in the destination country, and by extension, the degree to which local income is maximised.

A second criterion centres on how economic benefits are distributed. This is related to the spatial features of tourism. If production and consumption occur in geographically concentrated locales in a country, the economic impact of tourism will be spatially focused (Britton, 1982; Brohman, 1996; Pearce, 1995). The equitable social and regional spread of tourism benefits, in the form of income and employment, but also related aspects such as training and skills development in a given destination, is therefore taken as an important indicator of sustainability. Brohman (1996) notes that along with tourism's benefits, there also needs to be an even diffusion of the costs (such as more imports) associated with tourism.

Thirdly there are three interdependent dimensions to sustainability – economic, environmental/ecological and social (e.g. Stabler, 1997; Swanson and Barbier, 1992). When tourism activities take place in such a manner that economic gains accrued from it are to the benefit of the society at large, and to the benefit of the natural and social resources upon which tourism depend, the basis for sustainable tourism has been laid (e.g. V. Smith and Eadington, 1992).

Sustainability may also be said to be contingent upon sustained growth in tourism, in the form of tourist numbers, expenditure, investments and employment in tourism. All in all, 'sustainable development through tourism' may usefully be conceptualised as the outcome of tourism activities that bring tangible gains for the destination country and its society both in its present and future forms. It is based on (continued) growth and an equitable distribution of benefits and costs.

Globalisation, Tourism and Development

The concept of globalisation has emerged as a significant influence on academic scholarship over the past number of years, and has had wide-ranging effects on the way that tourism is analysed as sector. Nonetheless, with a few exceptions (e.g. Meethan, 2001; Wahab and Cooper, 2001) there has been limited systematic exploration of what tourism entails in the era of globalisation.

Two broad positions characterise the use of globalisation as analytical concept. The first sees it as a novel process arising in response to a number of forces and stimuli characteristic of a capitalist epoch in a particular historical juncture. The second questions the scope, scale, recentness and indeed existence of globalisation (e.g. Hirst and Thompson, 1999; Krugman, 1996). Discourse in the former tradition converges on two aspects. Globalisation is generally seen as a process that involves the compression of time and space dimensions (Mittelman, 1995) and is characterised by greater degree of interconnectivity between social groupings at different levels. Globalisation is also seen as a multiscalar process consisting of several dimensions. It refers in the first instance to an economic process whereby certain structural economic shifts – changes in the international financial system, the rise of the global telecommunications industry, comprehensive technological changes, and the increase and expansion of transnational corporations – are fashioning a distinctly different world economy, where events and decisions in one part of the world can significantly affect and shape other parts. This has an important impact on forms of authority and sovereignty. In some of the stronger formulations scholars designate the waning of the powers of the state and eventually its decline (e.g. Ohmae, 1995; Reich, 1991).

A second, counter view is represented by Hirst and Thompson (1999) who contend that the discourse on globalisation in essence relates to processes of economic, political and cultural internationalisation that have long been in forming. In this sense, rather than being a discrete process or event driven by its own logic and having far-reaching economic, and in particular political, global consequences as the consensus view seems to be, globalisation is not new, but simply an intensification of developments that have been taking place for a long time. Indeed, Hirst and Thompson (1999) maintain that much of what is provided as evidence for globalisation – economic and political integration, the increased power of transnational corporations, and the emergence of a 'global economy' – are old processes, or are less forceful than generally claimed by most authors. They argue that the present level of economic internationalisation is not exceptional, and that in several ways, the world economy was more integrated and interdependent in the era before the Second World War. In addition, they contend that there are very few truly transnational corporations, and the fact that international investment and financial flows mainly are between Western Europe, Japan and North America, debases claims of a truly global economy (Hirst and Thompson, 1999: 2; Sklair, 1995).

Notwithstanding, there is a prevailing understanding that there is an expansionary momentum to economic, social and political exchanges that transcend national borders and have certain consequences on economies, state structures and societies. Aside from having economic and political impacts, it also affects the cultural domain and shapes processes such as local identity construction (Castells, 1997). Cultural flows (e.g. through migration) are a contingent of globalisation that on the one level lead to a dynamic engagement between different cultures, and on another, to the fundamental transformation of affected locales (Appadurai, 1996). The growth in international travel as activity over the past two decades is closely tied to this wider thrust. Tourism is both an outcome of globalisation and a driving force of intensified global interaction. As noted by Fayos-Solà and Bueno (2001: 47) there are three features of contemporary tourism – the expansion of tourism demand internationally, increased similarities in tourism demand, and the concentration and convergence of tourism supply, in the form of tourism business mergers – that make it a quintessential aspect of globalisation.

As such globalisation has several dimensions through which an analysis of the link between tourism and development has to be reframed.

Globalisation, Culture and Consumption

There has been a more vigorous incorporation of culture as analytical and explanatory variable in tourism over the past number of years. There is today a greater understanding among scholars that tourism is a cultural affair, deeply locked into the changing nature and patterns of interaction, conduct and regulation within different societies, and that as an activity of consumption it provides important clues into the nature of the social complex (Zukin, 1995; Urry, 1995; Rojek and Urry, 1997).

A strong strand in the culture of tourism discourse draws from the critical tradition of the Frankfurt School and their work on the culture industry (e.g. Adorno, 1991; Marcuse, 2001). As first conceptualised by Adorno, the culture industry refers to the production of cultural goods for mass consumption in capitalist societies, a process that follows from the economic organisation of capitalism which is predicated upon the continued creation of goods for exchange and profit, rather than for fulfilling set uses (Featherstone, 1991; Bernstein, 1991). This involves the subjection of the cultural domain, which according to Adorno should have a higher value and intent, to the logic of capitalist production, with culture becoming commodified and marketable in the same way as other goods, and hence losing its higher value. Adorno (1991: 34) contends:

... exchange value exerts its power in a special way in the realm of cultural goods. For in the world of commodities this realm appears to be exempted from the power of exchange, to be in an immediate relationship with the goods, and it is this appearance in turn which alone gives cultural goods their exchange value. But they nevertheless simultaneously fall completely into the world of commodities, are produced for the market, and are aimed at the market. The appearance of immediacy is as strong as the compulsion of exchange is inexorable.

For theorists such as Adorno and Marcuse the development of the culture industry is a process that leads to a division between high culture (based upon culture as use item) and mass culture (based upon culture as exchange item). It depends on the manipulation of the masses and on a false sense of fulfilment (Bernstein, 1991: 8).

The theory of the culture industry draws attention to how culture is produced and reproduced for consumption. Building upon this, Baudrillard (1970) argues that the consumer society is one where consumption has become a fundamental component of modern living, and fulfils the function of keeping the capitalist system of production in place. The consumer society is a structure based upon the creation of signs and values that are attached to commodities. Agents such as the media continuously produce and reproduce and communicate signs and images that are consumed by people. Leisure, loosely defined as the availability of free time, is an important element of this system of signification. Similar to Veblen's (1912) notion of 'the leisure class', who are able to distinguish themselves by their ability to engage in leisure activities and for whom this accords respect (esteem), Baudrillard contends that leisure is 'a code of distinction'. There is a forced, contrived element to this, however, as people in truth are not free *not* to consume leisure. According to Baudrillard,

> [E]verywhere, we find in leisure and holidays the same eager moral and idealistic pursuit of accomplishment as in the sphere of work, the same **ethics of pressured performance** ... No one needs leisure, but all are charged to prove their freedom not to perform productive labour [Baudrillard, 1998: 155; 157 (bold in original)].

Seen in this way leisure and tourism consumption is oppressive and tyrannical. Due to its negative stance towards mass culture Adorno's theory on the culture industry has been criticised as elitist and deterministic (Bernstein, 1991). A different view is represented by Featherstone (1991) who notes that Adorno and other Frankfurt School theorists tend to overstate the power of manipulation in consumption and that they disregard the fact that different people respond to stimuli differently, and that consumers have own volition and choice. In this regard Urry (1995) argues that the increased ability to reflect upon the social environment is a key aspect of modernity/modern societies. This reflection, he argues, is both cognitive and normative, but can also be aesthetic. 'Aesthetic reflexivity' involves 'the proliferation of images and symbols operating at the level of feeling and consolidated around judgements of taste and distinction about different natures and societies' (Urry, 1995: 145).

The exercise of choice by consumers in modern-day consumer societies is reflected in the emergence of manifold lifestyles. 'Lifestyle' is both a marker of social status and position (Sobel, 1982: 8), and an expression of social identity and individuality in the consumer society. Featherstone (1991: 86) for instance argues:

> Rather than unreflexively adopting a lifestyle, through tradition or habit, the new heroes of consumer culture make lifestyle a life project and display their individuality and sense of style in the particularity of the assemblage of goods, clothes, practices, experiences, appearance and bodily dispositions they design together into a lifestyle.

This aspect of individuality and self-consciousness in consumption makes it the embodiment of the post-modern condition, where meanings, norms, and by extension social relations, are not fixed (Featherstone, 1991). Tourism, in this frame, is a form of expression in the modern consumer society. For some it is a quintessential feature of the post-modern lifestyle. Tourism offers an escape, a transcendence from the everyday, and a chance to explore the 'Other' (Zukin, 1995; Craik, 1997; MacCannell, 1992).

This view of consumption, and tourism as a subset of it, is a clear break from the Frankfurt School and emphasises rather tourists' independent facility. These two contrasting perspectives in tourism theory, however, are additionally significant for how they frame further tourism analyses. First, underlying the division over whether tourists are independent actors who select from an array of available tourist products, or are manipulated by capitalist agents, is a deeper debate regarding the producer-consumer nexus, and the exercise of power. In Baudrillard's formulation of leisure, for instance, leisure, and relatedly, tourism consumption, is a social and cultural activity that feeds into and sustains, but is subordinate to a larger system of production. The 'production of consumption' postulate encapsulated in the Frankfurt School tradition (Featherstone, 1991) suggests that tourism producers exercise considerable degrees of influence, indeed control over consumers. If, however, tourism consumption is seen as an individualised, autonomous or at its most extreme, a post-modern articulation, it is the ability of consumers to choose that shapes tourism as an activity and sector. The issue of who influences whom is a complex debate in tourism analysis that has different implications for different facets of tourism.

Globalisation and International Tourism Production

Differing viewpoints on the nature of power in tourism also extend to the production domain. On the one hand power relations among different sets of producers determine tourism outcomes to a significant extent. Increased mergers and acquisitions and trends towards homogenisation over the past number of years have consolidated the influence of major transnational corporations in the global tourism production system. On the other hand, the way that different tourism forms and markets are analysed, and the factors that are attributed to their development, is subject to particular understandings of where power lies in the producer-consumer nexus. This is evident, for instance, in debates on changes in tourism production, and contended shifts from Fordism to post- and neo-Fordism.

Fordism, neo- and post-Fordism Recent years have seen important developments in scholarship that see tourism as a manifestation of neo-Fordism or flexible specialisation. The discourse on neo-Fordism maintains that the contemporary era is characterised by distinctly different forms of production, accumulation and management than had been the case in the earlier part of the twentieth century. Fordism refers to a mode of capitalist accumulation and regulation that has several key bases: the creation of economies of scale through the mass production of goods (particularly in the car and electronics industries), produced for mass consumption. As a mode of regulation, Fordism usually dovetailed with the implementation of Keynesian economic practices, the expansion of the welfare state, and economic corporatism (Esser and Hirsch, 1989). Industrial production moreover, was driven by large centrally-organised corporations (Bernard, 1994). Labour within the Fordist mode was usually of a functional, highly specialised nature.

There has been a steady decline in this form of production and institutionalisation in Western Europe, Japan and the United States since the 1970s. While the wholesale eclipse of Fordism, and the existence of post-Fordism is disputed (for an overview see Amin, 1994), many advanced economies are increasingly based on systems of 'flexible accumulation and differentiation' (Parsdorfer and Cernay, 1999: 19), with production and decision-making not centralised in one firm, but spread among different sectors of a firm, and across firms. This decentralisation of large corporations is paralleled with the growth of medium and smaller companies as production units. According to Borja and Castells (1997: 52) concomitant changes in information technology have given significance to economies,

> in which increases in productivity do not depend on a quantitative increase in the factors of production (capital, labour and natural resources) but rather on the application of knowledge and information to management, production and distribution, both in process and in products.

Some contend that the impact on firms is that information technology and microelectronics are applied to every level of the production process; at the same time the trade and transmission of information has become both necessary, and easier. Linkages that are established among and across (large and small) firms produce networks of production, so constituting a new geography of capitalism (e.g. Brenner, 1998; Paul, 2002). The move towards neo- or post-Fordism – based on the creation of economies of scope, rather than scale, decentralisation and flexibility – are seen to be important elements of this.

While changes from Fordism to neo- or post-Fordism are generally viewed within manufacturing, shifts in the production and consumption of services are also attributed towards alterations in Fordist regimes of accumulation and regulation. This is also true in analyses of global tourism. Within tourism Fordism is usually associated with mass tourism – the wholesale creation of standard, packaged tourist products (the all-inclusive beach or resort packages sold to the Caribbean or Mediterranean are good examples) by large firms. Such firms practise vertical and horizontal integration, seeking to increase their size relative to other firms and to establish industrial dominance. In the hotel sector this most commonly takes place through the extension of subsidiaries. In this manner some of the world's largest hotel chains (e.g. Best Western, Accor, Sheraton and Hilton) have a commanding share of the global resort market. Such firms fortify their market eminence through aggressive and comprehensive marketing and branding. The advent of information technology and advance booking networks such as Computer Reservation Systems (CRS) and Global Distribution Systems (GDS) have enabled very large firms to strengthen their global position.

Lowered production costs and narrower profit margins necessitate higher volumes and spatial concentration. As such Fordist practices are generally associated with high-impact, ecologically damaging tourism (Mowforth and Munt, 1998) that in the resort model, establish enclaves that are cut off from the remainder of host societies, both in the procurement of tourist products and in tourists' contact with hosts (e.g. Britton, 1982). In the Fordist frame, in addition, labour is generally employed to satisfy fixed production schedules. Aspects such as worker training and the pliant use of labour are limited (Ioannides and Debbage, 1998). In this context, Fordist or mass tourism is generally viewed to possess all the negative features criticised by proponents of alternative or sustainable tourism discussed above.

Indeed, there is a close connection between purported shifts towards neo- or post-Fordism in tourism and changed consciousness regarding desirable tourist practices over the past two decades. Many authors have explained the rise and popularity of alternative tourist forms as the direct consequence of changes in consumption patterns. According to some (e.g. Poon, 1993) this is related to changes towards neo-Fordist consumption in Western societies. Urry (1995: 151) characterises such changes as a greater degree of individualisation; a greater preference for smaller/non-mass forms of consumption; and consumption being less about serving a function, but undertaken for its aesthetic value.

Many authors (e.g. Ioannides and Debbage, 1998; Gottdiener, 2000) argue that shifts in consumer tastes have in turn prompted changes in what tourism producers offer. From a production aspect, this involves a greater degree of market segmentation and of lifestyle marketing. Where the production of the mass tourist product focused on standardisation (the creation and selling of a set product), the establishment of economies of scale and horizontal and vertical integration, neo-Fordism is characterised by flexible production schedules and goods and niche marketing (Ioannides and Debbage, 1998: 102). Rather than the beach-hotel-charter flight product common to mass or Fordist tourism, neo-or post-Fordism is characterised by multiple goods produced by a variety of firms (supposedly) to the satisfaction of individual tourists' desires. While in Fordist tourism, producers dominate consumers, in neo- or post-Fordism it is the other way around. The emphasis is on the provision of a plurality of tourist products to meet the demands of a heterogeneous body of consumers. In industrial form, neo/post-Fordism also substantially differs from Fordism. Vertical disintegration, the focusing of production activities on only the final product, and outsourcing or subcontracting secondary activities to outside firms, is seen to be an increased consequence of flexible specialisation (Mowforth and Munt, 1998). The adaptation of certain Fordist techniques, such as franchising in the place of subsidiarising, means more flexible ownership structures, allowing firms to create niche brands aimed at capturing different subsets of consumers. In the hotel sector, for instance, many larger hotels have calibrated their product into different brands, with some targeted at the higher end, and others the lower end of the market. The range of differential hotel standards linked to the global Accor brand is a good example of this. In South Africa, some of the largest domestic hotel groups have also differentiated their brand, offering both luxurious, boutique hotels that are more expensive, and a range of basic, serviced hotels aimed at lower-yielding clients (see discussion in Chapter 4). It is today also a common international practice for hotels to have laundry, cleaning and even gastronomy services outsourced. In addition, the supple use of CRS and GDS enable smaller intermediaries and producers to enter the international tourism market, where since the 1960s large multinational corporations have been dominant (Williams and Shaw, 1998).

Consolidation and homogenisation The contended shift from Fordism to neo- or post-Fordism in tourism is encased in a specific grasp of the link between producers and consumers. And while analysing international tourism from the theoretical vantage point of flexibility has gained favour among scholars over the past few years, this disregards the fact that mass forms of tourism production and consumption remain predominant, and still constitute the larger economy (Ioannides and Debbage, 1998; Shaw and Williams, 2002). Moreover, if anything, globalisation has had the effect of increasing the significance in international tourism of larger, often transnational corporations. This is underscored by the extensive degree of consolidation among larger firms over the past decade. The trend towards very large travel firms merging, or buying up smaller firms has been particularly marked in the tour operator sector (Ioannides, 1998). In recent years, the West European market has become increasingly integrated and dominated by multinationals. For example, in 2000 Preussag, the owner of German operator Tui bought up the British Thomson Group, so forming the largest tour operator in Western Europe. Later that year it continued its positioning in the West European market by acquiring a 34,4 per cent share in Nouvelles Frontierès, the largest travel and tour operator in France (FVW Online, 11 October 2000). Tui has continued its path of consolidation to become the world's leading tour operator. In 2004 the Tui Group – which encompasses tourism business, shipping and other transport activities – saw a collective turnover of 180 billion Euro. The firm is also Europe's top leisure hotelier, owning in 2004 more than 163 000 beds in 285 hotels.

In the airline sector horizontal mergers have been a long-standing trend. In the 1990s, for instance British Airways gained part ownership of several other, smaller European airlines. The impact of 9/11 had been particularly severe on some airlines, and the airline sector had since been considerably reshaped. One of the most significant horizontal mergers was that between Air France and the Dutch airline, KLM during 2004. This had not only produced one of the largest air operators, but also created one of the largest distribution networks and cooperation alliances. More recently, during the first quarter of 2005 Lufthansa, the German national carrier acquired Swiss International Air Lines (formerly Swissair), a carrier that had been harshly affected by the turmoil created after 9/11. The European aviation market had seen significant restructuring since 2001. A generally more competitive environment following in the wake of 9/11, as confidence in air travel declined for a while, and the strong growth and subsequent success of low-cost airlines such as Rynair or Easy Jet has prompted a strong movement among some of Europe's largest national carriers to consolidate their positions. While this has involved the buy-up of financially weaker firms, it has also entailed an attempt to extend market share through the establishment of airline alliances.

Horizontal mergers are key mechanisms by which firms seek to improve their competitive advantage and gain market share. Other motivations include acquiring access to other firms' technology, augmenting research and development divisions and broadening product offer (Shaw and Williams, 2004). Globally, increased trends towards horizontal mergers in particularly the tour operator sector had led to the emergence of a few dominant firms. In specific markets such tour operators can have a significant influence on the types of product that are sold and patterns of consumption (Britton, 1991). Chapter 4 discusses how consolidation in both South Africa's tour operator sector and in that of key source overseas markets, shapes the basis of competition, with typically, large firms having more weight. In the case of South Africa the dominance of certain tour operators extends to the larger production system and impacts on aspects such as tourism prices in the hotel and car rental sector.

In a wider context trends of consolidation have, amongst others, had important homogenising influences on international tourism, since, for the transnational corporations, catering for the post-modern tourist still means standardisation. Paradoxically, therefore, as tourists are increasingly able to travel to many different parts of the globe, and with the purpose of exploring the less known, the 'Other', or that which is different, what is offered as tourist product is increasingly similar all over the world. Contexts and landscapes may for instance change, but the concepts are very similar. Such a dynamic is evident in representations of South Africa, where most international tour operators continue to project a staid tourist image of the country (Chapter 5).

Strong trends toward homogenisation show out the shortcomings of adopting a polarised view of Fordism and neo/post-Fordism in tourism. Many practices that generally are deemed neo or post-Fordist in character also exist in Fordist forms (Ioannides and Debbage, 1998; Torres, 2002). Flexibility in typical Fordist markets, such as in the expanded provision of product choices or elements of alternative tourism (e.g. a visit to a cultural village as part of a package tour) indicates that rather than being in decline, Fordism is practised in an adapted form in today's global market. Mass tourism mostly displays elements of both Fordism and neo/post-Fordism with the overall mass tourist product containing clusters of niche products (e.g. Ritzer, 1998).

Tourist production forms have been significantly influenced by factors of globalisation. Regardless of whether the impetus for changes in production lie in changed consumption patterns, or whether it is producers proactively shaping consumption, an important effect of globalisation is that it has brought the producer-consumer nexus even closer. For instance, the time taken to travel to a destination is much less, which means that more engagement can take place between consumers and (local) producers, and the proliferation of media coverage of the world's destinations means that visual consumption is possible for a far greater number of people. In addition, factors of globalisation, particularly changes in the availability and extent of technology, enable firms to ply a variety of production means and to access highly differential markets. Globalisation has an important influence on the shape of global tourism production and consumption.

Globalisation, Tourism Policy and Governance

One of the major components of the book is an analysis of governance in the global tourism system and its relation to tourism development. The focus is on forms of self-regulation within the production system (Chapter 4), the impact of overarching institutions of regulation and on the role of the state (Chapter 6).

Changing objectives of governance and tourism policy-making To date, both actors and structures of regulation have received scant attention in tourism analysis (Pearce, 1995). The role of the state, in particular, has been neglected (Richter, 1989; Clancy, 1999; C. Hall, 1994b). The state is an important element of tourism governance, both in a national context – through tourism policy making – and at an international level – as a participant in global regulatory regimes. Shaw and Williams (2004: 36-40) identify several means through which the state is a pivotal agent of regulation. It is a major point of intercession with the global economy which involves creating the framework within which firms operate and engage with others and in which international movement can occur. The state also helps to shape tourism production and consumption, both by providing the legal and policy frame (through consumer and labour legislation) and in shaping the wider environments (through macro-economic policies or political goals) within which tourism activities occur.

In the era of globalisation both the mediating influence of the state and the goals the state pursues, have changed. Rather than signifying the demise of the state, as argued by some, it suggests that the state had reoriented itself in the global political economy to contend with new forms of constrictions (Strange, 1996; Weiss, 1998). Perhaps one of the most significant manifestations of this is the strong emphasis that has come to be placed on raising the competitiveness of a given location and changed governance objectives that are tied to this. Cerny (1990; 2003) has characterised changing goals for the national state in the face of the contraction of its regulatory, productive and redistributive powers and functions, as the rise of the competition state, where national policy-making and regulatory regimes are geared towards positioning a given state favourably in the global economy. The residual state is one that adapts to an international environment which offers more limited opportunities for the state to fulfil its regulatory and arbitrating functions (Cerny, 2003). But challenges brought on by globalisation to the traditional powers of the state have also led to a fundamental recalibration of political authority, with government actors on a sub-national level emerging as new loci of power (e.g. Brenner, Jessop, Jones and Macleod, 2003). Brenner (2004) contends that this has led to a 'rescaling' of the national state with sub-national policy-making becoming the new domain through which the state institutionally engages with the international system. Shaped by the dominance of the discourse of neo-liberalism, urban, regional and national authorities are focused on increasing the economic and other attractiveness of their areas.[9] Harvey (1989) defined this as the shift from managerialism to entrepreneurialism among governance actors. Entrepreneurial governance takes various forms, and common policies and strategies that are undertaken may include Local Economic Development initiatives, the promotion of certain economic activities as key competitive sectors and efforts to (re-)image or (re-)brand a city to increase its allure to potential investors. Tourism usually plays an important role in this.

Tourism is a key focus of the 'entrepreneurial city' (Jessop, 1997) and 'tourism enhancement' has become an important Local Economic Development and urban regeneration strategy in many regions (Law, 1994; Beauregard, 1998). A common feature is the development of urban theme or entertainment parks or the redevelopment of harbour areas into tourist destinations (Fainstein and Judd, 1999). As will be discussed in Chapter 3, the Waterfront development of South Africa – the refurbishment of the dilapidated and underused harbour on Cape Town's Atlantic seaboard – has become one of the key elements of the country's tourist product. A rising body of literature criticises such developments that take place in most international cities, as the 'themisation of public space' (e.g. Zukin, 1995; Craik, 1997; Ritzer and Liska, 1997), geared towards voyeuristic tourist consumption (Marks and Bezzoli, 2001). Nonetheless, many public policies aim at developing themed leisure sites as an aspect of tourism development (Beauregard, 1998).

Second, the economic, infrastructural and publicity spin-offs that the hosting of mega-events such as the Olympic Games, or other major sports events are perceived to hold for a city or country, makes bidding for it an increasingly common aspect of government policies (Black and Van der Westhuizen, 2004; Chalip and Leyns, 2002). The focus is mainly on luring the global capital tied to such events – most notably in the form of multinational broadcasting firms – and on getting global exposure. As a whole the sport spectator industry – in markets such as the USA this is mainly centred on baseball and American football, while in Europe and other parts of the world football (or soccer) is the largest spectator sport – has become extensively tied to tourism and tourism development policies (Euchner, 1999).

The so-called Meetings, Incentive, Conferences and Exhibitions (MICE) market is a further focus of entrepreneurial governance policies (Fainstein and Judd, 1999). Increased travel for purposes other than leisure, such as business or the attendance of conferences, and the expansion of such travel over international boundaries, has contributed to the growth of the international MICE market. In an effort to capture this market, and also as a means to boost development many cities are attempting to develop themselves into convention cities, and the competition for the international MICE market is very intense (Judd, 1999; Fainstein and Gladstone, 1999). While the construction of large, national convention centres has been a common activity in Western Europe and North America since the late 1980s, an increasing awareness of the economic value of travel tied to meetings or conferences, has produced a more intense pursuit of the capital linked to such travel (Weber and Chon, 2002). Today, MICE has developed into an industry in its own right, with diversification of specialist producers – such as event organisers – globalised markets and professional standardisation characterising it. It has also become more extensively influenced by large multinational firms who dominate the global provision of MICE services. One example of a firm that is influential in the European MICE market is the Dutch group, Amsterdam RAI. This firm specialises in organising and hosting conferences and exhibitions on behalf of third parties. It is active in much of Northern Europe and in key Asian markets such as Bangkok and Turkey. In 2000 it expanded into the South African market when it was selected to build and operate the Cape Town International Convention Centre. Most cities and countries seriously pursuing the development of a strong tourism sector, allocate some public resources to the building out of the local MICE sector, and the infrastructure tied to that. In the South African case, it is for instance significant that the country's three largest and economically most important cities (Johannesburg, Cape Town and Durban) have all invested considerable volumes in the construction of convention centres since the late 1990s.

Overall, there is a strong convergence in urban, regional and national policy-making about the need to raise such areas' competitiveness. Furthermore, notions about the commodification of culture and leisure and variation in the consumption of cultural and leisure goods, have led governance in cities to be increasingly geared towards making them sites of consumption and at capturing the capital tied to cultural commodities (Sassen and Roost, 1999). This is also true at national levels, where to a significant degree, tourism development in national policies aims at profiling the distinctiveness of a country vis-à-vis others.

While all of these various factors are widely viewed as important elements in tourism development, there has been little in the way in tourism analysis of systematically investigating the wider structural motivations for the adoption of such tourism policies nor what consequences such policies could have. With respect to sport mega-events, for instance, it is widely accepted that the expected economic returns seldom materialise, with costs often far outweighing revenue (e.g. in the 1976 Montreal Olympics, the 1994 Lillehammer Winter Olympics, and the 1996 Atlanta Games) (Teigland, 1999; Hiller, 2000). The tourism consequences of such events are also not well known (Hiller, 2000).

Further, despite the similarities in tourism development objectives across developed and developing contexts, and the ubiquity today of policies aimed at making destinations leisure capitals, developing countries often do not share extensively in the global market. Instead, they remain in what Turner and Ash (1975) have designated as the international 'pleasure periphery', where they stand separate from the industrialised core, but are used for its leisure pursuits. Increasingly, under today's logic of competitiveness, not being part of this, even peripherally, is simply not an option for governments. It is within this framework that tourism development pursuits should be analysed.

Tourism institutions On a broader level, globalisation has had important effects on the institutional framework of tourism. In the first instance, most international tourism governance has traditionally taken place through intergovernmental organisations (see the overview in Chapter 6 of the organisations that make up international tourism regulation). The state has therefore been one of the prime tourism mediators on an international level. On a national level states also develop several institutional measures for the domestic regulation of tourism. Globalisation however has started to reduce states' participation in many of the most important international regulatory institutions.

Second, a range of new institutional actors that straddle different policy spheres (i.e. local, national, international) is present in tourism planning, policy-making and implementation. This can be seen in the composition of national Destination Marketing Organisations, or urban boosterist projects that usually are public-private initiatives. C. Hall (2001) notes that tourism is a highly distinctive 'intermestic' policy issue, i.e. it overlaps various tiers of governance, and importantly, requires coordination and formulation at all of these levels.

Third, globalisation produces the need for the establishment of 'international and supranational regimes to govern particular fields of action' (C. Hall, 2001: 23). In global tourism the international aviation regime has long been the most significant aspect of tourism regulation (Clancy, 2002b). Since the end of the 1990s, however, the liberalisation of trade in services under the General Agreement on Services (GATS) of the World Trade Organisation has become an important factor, not only in global tourism governance, but also production (Fayos-Solà and Bueno, 2001). Chapter 6 focuses on how global tourism will be impacted on by changed governance structures.

Although not always readily apparent, the institutional context within which tourism production takes place is very important. Institutions to a large degree shape the contours of tourism, and have a significant influence on production and development outcomes.

Given that tourism is a multifaceted activity that straddles many different sectors, institutions – both state and non-state – play a central role of regulation and coordination in the tourism system. Such institutions also have fundamental impacts on the tourism production process, either as producers themselves, or as sources of pressure, lobbying, or harmonisation in the tourism system. As such, institutions both directly and indirectly determine the parameters within which tourism as an activity takes place, and relatedly, influence the developmental consequences of tourism.

Conclusion

Tourism and its developmental impact can be viewed from several theoretical vantages. There are three main theoretical approaches to international tourism.

Traditionally modernisation and dependency perspectives have dominated tourism scholarship, although tourism has increasingly been framed within emerging discourses of alternative, sustainable and community tourism. None of these theoretical bodies provides satisfactory sets of tools with which to analyse tourism's role in development in the contemporary era. Globalisation has had major impacts on global forms of tourism production and consumption and has come to significantly reshape the relationship between tourism and development. The environment within which national tourism policy making occurs, for instance, has been affected in important ways. The global governance of tourism, further, has to be viewed with respect to the continuous interaction that occurs between actors at local, global and intermediate levels and the challenges that arise from such a complex form of engagement.

Notes

[1] Rostow proposes that the developmental process is a linear, progressive one, whereby all societies characteristically evolve from a traditional to a modern state (Rostow, 1960: 2). He postulates five stages of growth – the traditional society; the preconditions for take-off; the take-off; the drive to maturity; and the age of high mass consumption (Rostow, 1960). Traditional societies have low levels of industrialisation and economic production and interaction. They are highly stratified and hierarchical, with restricted upward social mobility. Social status is often achieved through ascription rather than performance, and authority usually lies with large agricultural (land)owners. The second stage of growth starts with a loosening of the cultural and social institutions that preclude any economic advancement in traditional societies. According to Rostow this transition towards modernisation may arise either endogenously with the creation and consolidation of centralised political authority in the form of a nation-state, or, in the case of colonialism, for example, may be induced by the entrance of more developed societies into traditional environments. The third stage of take-off involves the expansion of economic activities, technological developments, and increased income and savings that finance further development. The fourth stage sees a consolidation of this economic expansion. Rostow defines this stage of maturity as 'the stage in which an economy demonstrates the capacity to move beyond the original industries which powered its take-off and to absorb and to apply over a very wide range of its resources the most advanced fruits of modern technology' (p10). This is eclipsed by the final stage of high mass consumption, characterised by high levels of income and consumption (beyond basic needs such as food or shelter), and a growth in both the urban, and services-sector population. Modern societies are marked by technological advance and a high degree of economic integration. They are characterised by an authority structure where a plurality of social bodies vie for economic and physical resources. This makes for a greater level of competition and allows for social achievement through performance. These features, in turn create an environment of constant change and progress (Weiner, 1966).

[2] The dependency perspective derives from Marxist theory. In the earlier part of the twentieth century Immanuel Wallerstein built on the Marxist tradition to postulate a world-system. This is a concept that describes the economic and political division of power among states in the world. The world-system is composed of two main structures: a capitalist core, characterised by an integrated economy and high productivity; and a

periphery, where capitalist development is not as penetrated. The world-system consists of a division of labour where the core mainly produces manufactured goods and the periphery mainly raw materials, and where there is an exchange of such commodities between the two. In the case of the periphery, those economic sectors involved in the production of raw materials are externally focused, and poorly integrated with the remainder of the home sectors. There is generally a high level of reliance on imports from the core. In the 1960s and 1970s a number of theorists further developed Wallerstein's core-periphery postulate, and formulated the dependency theory. First geared towards explaining economic underdevelopment in South America (e.g Frank, 1967) the dependency theory had gained broad currency by the 1970s. Dependency theorists hold that the international political and economic system is characterised by a number of core capitalist countries that dominate and direct activities in this system, and countries in the periphery who, through (characteristically) dependent economic relations with the core are drawn into the system. This prevents periphery countries from developing sovereign economic bases upon which development can occur (Frank, 1967; Valenzuela and Valenzuela, 1978).

[3] This is despite the fact that the bulk of tourist activity and earnings in most countries of the South are generated by domestic and regional tourism. Ghimire (2001: 1) for instance notes that in 1998, 55 per cent of tourism in the Association of Southeast Nations (ASEAN) region, 73 per cent of Southern African tourism, and more than 70 per cent of tourist activity in the Mercosur area, originated from within the respective regions.

[4] Both the modernisation and dependency approaches can be criticised on a number of counts. First, by claiming that development involves the shift from tradition to modernity, a process that is seen as linear and natural, or, one that could be induced through exogenous stimuli such as international tourism, the modernisation approach reduces development to the attainment of certain cultural systems and values. In its most vulgar form it equates economic advance with westernisation. Similarly, the core-periphery model that forms the basis of the dependency perspective is a simplified conception of international economic and social exchange, particularly in countries of the South, where societies are portrayed as dependent and reactive. Its depiction of the international capitalist system in addition, does not fully capture the complexity of it, which has come to be defined less by a crude functional division between 'developed' and 'developing' and a one-ward flow of production and goods, and is instead characterised by a greater degree of interdependency. Finally, as argued by Opperman (1993), by focusing exclusively on mass and international tourism, the dependency perspective overlooks important components of many countries' tourism markets (e.g. free, independent travellers).

[5] Critics charge that there exists as many definitions for the concept as possible strategies. In addition, dominant conceptions of sustainable development often do not take account of the influence of inherently unequal social relations within and among societies, causing 'sustainability' to be an ever-elusive goal (Blowers and Pain, 1999; Mowforth and Munt, 1998).

[6] The distinction between mass and alternative tourism is not clear-cut however. Mass tourist forms such as all-inclusive beach vacation packages may also be said to be spatially concentrated. Similarly, many of the tourist products generally subsumed under the term alternative tourism, such as safari or nature-based tours, can also be sold as part of a mass tourist package. Alternative tourism seeks to distinguish itself on the basis that it is founded on certain ethical and practical principles that are deficient in mass tourism, and moreover a response to the shortcomings of mass tourism.

[7] Richtersveld, a large mountainous desert biome, and populated mainly by communities of Nama descent, was first established by the South African government in 1991,

initially with the aim of extending the national conservation system without the government having to incur large investment costs.

8 Although, since its establishment very little joint or co-management has in fact occurred in the park (e.g Boonzaaier, 1996).

9 One strand of the globalisation discourse focuses on the effect of globalisation on the geography of international capitalism, and, specifically, the salience of urban regions and cities in the world economy. The *world city/global city* perspective is a broad-spanning theoretical frame and set of propositions that mainly derive from the field of economic geography. World city/global city theorists propose that shifts in the international economy is bringing about the territorial re-organisation of the world, with cities emerging as new economic centres, replacing the nation-state as unit and actor within the world economy (e.g. Friedmann and Wolff, 1982; Sassen, 1991, 1993). They posit a hierarchical scaling of cities, based on their level of incorporation into the world economy. *World or global cities* are identified as urban regions that hold large shares of world production activities, transnational corporations and financial institutions and consequently form industrial and technological nuclei in the international system (Sassen, 1991). Economic, technological, financial and transport linkages among these centres, it is argued, so constitute the global economy (Brenner, 1998), which may be typified as consisting of 'both a worldwide net of corporations and a global network of cities' (Feagin and Smith, 1987: 3). Sassen (1991, 1993) contends that global cities occupy a command position in the global economy. In addition, she argues that aside from constituting sites of international production, global cities such as New York, London and Tokyo also offer large consumer markets. World/global city theorists essentially propose a power shift in the international economic system, away from the nation-state as locus of decision-making to urban regions. According to Jessop (1997) this leads to the emergence of 'entrepeneurial cities', with regional and local authorities replacing national authorities as new power sites for economic development.

Chapter 3

South Africa's Tourist Sector
Patterns, Parameters and Paradoxes

Introduction

In March 2003, while many of the world's largest tourist destinations still suffered extensive setbacks from the September 11th attacks on the US World Trade Center, South African Tourism, the national tourism promotion agency proclaimed the country as 'the world's fastest-growing destination'. The reason was that while global tourism had fallen and international arrivals in regions such as the Americas had declined by 13m since 2001, as a direct consequence of the attacks, tourist arrivals from South Africa's main overseas markets (predominantly from Western Europe) had risen during 2002. In total, international arrivals increased by 20 per cent. According to the South African government, this heralded a new era for tourism growth.

This had followed a worrying period for the country's tourism sector, when after an initial boom in the mid-1990s with the end of institutionalised apartheid, the pace of growth had slackened. By the end of that decade tourism authorities had resigned themselves to a sector that seemingly had expanded too rapidly, and while not contracting, had started to plateau off.

Politically, the government had invested a great deal in tourism. It is seen as an important conduit through which foreign reserves could be increased, foreign and domestic investment boosted, and, given the relatively lower entry costs, employment created (DEAT, 1996). Tourism is also seen as an effective means through which South Africa could successfully enter and compete in the international economic system (DEATT, 2001). In all, it is regarded as a key catalyst for the economic growth that the government would like to attain to meet the country's developmental imperatives.

The unforeseen bolster following 9/11 emphasises the unpredictable nature of global tourism and throws into relief some of the most important aspects affecting South African tourism. Here is a country that possesses over factors such as natural beauty and an attractive landscape, and that had used these to establish itself favourably against other competitor destinations. Qualities such as exoticism – as an African location – and a unique political history further distinguish it as a tourism locale. Yet South Africa has been subjected to the uneven rhythms of global tourism, and while it was political stability and distance from terrorist campaigns that advanced its popularity as an arrivals destination post-9/11, it was precisely the presence of these factors that stymied growth only a few years before:

between 1998 and 2000, for instance, a series of more than 20 bomb blasts linked to a domestic vigilante group, some of them at South Africa's prime international tourist attractions, was one of the factors that negatively affected the country's tourist sector.

The ebb and flow of South African tourism over the past ten years is very similar to the patterns seen in many other developing countries who along with having to contend with the capricious effects of exogenous factors, also have to negotiate the unpredictability of outcomes in the global tourism production system.[1] Unequal power relations exist among producers within this system and generally it is developing countries that have less recourse to influence the direction of producer interaction.

This chapter provides an overview of the South African tourism sector and its location in the global system. It focuses on the key growth and policy trends that have characterised the sector since 1994 and the various obstacles the sector had faced. Tourism policy places great emphasis on increasing South Africa's share of the world market, while at the same time it aims to develop a sector that contributes to the country's economic development and enables economic and social empowerment and upliftment. Strictures set by its location in the larger international system and the influence of external factors have however meant that the government has been significantly constrained in the attainment of its policy goals. The context within which tourism development occurs furthermore – contending with the spatial, economic and racial imprint left by apartheid planning – constitutes a further difficulty.

The first part of the chapter sketches the background to South Africa's post-apartheid tourism development and reviews central policy objectives. The second part reviews patterns in the country's international tourism markets and the parameters that have shaped tourism growth. The third discusses some of the main opportunities and challenges for further development.

Tourism in Post-Apartheid South Africa

The Context

As a country South Africa is characterised by many distinctions – concerning its topography and ecology and its historical, political and social features – that set it apart from many other countries, and provide it with many unique tourist attractions.

Geographically, the country's location at the southern end of the African continent and at the confluence of two major oceans has led to, in recent years state and business entities setting out to market the country as the 'gateway to Africa'. This is in marked contrast to the apartheid era when, as part of the apartheid ideology, authorities sought to develop South Africa as an European enclave in the African continent. Their orientation, and up until the mid-1980s when large-scale international sanctions were imposed on the country, political links were predominantly with Western Europe and North America. The end of apartheid has seen greater emphasis being placed within South Africa on establishing firm diplomatic and economic linkages with African counterparts and on promoting an international standing as an African country.

Topographically the country has four major landscapes: a vast expanse of arid and semi-arid plains that constitutes the interior, and covers the largest area of the country's 1 219 912 km²; a narrow coastal strip that extends from the Atlantic Ocean in the west and southwest of the country to the Indian Ocean in the east; a large series of mountain belts – the escarpment – that run parallel to the coastline and separates the coast from the interior; and an extensive sub-tropical region that covers the northeast expanses of the country. Along the southwest a Mediterranean climate reigns with mild winters and regular winter rainfall. The interior is mainly drier with a harsher climate, while the north and eastern parts of the country have more temperate climates. Together these geographic and climatic features significantly determine human settlement and economic activity, with the vast, dry interior (the Karoo and Kalahari regions) being sparsely populated.

The political transformation that took place with the end of institutionalised apartheid (signified with the holding of the first democratic elections in April 1994) also had geographical bearing, as the establishment of a quasi- or weak federal political system, constituted of a central government and sub-central or provincial entities, led to political boundaries within the country being reshaped. From the four provinces (the Cape Province, Natal, Witwatersrand and the Orange Free State) that were created during the earlier part of the twentieth century, nine new provinces came into existence after 1994 (see Figure 3.1 below). As laid out in the post-apartheid Constitution (Republic of South Africa, 1996) the provinces share a number of fiscal and other concurrent functions with the national government. Tourism is one such sphere where provincial governments have limited autonomy and legislative capacities.

The country has a number of geographical features that provide it with a unique placing in the global tourism market. The Western Cape province, for instance, is distinguished by its natural vegetation, fynbos. Fynbos mainly consists of small shrubs and herbaceous plants and bulbs (most famous of which is the protea flower). This vegetation is endemic to the southwestern Cape region; it indeed uniquely occurs here. The Cape Floristic Region covers 35 per cent of the Western Cape and has the richest known density of flora in the world (Wesgro/KPMG, 1998). The vegetation, along with other physical features such as Cape Agulhas (the southernmost point of the African continent) and the province's mountain ranges, constitute important natural attractions to visitors. On the whole, as will be discussed at greater length below, the Western Cape is one of South Africa's prime international tourist regions. Other major regions include Mpumalanga (which houses most of the country's state and private game reserves, and where the vast Kruger National Park is located), Kwazulu-Natal, and Gauteng. Johannesburg, Durban and Cape Town, the most populous and economically largest urban regions, are also the country's three main tourist cities.

The country has sought to gain a great deal of international mileage from its recent political past and relatively peaceful transition to democracy since the early 1990s. This has found reflection in a burly post-apartheid foreign policy orientation and attempts to promote itself as a global leader. Most of this is built on a strong moral identity and positioning as a leading example of African democratisation. This has also strongly infused the development of South Africa's tourism sector and determined the tone of its international expansion since 1994.

Figure 3.1 Political geography of South Africa

As in most other developing countries, tourism has gained a great deal of attention in post-apartheid South Africa.[2] Unlike many others, however, the context within which tourism development is being pursued is one where the government seeks to help engender the emergence of a new society. Post-apartheid governance has primarily been concerned with addressing some of the stark socio-political and socio-economic impacts of apartheid legislation and planning. Poverty alleviation, economic growth, employment creation, development, and of late, empowerment have been some of the principal goals of national governance since 1994 and have found reflection in most policy documents. Alongside this, more comprehensive social objectives have included nation building, racial integration and social cohesion.

As such tourism development goals have been of a very particular nature. First, recognising that tourism can contribute to economic development, the government has sought to build out the sector. This has included expanding the existing physical, financial and business infrastructure, for while tourism during the apartheid era was rather limited in its international and domestic penetration (for the former due to the levying of sanctions in the mid-1980s, and for the latter, due to an active focus on the white population), South Africa had still built up a sizeable sector, that internationally, carried a fair level of brand awareness. In this way several attractions (such as Table Mountain, Kruger National Park, Cape Point) have long been marketed internationally, often by large South African hotel firms, and have become important tourism icons. On such available visibility and existing resources and capital, the government was keen to develop a sector that could capitalise on the upswing that had been experienced globally.

Tourism development policy is encapsulated in the national *White Paper on the Development and Promotion of Tourism in South Africa* (DEAT, 1996).[3] Although dated, this White Paper remains the core expression of the government's central tourism objectives. It attempts to formulate a tourism policy through which both economic growth and development can be attained in South Africa. Tourism is seen as a crucial means through which the South African government's economic and social development objectives, contained in the Reconstruction and Development Programme (specifically, meeting basic needs, developing human resources, building the economy, and the democratisation of state and society) (Republic of South Africa, 1994) can be attained.[4] A key objective of the national policy is to foster 'responsible tourism', defined as,

> tourism that promotes responsibility to the environment through its sustainable use; responsibility to involve local communities in the tourism industry; responsibility for the safety and security of visitors and responsible government, employees, employers, unions and local communities (DEAT, 1996).

Towards this, the following principles underlie national policy:

- that tourism should be private-sector driven, although the government should facilitate tourism development by ensuring an enabling environment;
- that tourism growth and development should be based on 'effective community development';
- 'sustainable environmental practices' should direct tourism development;
- co-operation between stakeholders nationally and within the Southern African region should steer targets and programmes;
- and that tourism should be a means to economically empower 'previously neglected communities', and in particular women (DEAT, 1996).

At the same time the government wants to transform the tourism sector. This mainly entails increasing the access of groups previously excluded, not only from tourism production, but also consumption, and of enlarging the developmental impact of tourism. In the apartheid era tourist activities were mainly undertaken by white, middle-to-upper income groups (Koch and Massyn, 2001). Post-apartheid policy has been focused on increasing tourist consumption by blacks, and particularly to encourage the emergence of black tourism producers.

In 2002 these goals were articulated in the government's 'Responsible Tourism Guidelines' (DEAT, 2002a), a document that sought to lay out ways of reaching the objectives of the 1996 White Paper in terms of the 'triple bottom line of sustainable development', (i.e. economic, environmental and social sustainability). Guidelines are provided to the private sector towards practising responsible tourism and providing opportunities to local communities. These are: to establish partnerships and joint ventures with communities in which the latter have meaningful participation and equity; to buy and use as far as possible locally made goods and services available within a 50km radius (this is to increase by 20 per cent over three years); and to recruit and employ staff as far as possible from local communities (i.e. within 20km of the enterprise) (DEAT, 2002a).

The distribution of tourism's benefits has been quite restricted with few available opportunities for previously excluded groups. This partly stems from a very particular spatial patterning of tourism development prior to 1994. Thus, as a further goal the government has set out to spread the economic impact of tourism. This has been conceptualised in several different ways, but has centred on encouraging the development of new products that, in the context of South Africa's traditional icons, posed alternative options and easier access for the country's black population. The promotion of 'township' and cultural tourism has been one of the main vehicles in this regard (DEAT, 2002b). Yet biases attached to township tours, incongruity between the preferences of international tourists, who have been the main target group of promotional campaigns, and product offers and often inadequate support by the government has meant that limited developmental success has to date been attained with this form of tourism (see for instance Goudie, Khan and Kilian, 1999; Thomas, 2005).

In the same way, tourism's spatial structure has not changed significantly over the past decade and travel flows have remained roughly the same. As the discussion later in the chapter and other parts of the book will show this is largely due to factors such as limited international promotional campaigns and the entrenchment of a specific destination image, and a lack of investment in lesser-visited tourism locales.

One area where South Africa has had a measure of success, and which impacts in an important way on its tourism sector, is its involvement in campaigns to host major international events. Since 1994 the country has hosted or bid to host a series of high profile events. This includes its hosting of the World Conference Against Racism, Racial Intolerance, Xenophobia and Related Intolerance in 2001 and the World Summit on Sustainable Development in 2002. Both UN conferences, they constituted a means for the country not only to attempt to position itself in the global MICE market, but also in the context of some of its larger foreign policy goals, enabled the country to showcase itself diplomatically.[5]

A political motivation also underlies South Africa's attempts to host large (or mega-) sports events. Sport has long been targeted as an important social force (Black and Nauright, 1998; Aleghi, 2004) and South Africa's hosting of and victory in the Rugby World Cup of 1995 and the Africa Cup of Nations the following year came at an important time in the country's nation-building project. A strong attempt to utilise the political spin-offs of mega-events also account for the country's bids to host the FIFA World Cup in 2006 and 2010 (Cornelissen, 2004b) and the failed bid for the 2004 Olympic Games (e.g. Hiller, 2000; Swart and Bob, 2004). Economic considerations and projections about a high level of international publicity, additional foreign and domestic investment and growth in strategic sectors such as tourism, were also key incentives.

To date, however, South Africa's experience in the holding of such events has shown that political factors can often overly direct their process and outcomes. For instance, South Africa's co-hosting of the 2003 Cricket World Cup with Zimbabwe and Kenya was geared to provide the other two African countries some opportunity to share in the economic and tourism benefits. However, a political fracas surrounding Zimbabwe and recent terror attacks in Kenya, leading to the cancellation of some of their scheduled matches, meant that much of the expected economic spin-offs did not materialise for these two countries (see fuller discussion in Chapter 7).

Sustained activity around mega-events over the past number of years seems to indicate that South Africa is driving a distinct strategy, aiming to participate as far as possible in the global mega-events industry. This could be beneficial for the country's tourism sector if it is orchestrated through a programme that encompasses targeted infrastructure development and investments. Market considerations, rather than political goals should be the prime determinants. Chapter 7 focuses more extensively on sport mega-events and their tourism facets.

Patterns in the South African Sector

The South African sector has without question experienced rapid growth over the past decade. The most important developments have occurred in its international sector, although domestic tourism has also seen significant expansion. Domestic tourism is indeed the mainstay of the South African tourism system. Up to 49 million domestic trips are undertaken, accounting for R47bn in tourist receipts (SA Tourism, 2004). International tourism is however a higher yield component, contributing R53.9bn in tourist receipts in 2003. It is in acknowledgement of this that post-apartheid policy has tended to place greater emphasis on international tourism development. Since this book is an analysis of South Africa's location in the global tourism system, its main focus is on the country's international markets. This is not to understate the importance of domestic tourism, which is in many regards the bedrock of the South African tourism economy.

The global context within which tourism growth in South Africa had occurred since 1994, was a major factor in this sector's expansion.

Trends in global tourism In world terms, international tourist arrivals have billowed over the past two decades. It indeed has more than doubled since 1985, from 327 million to 657 million in 1999 (WTO, 2000). The vast majority of international travel is intra-continental. Eighty-seven per cent of all European travel in 1998, for instance, was within the European continent (WTO, 2000). For long-haul international tourism, the direction of travel is overwhelmingly North-North, between the European continent and North America. Europe and North America account for the largest share of international tourist arrivals (WTO, 2000). These two regions also generate the greatest volume of international travel.

High growth in global tourism helped the South African sector to expand after 1994. The country also benefited from the so-called 'Mandela syndrome' – a high level of curiosity among potential visitors over the end of apartheid and the country's political transformation, strengthened by the prominence of former president Nelson Mandela. This had translated into significant development. In 1986, for instance, international tourist arrivals to South Africa tallied 645 000, or 0.2 per cent of world arrivals. By 2002 international visitor numbers to South Africa had risen to 6.42 million. In global terms, however, South Africa is a small player, taking less than one per cent of arrivals and ranking below the 40 top tourism earners.

South Africa as an African destination Within Africa, South Africa has become the main destination for international tourists, in 2002 receiving close to one-quarter of all arrivals. Africa's share of international tourism has risen over the past number of years; even so it is quite small, representing only 4.1 per cent of all international tourism in 2002. Table 3.1 illustrates Africa's position vis-à-vis other regional destinations.

Table 3.1 World tourism patterns

Region	Share of international tourist arrivals (%)				Share of international outbound tourism (%)			
	1990	1995	1999	2002	1990	1995	1999	2002
Africa	3.3	3.6	4.2	4.1	2.6	2.4	2.5	2.4
Americas	20.4	19.5	19.3	16.3	21.8	19.5	19.4	17.1
East Asia/Pacific	11.9	14.3	14.3	17.9	12.3	15.1	14.4	18.7
Europe	61.7	59.7	58.7	56.9	55.1	53.7	54.7	57.6
Middle East	2.0	2.2	2.7	4.0	1.4	1.3	1.4	2.3
South Asia	0.7	0.7	0.8	0.8	0.7	0.8	0.8	
Other countries*					6.1	7.2	6.7	1.9

* Country of origin not specified

Source: World Tourism Organisation, 2003

The main tourist attracting regions are Southern, Northern and East Africa. There has been a shift in balance among these regions over the past half-decade, as North and Southern Africa's share of continental tourism have steadily risen and that of East Africa has progressively fallen. Three countries however dominate the international tourism market for Africa. These are South Africa, Tunisia and Morocco. In 2002 they accounted for more than half of all international arrivals to the continent. Up until 2000 Zimbabwe was the fourth largest African destination (receiving in that year seven per cent of international arrivals), but the country's tourism sector has since rapidly declined. The reasons for this are discussed below.

South Africa's position as the top continental tourism destination marks a significant change from the previous two decades, when the country's international pariah status and related economic and diplomatic sanctions curtailed tourist numbers.

While its position as an African destination was underplayed during the apartheid era, South Africa has sought to capitalise on its geographical location since 1994. This has included accentuating its exoticism as an African destination to international markets, although this strategy had tended to go awry in the recent past, as the predominant tourist image of the African continent – emphasising negatives such as crime, poverty and political instability – often tended to detract, rather than promote tourism to the continent (Chapter 5). Negative international tourist imaging could have severe impacts on travel flows. This is demonstrated in the sharp downturn that Zimbabwe's tourism sector has seen in recent years due to the political standoff between the governing party, ZANU-PF and opposition groups, mainly led by the Movement for Democratic Change (MDC). Since the end of 1999 Zimbabwe has experienced a series of incidents that by 2001 had deepened into a political crisis. The wider context of the crisis is the emergence and steady growth of political opposition to the ZANU-PF regime and increased pressures for political change. This is partly built around conflict about a controversial land reform programme instituted by ZANU-PF which has entailed the expropriation and transfer of white-owned farms to black residents. The impact on Zimbabwe tourism has been severe, with tourist arrivals falling by more than one-tenth in 2000 (WTO, 2001). The sector has as yet had little recovery.

The case of Zimbabwe underlines the fact that the external environment in which national tourism systems functions can have a very significant impact on this system. Several international examples exist of the effect of exogenous factors such as political instability, crime and terrorism on the tourism system. Central to all of these is that risk, perceptions of risk, or the potential of risk significantly affect tourist demand and behaviour. Seddighi et al. (2001: 182) for instance argue:

> the way that bombings, coup d'etats, armed attacks, civil wars, attacks on tourists or even the probability of such occurrences, are perceived by tourists is the determinant factor which modulates tourist visitation and the travel behaviour of prospective holidaymakers.

In a comprehensive review of studies on the impact of terrorism and political instability, Sönmez (1998) highlights how tourists may be affected: by deciding not to travel; by travelling to another country ('destination substitution'); and by adopting risk-aversive travel patterns and behaviour in the affected destination.[6] Crime in destination countries is another factor that influences the tourism system and as discussed below, has played a major role in curbing tourist arrivals in South Africa.

South Africa's tourist sector is deeply locked into the wider travel circuit of Southern Africa. Most international tour packages, for instance, combine several Southern African destinations. For the most part this involves foreign tourists travelling from one principal attraction or location to another in the region. Such travel is generally built around core nature-based sites and large state-owned or private game reserves. Since the 1980s, the growing popularity of eco- and adventure tourism had led destinations such as Botswana, Malawi, Zambia, Zimbabwe and Tanzania to develop sizeable nature-based tourism economies, predominantly through strong linkages with overseas tour operators. These countries had for instance been able to establish themselves as prime international destinations for group-based, overland travel. This form of travel links various localities in Southern Africa and is generally sold by specialist operators. Since the end of apartheid, the Southern African travel circuit, as it is packaged and sold by tour operators, has become extended through the addition of a multitude of sites in South Africa.

Of late, South Africa has become the central tourism node within the Southern African region as overseas tour operators have on an increasing basis designed travel packages around destinations in the country. One of the key reasons is its level of infrastructural development and a relatively sophisticated transport network. An aggressive strategy by the national carrier, South African Airways (SAA), to establish itself continentally and the growth of Johannesburg International Airport has furthered the emergence of the country as a transportation hub for the remainder of the continent. Many connections between African capitals and other international locales now occur through Johannesburg. For instance, through subsidiaries of the South African carrier, SA Airlink and SA Express, flights exist to most Southern African capitals and other regional locations.

One of the most important continental linkages was created by the end of the 1990s with the establishment of a strategic partnership between SAA and the national carriers of Tanzania and Uganda who together founded SA Alliance Air. This alliance provides the South African airline with the infrastructure to operate to East African destinations. In this manner SAA is able to offer a broader network of African destinations to overseas visitors, and strengthen its position as regional carrier. In October 2000 SAA announced measures to extend its operations in East Africa through the introduction of three new flights per week to Entebbe, Uganda, and the increase of its flights to Zimbabwe. The latter action follows the cancellation of direct flights to Harare, the Zimbabwean capital by many major international carriers (such as Lufthansa) in the recent past.

SAA has also sought to extend its capacity to West Africa. While the West African region attracts far fewer international leisure tourist arrivals, it is an increasingly important business location, particularly for South African firms. Private sector expansion into West Africa has been accompanied by a greater penetration by SAA into the region with, over the years, flights introduced from Johannesburg to Cote d'Ivoire (Abidjan), Ghana (Accra) and Nigeria (Lagos). In 2004 SAA indicated its intention to enlarge its West African route network with the initiation of flights to the Malian capital, Bamako.

Despite such forms of expansion on the part of the South African carrier, civil aviation within Africa is notoriously underdeveloped. Few intra-continental flight connections exist and air transport between destinations is often very expensive. Factors that account for this include the design of infrastructure and transport routes by imperial powers overwhelmingly to serve colonial goals during the colonial era (which often meant the construction of roads and the development of ports with the sole aim of transporting raw materials and other resources from the African country to Western Europe), and in the post-independence era, a lack of interest and/or capital among African governments to strengthen intra-continental infrastructure linkages. Conflict in several parts of the continent have in addition severed some existing air transport ties (Ethiopian Airlines is one of the major African carriers whose service provision had vastly declined over the past years) or has hampered the progress of deepened connections. This means a major constraint on one of the supply facets of international travel and tourism to the continent, and the dominance of continental air transport by a few, usually external airlines. This creates, for instance, the absurd situation where travel between two neighbouring or proximate African locations takes place via an European hub (travelling from one capital to another in West Africa with Air France, for example, occurs most directly through a stopover in Paris; similarly few direct links exist between locations in Central, or East Africa). The consequence of this is that international tourism travel routes within the continent are fairly rigid. As early as 1986, concerned by a possible over-dependence on international tourism by African countries, and a lack of capacity by these countries to direct tourism travel favourable to their own economies, the United Nations Economic Commission for Africa (ECA) adopted a declaration to foster domestic and intra-regional tourism within the continent. Similar goals have in recent years been set by the African Union (formerly the Organisation of African Unity (OAU)). Yet tourism trade among African countries continues to be hampered by weak economies and the prohibitive costs of establishing aviation links.

It is within this context that South Africa's efforts to entrench itself as continental transport hub are significant. Even though this has meant some financial gains for the national carrier, there have been some important costs attached to this strategy. From a tourism perspective this has often meant that the country's international image has become centrally tied to that of the wider continent. Negative events in the Southern African region often affect the country's own tourism sector. Events in Zimbabwe over the past five years, for instance, had led South Africa, along with other Southern African states such as Botswana and Zambia to experience destination substitution effects.

The Southern African region also impacts on the country's tourism sector in another way, through collective tourism regulation within the Southern African Development Community (SADC), the regional intergovernmental organisation.[7] Through its tourism directorate, the SADC aims to homogenise tourism activities in the Southern African region. This entails the drafting of common tourism development goals (articulated in a Tourism Protocol), the pooling of tourism resources and collaboration on tourism production and marketing. The latter occurs through a marketing agency, the Regional Tourism Organisation of Southern Africa (RETOSA). Within the frame of the SADC, agreements on a common regional visa regime have been drawn up.

A further important regional initiative has been the establishment of transfrontier conservation parks or areas, where countries who share overlapping national parks, have bilaterally contracted to jointly manage these parks as single units and to remove physical and legal restrictions on the movement of human beings and animals within these parks. These entities are conceptually different – a transfrontier park is an area where different governments co-operate to manage conservation and other resources, and where physical barriers to human and animal movement between two separate parks are removed, while on the other hand, a transfrontier conservation area (TCA) is one where conservation activities of different statuses border each other (e.g. a national park bordering a private game reserve), and where countries or stakeholders agree to co-operate on common objectives, but international boundaries and limitations on movement remain intact. However both entities are manifestations of a particular approach to nature and wildlife management known as Transboundary Natural Resource Management (TBNRM). Marrying an array of ecological, environmentalist and economic discourses (see for instance Wolmer, 2003), TBNRM refers essentially to conservation programmes across national boundaries and that involves more than one government.

Objectives behind TBNRM are plentiful, but include goals such as rationalising natural resource use, obviating the impact on nature and wildlife of 'artificial' political borders, and as means to reduce conflict (the concept of 'peace parks' is for instance often associated with TBNRM, suggesting that through cooperation interstate divisions may be offset).[8]

In Southern Africa TBNRM has become an additional leg of regional initiatives aimed at pooling resources and drawing collective benefit from joint efforts. Combining nature conservation and tourism promotion is a key aim of such initiatives. SADC member states have for instance undertaken to establish a free trade area (FTA). Regional trade integration, including tourism trade, is the objective of the FTA. The 1999 SADC Protocol on Wildlife Conservation and Law Enforcement makes provision for cooperation on joint utilisation of wildlife resources. Further, the South African government, through its Spatial Development Initiative (SDI) programme, has also aimed to use infrastructural development to promote economic growth in the region. In one of the flagship SDI programmes, the Maputo Development Corridor, which entails the improvement of transport linkages and through that, an economic activity corridor between South Africa and

Mozambique, promoting local tourism development is a central goal (see for instance Rogerson, 2001; Söderbaum and Taylor, 2003).

Since the late 1990s three transfrontier parks have been established in Southern Africa – the Kgalagadi Tranfrontier Park between South Africa and Botswana (that merges the Kalahari Gemsbok National Park and the Gemsbok National Park), the Great Limpopo Transfrontier Park (that joins bordering parks and pristine ecological areas in South Africa, Zimbabwe and Mozambique) and the !Ais-!Ais/Richtersveld Transfrontier Park between Namibia and South Africa. Two transfrontier conservation areas have also been established, the Lubombo Transfrontier Conservation Area which joins several smaller conservation areas in SA, Swaziland and Mozambique, and the Maloti-Drakensberg Transfrontier Conservation Area between Lesotho and SA.[9]

While very large in scale and ambition the three tranfrontier parks have not lived up to many of the tourism development expectations. In the case of the Great Limpopo Transfrontier Park, for instance, a lack of proper conceptualisation and planning by state authorities has meant that the establishment of eco-tourism and community-based programmes has been slow. In more recent times political instability in Zimbabwe and mistrust on the part of the ZANU-PF government of the involvement of western donors and agencies (the USAID and the Peace Parks Foundation, an organisation set up by a wealthy South African, have been two of the park's important funders) has become a threat to the further expansion of initiatives in the park (Wolmer, 2003).

The !Ais-!Ais/Richtersveld Transfrontier Park, established in 2003 and adjoining the !Ais-!Ais Hotspring Game Park in Namibia with the Richtersveld National Park in SA, effectively aims to combine models of regional, transborder conservation with that of community conservation. As discussed in Chapter 2, the Richtersveld National Park is one of the largest and oldest cases of CBNRM in South Africa. Richtersveld itself however has been slow to deliver on many of the ambitious tourism development goals. Two factors have been responsible for this. First, the communal body initially set up to manage Richtersveld alongside SANParks has not been fully accepted by the entire community. Discord within the community on development programmes has hampered the progress of many tourism ventures. Second, the Richtersveld community has continually been embroiled in a land claim with the state. Part of their claim is for ownership over a major state-owned diamond mining operation. An extended legal conflict between the two parties on the one hand, and the lucrative compensation claimed for by the community (a total of 2.5bn Rand) on the other, have been complicating factors in the initiation of tourism development programmes. The complexities surrounding the CBNRM on a domestic level, has filtered into many of the regional objectives of the Transfrontier Park. The park is an example of the difficulties of combining regional and community conservation management models.

The South African international tourist product The South African tourist product is highly distinctive. This is firstly due to South Africa's position as a long-haul tourist destination. The distance, time and costs involved in travelling to South Africa mean that the market tends to be smaller than for short- or medium-haul destinations. South Africa's second distinction lies in its status as an African country, and the touristic appeal that is linked to this. The idiosyncrasies of South Africa's social and political history moreover makes it a very paradoxical destination: the fundamental attraction of the country resides in its geographical location on the African continent, and the opportunity it presents to the tourist who is interested in viewing and experiencing uniquely African features (in sum the vastly different landscape, peoples and cultures, and the wildlife). In this scheme South Africa is an exotic destination that offers the tourist the possibility to become an explorer and in many ways to refashion a romantic pioneering era. Historically, however, economic, political and social development of the country, to which the development and attraction of South Africa as an international tourist destination was closely related, tended to emphasise a distinct non-Africanness, a certain European familiarity about the destination. As a consequence the South African tourist product was one that was founded upon certain attractions, and the reputation of being 'a little Europe in Africa'. The political changes in the beginning of the 1990s have however meant that this needed to be altered.

Numerous characteristics set the country apart from many other international tourist destinations. First, since its attraction centres around natural, physical and social features such as landscape, wildlife and culture, the exploration of these forms a key component of the tourist product. Secondly, travellers spend a longer period of time in the country (on average two to three weeks).

Despite its otherwise natural appeal, South Africa is not regarded and sold as a large beach or resort destination. When leisure and vacationing do take place along the country's coastal regions, this is usually over a short period of time, and as part of visitors' larger tour of the country. This is in contrast to other African destinations, particularly North Africa, parts of southeast and East Africa (particularly Mozambique, Kenya, Tanzania and Zanzibar), and parts of West Africa where the sort of infrastructure for so-called stay-put vacationing has been well developed. This type of market has only been rudimentarily developed in South Africa, particularly along the country's east coast in centres such as East London and particularly Durban. It had picked up after 1994 when, concomitant with the general surge in the South African international tourist market, wholesaler producers moved in and attempted to promote the country as a beach resort destination. Beach vacationing is however a very small component of South Africa's international tourist appeal.

Distinct from 'sun, sand, sea and hotel' destinations such as the Caribbean or the Balearic Islands, tourism in South Africa is thus characteristically not linked to one locale. Instead travel is an important aspect of the country's tourist product. In this regard South Africa is highly comparable to destinations such as Australia, South America, other parts of Africa, or the United States of America.

Table 3.2 South Africa's ten main international tourist attractions

Ranking	Attraction	Location
1	Victoria and Alfred Waterfront	Cape Town, Western Cape
2	Table Mountain	Cape Town, Western Cape
3	Cape Point	Cape Town, Western Cape
4	Wine Route	Winelands, Western Cape
5	Garden Route	Western Cape
6	Kirstenbosch Botanical Garden	Cape Town, Western Cape
7	Ostrich farms	Little Karoo district, Western Cape
8	Robben Island	Off Cape Town coast, Western Cape
9	Sights in Pretoria, e.g. Union Buildings (site of government)	Pretoria, Gauteng
10	Kruger National Park	Mpumalanga province

Source: South African Tourism (2000)

South African Tourism conducts biannual surveys on the travel and spending patterns and preferences of international tourists to the country. These surveys indicate that the Western Cape (the southernmost province) is very popular among international tourists. Eight of the ten main national tourist attractions as listed by international tourists are found in this province. The country's primary attractions are shown in Table 3.2.

Given the centrality of the Western Cape in tourists' ranking, international marketing makes extensive use of core tourism features found in this province (such as Table Mountain and Kirstenbosch Botanical Garden in Cape Town, the wider Cape Peninsula, and wine routes located close to the Cape metropolis). In recent years, the Victoria and Alfred Waterfront, an entertainment and leisure waterfront development, and Robben Island, where political prisoners, and most famously Nelson Mandela were incarcerated during the apartheid era, have become key international attractions.

South Africa's international tourism markets It is customary to regard 1995 as a watershed in South Africa's tourism industry. In this year international tourism increased dramatically for the first time, when total arrivals into the country rose by 22.3 per cent. As shown in Figure 3.2 the country's international market has maintained a high level of growth, although, as will be discussed later, it has been marked by a great degree of flux in the recent past.

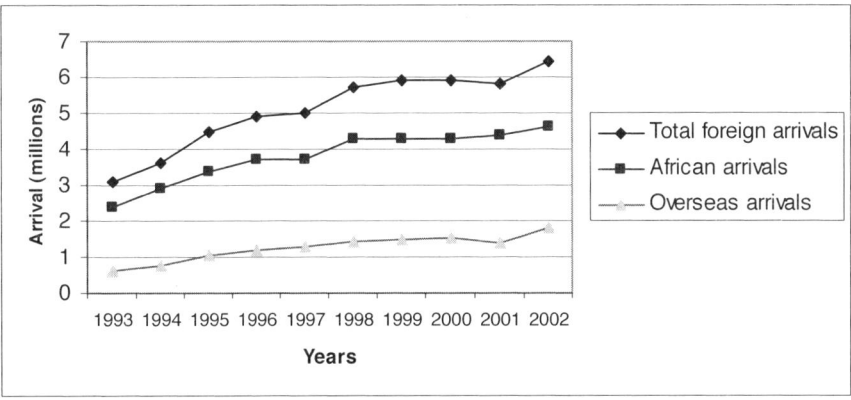

Figure 3.2 Foreign tourist arrivals in South Africa, 1993-2002
Source: Statistics South Africa, various years

It is however useful to break South Africa's international tourism markets down into its component parts. Statistically, a distinction is made between international tourists who stem from Africa and those whose country of origin is outside the African continent, and who usually arrive by air or ship. African arrivals indeed make up the greatest share of all foreign arrivals into South Africa,[10] as is illustrated in Table 3.3.

Table 3.3 Breakdown of South Africa's tourist markets, 1993-2002

Year	Total international arrivals (number)	Overseas arrivals		African arrivals	
		Number	Share of total (%)	Number	Share of total (%)
1993	3 093 183	618 637	20.0	2 474 546	80.0
1994	3 668 956	704 439	19.2	2 964 516	80.8
1995	4 488 272	1 072 697	23.9	3 415 575	76.1
1996	4 944 430	1 171 829	23.7	3 772 601	76.3
1997	4 976 349	1 273 945	25.6	3 702 404	74.4
1998	5 732 039	1 427 277	24.9	4 304 762	75.1
1999	5 917 700	1 491 260	25.2	4 426 440	74.8
2000	5 900 000	1 528 100	25.9	4 371 900	74.1
2001	5 787 368	1 502 090	26*	4 134 141	71*
2002	6 429 583	1 803 887	28*	4 455 971	69*

* Difference accounted for by unspecified entries
Source: Statistics South Africa

The number and share of overseas tourists to SA has steadily increased, while the share of African arrivals has decreased between 1993 and 2002. The overseas segment has enjoyed a greater rate of increase in this nine-year period.

Most of South Africa's African visitors stem from its six neighbouring countries – Botswana, Lesotho, Mozambique, Namibia, Swaziland and Zimbabwe. Of these, Lesotho is the single largest source for international arrivals (DEAT, 2001). The official statistics on foreign arrivals in South Africa have to be read with caution, however. With regard to the Africa arrival category, Statistics South Africa does not differentiate between those short term (usually daily) visitors who generally cross the borders into South Africa to shop, sell goods, or seek employment, and those who intend to engage in tourist activities. As such the vast majority of African arrivals are not tourists in the true sense. Where African visitors do engage in tourist activities, their travelling and spending patterns differ markedly from those of overseas visitors. Overseas visitors tend to stay longer, and to spend more money. African visitors, on the other hand, tend to come for the purpose of visiting friends and relatives, or to do business, and hence do not contribute as much to the various tourist sectors, such as accommodation (SATOUR, 1998; 2000). As a consequence less tourism revenue is generated by African arrivals than overseas arrivals.

The most important source markets for overseas visitors are the United Kingdom, the United States, Germany, Italy, the Netherlands and France. The United Kingdom and Germany are traditionally the two prime source markets for overseas tourists to South Africa, as is illustrated in Table 3.4.

Table 3.4 Trends in SA's main overseas markets, selected years: Number of arrivals by origin and share of total overseas arrivals

Origin	1993		1995		1998		2002	
	Number	Share (%)	Number	Share (%)	Number	Share (%)	Number	Share (%)
United Kingdom	148 868	24	243 621	22.7	321 281	22.5	442 910	24.5
Germany	104 764	17.4	168 186	15.7	195 878	13.7	248 990	13.8
Netherlands	19 578	3.2	47 068	4.4	83 022	5.8	110 389	6.11
France	25 548	4.1	53 492	4.9	72 994	5.1	112 078	6.21
Italy	17 649	2.8	27 491	2.6	37 204	2.6	47 756	2.64
Europe (other)	96 393	15.6	157 681	14.7	239 886	16.8	288 621	15.9
United States	62 430	10	103 466	9.6	166 071	11.6	170 611	9.45
Canada	12 760	2.1	20 888	1.9	27 544	1.9	33 684	1.9
Total		79.2		76.5		80		81

Source: Statistics South Africa, selected years

Other significant, albeit smaller, overseas source markets include Switzerland, Sweden, Austria, Spain and Belgium in Western Europe, and the Pacific countries of Australia and Japan. Within Central and South America (which only account for three per cent of overseas visitors to South Africa) Argentina and Brazil are the two prime source markets. Over the five-year period between 1993 and 1998, foreign arrivals from the United States and Netherlands have consistently shown the greatest increase.

The country has three broad consumer segments for international tourism: those who go for the purpose of leisure or vacation; those whose visit to the country is business-motivated; and those who primarily visit friends and relatives (the VFR segment). Crosscutting these, and constituting two further segments, are travellers who are first time visitors, and those who are repeater visitors. The leisure and travel patterns of the two latter groups markedly differ. First time visitors are more likely to make use of tour operator services, and visit the main tourist locations, while repeater visitors (many of whom cross-cut with the VFR and business market segments) will go to different, new or less well known locations. A leisure motivation however underlies all of the five consumer segments.

A further distinction can be made with regard to the types of accommodation used by consumers. This consists of an 'upmarket' or luxury segment which includes three, four or five star lodges, guest houses and hotels, and a 'budget' segment which includes backpacker and less expensive (and usually lower-graded) hotels and guest houses. In general tourists who constitute the upmarket or luxury segment fall into an above-average income category and tend to be older. The budget segment tends to be younger.

Given the 'nature, wildlife and culture' appeal of South Africa, and the characteristics of the country's international consumer segments, the country's overall tourist product is highly varied. Table 3.5 summarises the main South African international market segments.

Surveys of overseas tourists' profiles yield a diverse range of preferences and travel patterns. In the case of German and British tourists, for instance, different travel motivations and behaviour translate into highly dissimilar markets (Table 3.6).

The German traveller market is a highly dynamic one. Germans are known for their proclivity to travel. In 1999, 48 million German people took at least one holiday trip of at least four overnight stays. This represents a travel propensity of 75.3 per cent (FUR, Reiseanalyse Aktuell, 2000).[11] These figures make Germans the most active travellers in Europe.[12] The majority of German and British tourists to South Africa are holiday-makers, although in both markets visiting relatives and friends is an important motivator for travel to South Africa. The strength of the VFR segment is due to historical political and social linkages between South Africa and the two countries. In the case of the United Kingdom these ties also extend to business interactions, and account for the higher proportion of visitors that come for business purposes.

Table 3.5 Main market segments in South African overseas tourism

Type of product/product segment	Type of consumer
Safari trips/visits – South Africa	First time; repeater; VFR; leisure; business; younger; older; all income levels. Included as basic component of all trips, operator packages.
Overland/camping trips – Southern Africa	First time; repeater; VFR; leisure; business; younger; all income levels.
Hunting trips/tours	Leisure travellers; older. Business travellers form a distinct niche.
Adventure/sport tours/trips	First time; repeater; VFR; leisure; younger; all income levels.
Golf tours	Upper income; business; repeaters
4 × 4 wheel drive tours	Particularly younger travellers
Cultural tourism	Particularly older, often repeater visitors
Study tours	All, but mainly higher income and older travellers
Visits to urban areas	All
Visits to rural areas	All
Visits linked to conferences, exhibitions, events (MICE)	Business, leisure, higher income

Source: Author survey of international tour operators, July-December 2000, $n=33$

Table 3.6 Profile of German and British tourists to South Africa

	United Kingdom		Germany	
	1998	2000	1998	2000
Main Purpose of visit (%)				
Holiday	44	52	55	60
Business/conference	17	14	15	15
Visiting friends/relatives	36	28	24	17
Number of nights in SA	21.5	19	19.7	21.3
% First-time visitors	44	43	59	60
Destinations visited (%)				
Other African countries	35	28	37	32
Gauteng province	39	36	82	39
Western Cape province	70	70	45	78
Kwazulu-Natal	25	24	29	28
Main attractions before visit	Climate Scenery VFR	VFR Climate Scenery Value for money	Scenery Climate Changes Wildlife	Scenery Wildlife Climate
Main disappointments after visit	Crime Service Infrastructure	Crime Service Infrastructure	Crime Infrastructure Service	Crime Service Poverty Dull cities

Source: SATOUR Summer Survey 1998, 2000

Opportunities and Challenges for South African Tourism

Growth and Economic Impact

In 1996 the national White Paper on tourism development and promotion had set the following specific growth targets:

- to raise tourism's contribution to GDP by eight per cent by 2000 and ten per cent by 2005;
- to maintain a 15 per cent increase in total visitor arrivals between the years 1996 and 2006;
- to create 1 million new jobs in tourism by 2005;

- to increase foreign exchange earnings from approximately 10bn Rand in 1996 to 40bn Rand by 2005;
- to increase the number of overseas arrivals to 2m by 2000 and African arrivals to 4m.

The accomplishment of these targets has been mixed. For instance, in 1996 the number of African arrivals was 3.8m. By 2000 this had increased to 4.3m. The number of overseas arrivals in 2000 was 1.6m, well short of its target. The rate of growth has been highly variable. Rather than the projected 15 per cent, tourist arrivals had grown at an average of roughly nine per cent between 1993 and 2002. This is well above the international average of three per cent, although, as shown in Figure 3.3 the pattern of growth has been highly erratic.

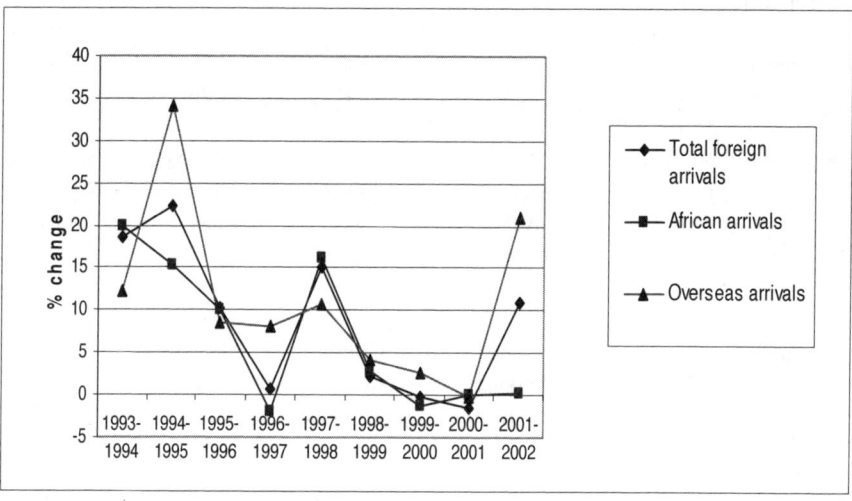

Figure 3.3 Percentage change in international arrivals, 1993-2002
Source: Statistics South Africa

Factors that account for this are varied. The decline in overseas arrivals at the end of the 1990s was linked to many causes. Widespread international publicity on the high level of violent crime in the country (Ferreira and Harmse, 2000) and negative perceptions of the course of development in South Africa have been important disincentives to the country's main overseas markets. Since the late 1990s in particular, the wearing off of the 'Mandela syndrome' and uncertainly about the political future of the country have contributed to the decrease in overseas arrivals. An exacerbating factor during that same period, particularly in prime tourist locations such as Cape Town, was a series of bomb blasts linked to a domestic vigilante group. Between 1998 and 2000 this group was believed to have been responsible for more than 20 bomb attacks in and around Cape Town (*Mail and Guardian*, 21 September 2000). A number of the city's major tourist locales, such as the Victoria and Alfred Waterfront, were targeted. All of these factors contributed to a levelling off in international tourist arrivals. This was a key concern for tourism authorities (*Business Day*, 5 September 2001).

Changes in global travel patterns following 9/11 have had a beneficial impact on the South African sector. The sharp increase in total foreign tourist arrivals in 2002 for instance, stems from a diversion in travel routing, mainly from the Americas. Growth in South Africa's two largest overseas markets, for example was high, with in 2002 year-on-year arrivals from Germany increasing by 22 per cent and from the United Kingdom with one-quarter. Similar levels of growth were seen in other established source markets in Europe (such as France and Italy), but also in smaller, newer markets, particularly from Asia.

A return of travel confidence and a revival in some of the world's major destinations (in 2003, for example, North America experienced 12 per cent growth) has however meant that this was short-lived. During the first eight months of that year South African tourist arrivals from its core European markets had once again declined by four per cent.

Further, a sustained appreciation of the South African Rand against other major currencies since 2002 has started to depress demand in overseas markets (Grant Thornton, 2004).[13] The African market is mainly comprised of the VFR and shopping segments. Given this, it is likely that the strengthening of the Rand over the past couple of years, coupled with downturn in their own domestic economies have deterred many African travellers.

Within this environment tourism's impact has also been varied. Overall, tourism's contribution to the national economy has grown. Using Tourism Satellite Account methodology, expansion in both the size of the tourism *industry* and the tourism *economy*[14] has occurred, as shown in Table 3.7.

Table 3.7 Gross economic impact of tourism in South Africa

	1998	2000	2010 (projection)
Tourism Industry Contribution to GDP (%)	2.6	3.6	5.3
Percentage of total employment	2.4	3.4	4.5
Tourism Economy Contribution to GDP (%)	8.2	7.9	13.4
Percentage of total employment	7.0	7.5	9.3

Source: WTTC, 1998; 2000

Distribution and Development

Impact has however been broad and disproportionate. Major producer sectors within the South African tourism economy have been unevenly affected. For instance, the hotel sector has seen rapid expansion in supply, but consistent low levels of occupancy (on average, 45-50% since 1994). This has caused reduced overall revenue, which in turn has affected hotels' employment and operating practices. Similar experiences have been made in the wider accommodation sector. The accommodation sector accounts for the largest proportion of international tourist expenditure once visitors reach their destination. As such accommodation statistics constitute a most ready and visible measure of tourism impact. The high degree of volatility experienced by the country's accommodation sector, however, points to irregular tourism impact.

In addition, strong regional and social variation occurs in the distribution of tourism impact. Far from providing the access and developmental opportunity that the government has aimed for, patterns of tourism activity in the country is highly concentrated, based mainly in the three metropolitan areas of Cape Town, Gauteng and Durban (Rogerson, 2002).

Skewed geographical impact: the example of the Western Cape The spatial unevenness of tourism can be illustrated through the example of the Western Cape. This province is the one of the premier tourist regions of the country, and given its prominence in the international market (Table 3.2), it is a particularly important component of the country's overall tourism sector. The South African Constitution proclaims tourism to be both a national and provincial competence. This means that although provincial governments are able to structure and legislate for provincial tourism programmes, this has to be in line with national programmes and policies. In the Western Cape the provincial policy-making process started with the promulgation of the Western Cape Tourism Act of 1997. This Act set out the aims and objectives for tourism in the province, and the institutions through which tourism promotion and development activities are cohered and regulated. Provincial policy is contained in the *White Paper on Sustainable Tourism Development and Promotion in the Western Cape* (DEATT, 2001). This White Paper aims to establish sustainable tourism in the province through continued growth, increased employment in tourism and through the development of a tourism sector that provides benefit to 'the whole population of the Western Cape' (DEATT, 2001). Its vision is to have the Western Cape become 'renowned as a premium world tourism area', by the year 2010 (DEATT, 2001).

The concept of 'responsible tourism' that informs the national tourism policy also underlies the provincial White Paper. It however articulates a more comprehensive set of goals that are aimed at addressing specific needs of the Western Cape. The provincial White Paper is an attempt to realise the projected economic potentials of tourism, and to meet the developmental imperatives of the province. It seeks to address historical inequities and imbalances in the provincial tourism sector, both in terms of what is produced, and who gains from tourism. Five principles form the basis of provincial tourism policy:

- **Social equity**. It is proposed that tourism should benefit the larger provincial populace, and should be inclusive of 'previously neglected or disadvantaged' population groups. Tourist products should also reflect the cultural diversity of the province.
- **Environmental integrity**. Tourism development should not be at the expense of the environment; conversely, the environment should be considered as an important tourism asset that needs to be judiciously developed and managed.
- **Economic empowerment**. Although regulation is needed to appropriately guide economic growth and to protect citizens, the environment and tourists, avid regulation of the tourist sector by the government must be avoided. Since there are many linkages with other economic sectors, the involvement of stakeholders from such sectors should be sought in decision-making. Finally, the participation of and ownership by 'emerging entrepreneurs', particularly small, medium and micro enterprises in tourism need to be actively encouraged and supported.
- **Co-operation and partnership**. The provincial government, tourism businesses, local communities, and the labour force all have different roles and responsibilities in tourism development. The development and promotion of tourism should be based on active collaboration between these various groups.
- **Sustainability**. Sustainability is a key objective but is also a guiding framework for tourism policy and actions. According to the White Paper tourism is economically sustainable if it provides a diversity of market opportunities and employment, and easier access to 'productive resources'.

It is institutionally sustainable when it involves co-operation between the public and private sectors, and local communities. The environmental sustainability of tourism is based on a balance between the protection of the environment and the beneficial use of the environment. Finally, the socially sustainability of tourism is based on the involvement and participation of host communities in tourism management (DEAAT, 2001).

A number of secondary principles underlie the strategies and actions put forward by the White Paper. The first is that tourism development has to be market-driven. The White Paper for instance states that, 'tourism development must be based on programmes and initiatives related to current and potential market trends and requirements' (p.30). Linked to that is the notion that all product development, marketing and market actions need to be targeted and focused. This firstly entails the identification and packaging of core attractions in the province, and the promotion of these through themes and an autonomous, well-disseminated provincial brand. Product development and offer should furthermore be directed at specific market segments. A final principle is to enhance the distribution of the benefits accrued from, and opportunities related to tourism. This is encapsulated in the strategic objective to,

> reduce the current pattern of over-concentration of tourism facilities and physical development by encouraging the proposed development of tourism in underdeveloped areas. This should be undertaken as an attempt to spread the availability of tourism facilities to a greater proportion of the province's population and to create job opportunities' (p.31).

Tied into this is the goal to foster and facilitate the greater involvement of the province's residents in both the development and management of the tourism sector, through a broad process of capacity building. Strategy 13 of the White Paper aims to 'promote entrepreneurship, with special emphasis on neglected communities', while strategy 14 proposes to 'improve (the) participation of local communities in tourism development'.

Product development and promotion are two of the key focus areas of Western Cape policy. The provincial White Paper sets out a framework for the development and marketing of tourism products. Its approach can be read as an attempt to foster tourism growth in the province through a more attractive and wider product offer that stresses the competitive advantage of the province over rival destinations and will hence attract more tourists to the province. Specifically, the following goals are laid out in the White Paper. Strategy 9 proposes to 'package tourism themes and attractions in the form of suggested routes and itineraries', whilst strategy 10 proposes to 'promote unique selling propositions and initiate special attraction programmes'.

Unpacking this, the strategies entail three facets: first, core physical, social and cultural attractions (termed 'magnets' or 'icons') have to be identified in each of the eight tourism regions of the province; second, cross-cutting tourism themes (e.g. scenery, wine and food, culture, sports), and tourism programmes (specifically proposed are heritage, eco-tourism, adventure, and events tourism programmes) have to be developed. Third, these attractions and themes have to be combined into single product offers that take the form of different tourist routes and itineraries. Tourist routes should all originate from Cape Town, the main urban area and radially extend into different parts of the province. The corollary of this is that tourists are encouraged to visit larger parts of the province (i.e. to spread the impact). All of this should be contingent with the development of a distinctive provincial tourism identity.

Product development should also be geared towards the economic and social empowerment of the province's previously disadvantaged groups. As such, the White Paper places a great deal of emphasis on the development of new, or alternative tourism products that dually are reflective of the cultural landscape of the province, and through which opportunities could be afforded to previously disadvantaged groups to enter the tourism sector as producers. Strategy 14 aims to improve the involvement of local communities in tourism development, through two means – the proactive identification and development of 'local assets that could complement the programmes' and goals described above, and the strengthening of 'the representation of local indigenous arts and cultural expressions' in the Western Cape tourism product offer (DEAAT, 2001: 43).

Another primary goal of the Western Cape policy is to diffuse the economic and developmental benefits of tourism. Through the encouragement, expansion and support of new products, people from previously disadvantaged backgrounds (termed 'emerging entrepreneurs') can be integrated into the main tourism system.

In spite of these various goals, there has been little success in enhancing the impact of tourism. Patterns of tourist supply and usage are geographically focused, with tourism activities mainly located in the more affluent parts of the Cape metropolis, and in some of the more prosperous regions adjacent to it, such as the Garden Route and the Winelands (see Figure 3.4 below). These areas therefore absorb most of the economic spin-offs of tourism.

This pattern partly arises from the prominence of these areas in South Africa's destination image, and the reinforcement of this by the promotional campaigns driven by international tour operators (Chapter 5) and national marketing agents (Visser, 2004).

Large-scale capital investments in the province over the past half-decade have however underpinned the geographical focus of tourism impact. Figure 3.5 indicates that major capital investments by the provincial state and the private sector since 1998 have followed general levels of tourist activity, with investments being most focused where tourist activity is most intense, i.e. in metropolitan Cape Town, the Garden Route and Winelands. There has been little in the way of large-scale demand stimulation in the regions where tourist activity is less dynamic. In all tourist development and value-adding through tourism investment converge in the areas of the province where tourism activity and impact is already highest (Cornelissen, 2005).

68   *The Global Tourism System*

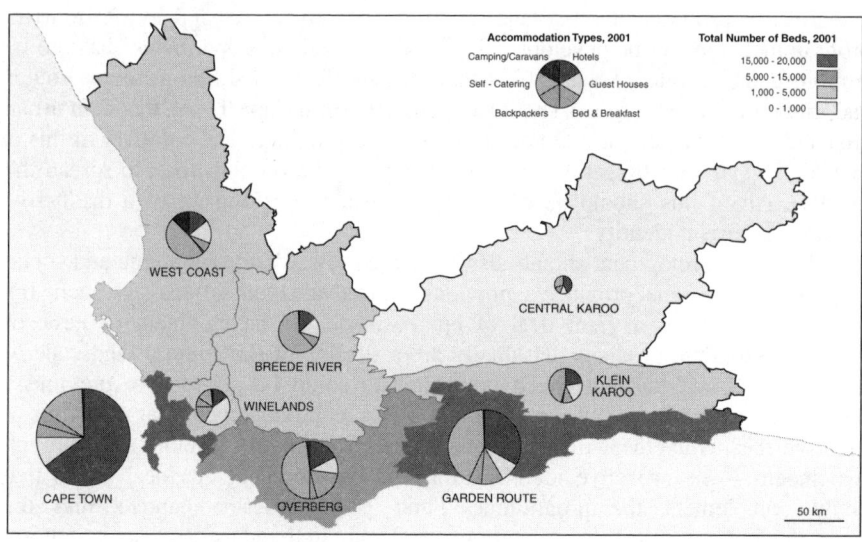

Figure 3.4 Spatial distribution of tourist accommodation in the Western Cape, 2001

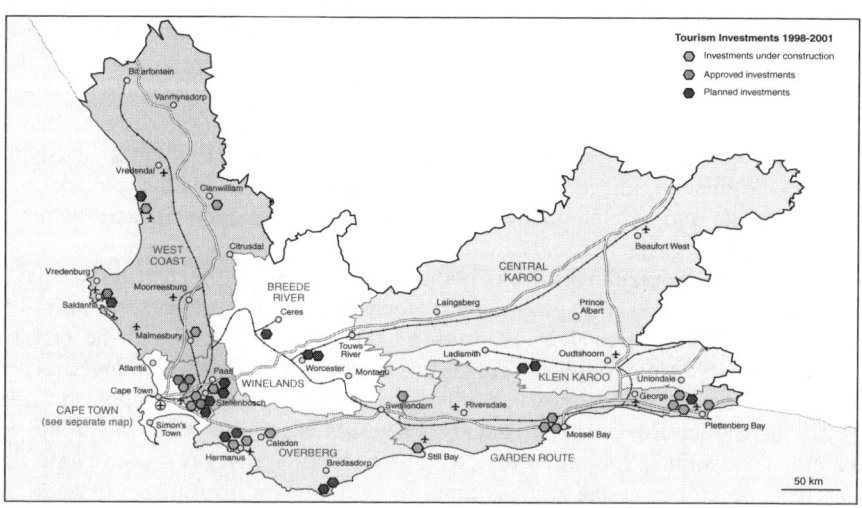

Figure 3.5 Major tourism investments in the Western Cape

A further feature of tourism investments in the province is a strong emphasis on only certain market segments – in general middle-to-high income international tourists, rather than the lower-income, domestic market. There is a particular targeting of the golf tourist market through a high level of golf-related development, mainly through the construction of golf complexes, i.e. the establishment of golf estates with residences (houses, apartments or villas) and/or hotels. By 2001 almost one-quarter of all tourist developments in the province were golf-related. In total, golf developments carried a value of R7.9bn, making these projects of the most extensive in the province. The combination of golf, hotel and residential investments – an integrated form of development – is a common and growing trend in real estate development internationally (Miles et al., 2000). International experience shows that two principal motivations underlie such developments from the perspective of investors – land use optimisation and profit maximisation. Close synergies between the three segments in terms of the primary market that is aimed at (i.e. wealthier, golf-playing clientele) enhances the return on investment and hence the attractiveness of such investments (Miles et al., 2000). In addition, diversification reduces the risk of financial loss. With this sort of development, investors in the Western Cape hence seem to be following an emergent tendency in international leisure development.

Given the high contingency costs that go along with golf tourism, this market generally consists of higher-income clientele. Since mainly five-star hotels, and middle- to high-income residences form part of these complexes, these can be seen as very exclusive developments. However, the fact that a number of golf-related property developments are also what are known as security complexes – security-controlled compounds with limited access points, suggests that some of these developments are specifically aimed at being exclusionary. In addition, in recent years, there has been increased censure of the negative ecological impacts of golf estates, which generally have high levels of water consumption. The exclusivity of such estates has also been widely criticised. The complex nature of the debate and the political controversies surrounding golf estate developments in South Africa, are discussed in greater detail in Chapter 7.

Given the current patterns of development and investments in the Western Cape, the developmental benefits of tourism – *inter alia* employment, training, skills development – are regionally focused. Similarly, and equally vital, the costs associated with tourism – such as seasonal variations in demand and its related effects on employment, revenue and training – are mainly borne by certain regions.

Such tourism development patterns seem to be in stark contrast to the goals of greater tourism access, empowerment and transformation that underlie the government's policy.

The trends in the Western Cape are indicative of the complexity of addressing two, often contending objectives, that of growth and equity, or distribution. This difficulty has been encountered in many other parts of the country. In all, impact distribution has not been an easy goal to attain.

Tourism Transformation and Empowerment

A further area in tourism transformation where there has been only partial change is in the ownership structure of the sector. Despite numerous state-led initiatives and programmes over the past number of years to improve the integration of black producers into the country's tourism system, production is still widely viewed as being white-dominated, under the direction of a few major white-owned corporations. The government's acknowledgement of the slow rate of change is encapsulated in a policy document that states that 'there has not been any significant progress in this area ... after our democratisation of 1994 (DEAT, 2000). A study commissioned in 2003 by the national Department of Environmental Affairs and Tourism showed that more than 80 per cent of management staff in listed tourism firms were white men, while only 6 per cent of listed firms were black-owned.

In recent years the government has sought to play a larger role in influencing the pace and nature of transformation. Often this has taken a very direct form. For instance, in 2003 the then minister of tourism announced that if a more 'reasonable approach' was not adopted towards employing tour guides the government would consider the imposition of a quota system (*Business Day*, 6 June 2003).

The government's attempts to transform the ownership structure in tourism should be seen within the wider context of its efforts to promote broad-based black economic empowerment (BEE), a wide-ranging set of objectives regarding blacks' access to and influence over the country's economy. BEE has followed a lengthy period of gestation, developing from a series of wide goals to a specific policy in August 2003 when the BEE Act (Republic of South Africa, 2003) was promulgated. This act sets out several standards against which economic empowerment in different sectors can be assessed. Criteria for black economic empowerment are set out with respect to ownership, management and control, employment equity, skills development, 'affirmative procurement', enterprise and social development. Different industries are encouraged to set sector-specific targets and timeframes against which to measure themselves in terms of the level of black equity ownership, management, employment, skills development and preferential procurement they make provision for.

The BEE Act is one in a line of different pieces of legislation that aim at extensive political and economic transformation in South Africa and that seek to concretise empowerment. In 1998 the South African government promulgated the Skills Development Act (Republic of South Africa, 1998a) with the purpose of setting a framework for in-service training and industry-specific education (see discussion in Chapter 6). In the same year, the Employment Equity Act (Republic of South Africa, 1998b) was adopted. This Act compels, inter alia, firms with a staff complement of 50 or larger, or those with an annual turnover of R5m or more, to ensure that their staff composition is representative of the broader demographic environment within which it functions. This also entails the provision of equal employment opportunity to individuals who had been disadvantaged under the apartheid system. The Employment Equity and BEE Acts designate three beneficiary or target categories – black people (a generic term that includes black

Africans, 'coloureds' and 'Indians'), women and disabled persons. Together, these various Acts constitute the legal foundation for a profound reshaping of economic ownership in South Africa. In recent years the wider BEE programme has come to be politically controversial as several high profile black figures have questioned the extent of its impact, and whether it is not to the benefit of a small minority.[15]

In the tourism sector attempts have been made to implement the provisions of the BEE Act. During 2004 a transformation steering committee was appointed, tasked with developing a number of key targets for black economic empowerment in the tourism sector. As an outcome, a Tourism BEE Charter and Scorecard was adopted at the end of that year. The scorecard comprises a set of quantitative measurements to assess the degree to which firms have complied with the requirements of transformation and to gauge their BEE status over a ten year period. Key BEE targets are that by 2014:

- more than one-third (36 per cent) of all firms should directly or indirectly be owned by black people;
- blacks should comprise 60 per cent of executive management boards;
- at least three-quarters of a firm's staff is comprised of black people, and that 45 per cent of this should be women;
- 75 per cent of expenditure on skills development should be targeted towards black employees;
- 50 per cent of expenditure on procurement should be on companies that are BEE compliant;
- one percent of revenue should be spent to facilitate enterprise development by black-owned SMMEs. This could include aspects such as twinning initiatives;
- one per cent of money spent on social and industry-specific developments (for example, as part of 'corporate citizenship' programmes and spent on education or community projects) should be aimed at developing local black tourism.

Several premises underlie the Tourism BEE Charter and Scorecard. One is that transformation will stimulate new entrants into the sector, and as a result, innovation and new products. This in turn, it is assumed, will help to stimulate demand in new markets. A second is that transformation will help to balance out the skewed nature of tourism impact across the nine provinces of South Africa. Overall, tourism transformation is regarded by the authorities as one of the means by which nation-building could be supported (DEAT, 2004).

It remains to be seen however whether the Tourism BEE Charter will produce the level of transformation envisaged. One of the challenges is to ensure compliance. The Charter recommends the establishment of a BEE Council to popularise, implement and monitor the BEE goals within the tourism sector. However, a degree of tension has developed between the government and large tourism producers in the South African system, with corporations viewing the government as too interventionist, and the government suspecting white businesses of deliberately seeking to limit the access of black producers. In truth, success with transformation has been slow due to the lack of available capital on the part of prospective black producers, some conceptual and institutional shortcomings on the part of state initiatives and programmes and a degree of resistance by established producers. Within this context, a heavy-handed, top-down approach – one that may arise through a zealous application of the Tourism BEE Charter – is likely to de-legitimise and hamper the process of transformation even more.

A further challenge is to steer transformation to be in line with changing global demand and the nuances of South Africa's main source markets. In this regard lessons can be taken from township tourism, which, for a long time regarded by South African tourism authorities as an important sector through which to integrate previously excluded and black producers, has shown little growth. Part of the reason is a strong perception in key source markets that South African townships are dangerous. At the height of the anti-apartheid struggle in the mid to late-1980s, most civil unrest and political violence were centred in the townships, while in the post-apartheid era domestic and international reporting about crime in townships have cast these areas very negatively. Concerns among overseas tourists about their safety, a general lack of exposure and knowledge about townships and their residents, and generally little interest in 'the township product' (mainly consisting of guided bus tours and brief visits to township sites such as formal or informal taverns) have meant that township tourism remains a very small component of South Africa's overall tourism economy.

One of the consequences of weak demand is that little opportunity exists for black producers. This is highlighted by Thomas (2005) who states that:

> (There is) an often perceived link between middle and higher-income foreign visitors (in particular overseas visitors) and 'township-tourism-service suppliers', which is easily interpreted as a link with 'informal' tourism services… Closer observation shows that links with local informal suppliers only exist in exceptional circumstances. While it is obvious that many overseas tourists are keen to get more acquainted with the explicitly 'African' part of South Africa's living, entertainment, recreational and general tourism environments, this usually happens through modern, well developed and serviced establishments located inside African-dominated township suburbs and community-orientated rural settlements. Although those establishments usually try their best to emphasise this link to the grassroots level, the business itself generally fulfils all the conditions of an established, first-economy business, just adapted to the style of the local environment.

In all, despite various attempts to make the tourism sector more representative and to create entry opportunities for black producers, the ethnic expansion of South Africa's tourism sector has taken place only very moderately. Too few financing opportunities or support by the government to this effect, and features related to the broader society, such as the lack of skills and human resource capacities, can hinder empowerment objectives. A drawback is that institutions that have been set up towards this goal have their own deficiencies that hamper skills development and training. Despite the objectives of the Skills Development Act to broaden, formalise and systematise training in different economic sectors, and the establishment of the Tourism, Hospitality and Sport Education and Training Authority (Theta) to monitor and accredit training and skills development in the tourism sector, this process has progressed very slowly. Theta is impeded by a lack of awareness among tourism producers of its aims and operations. In addition, logjams between the Department of Revenue, which is responsible for collecting skills levies from producers, and Theta, constrain the operations of the body (personal communication, Theta administrator, 29 March 2001).

Conclusion

Tourism has emerged as one of the important policy focus areas in post-apartheid South Africa. The country has indeed drawn benefit from a rapidly growing global sector, and a high level of curiosity about the political changes that had taken place since 1994. Yet expansion has been irregular as South Africa experienced both the negative and positive impacts of exogenous factors such as political instability and terrorism in competitor destinations, and perceptions around crime in its key source markets. Tourism's impact has also been uneven, as the spin-offs from tourism growth have been unequally distributed among different sectors and regions of the national tourism system. Transformation of the sector, and raising the access of previously excluded groups have long been key policy objectives, although little progress has been made with these so far. Although institutions and legal instruments have been developed to promote development, training and empowerment, they are impeded by several factors. Innovative ways need to be found to foster skills development, transfer and eventual economic empowerment. The difficulties related to this means that it will be a long-term process. This however remains at the core of developing a sustainable sector. Other factors relate to South Africa's location in the global sector. These include the specific nature of interaction in the tourism production system and how relations of leverage and influence determine tourism outcomes; how the construction of the country's tourist image impact on travel flows; and finally, how the national, international and regional regulation and governance of tourism shape and sometimes constrict growth. It is to an analysis of these that the following chapters now turn.

Notes

[1] Natural disasters, social factors such as hygiene levels, and political instability, terrorism or crime exercise major influences on international tourist travel flows. Macroeconomic factors such as changes in disposable income in source markets, and falling or rising exchange rates also are important exogenous determinants of demand.

[2] Tourism development has featured prominently on the policy agenda of the post-apartheid government from an early stage. This is not to over accentuate, however, the importance given to tourism. It has only really been towards the end of the 1990s when priority was given to it as an economic sector and major macro-economic policies started to incorporate tourism (Rogerson and Visser, 2004).

[3] The national policy framework is provided by the 1996 White Paper and the Tourism Act of 1993. Together, these outline several development objectives and strategies and the institutional frame within which tourism development should take place. The Tourism Act of 1993 (amended in 1996 and 2000) saw the establishment of the South

African Tourism Board (SATOUR), a statutory body responsible for the promotion of tourism in, and to South Africa. Since the late 1990s, the membership and composition of this body have been significantly transformed in an attempt for it to be more reflective of the larger South African population. In 2000 the body's name was changed to South African Tourism.

[4] The Reconstruction and Development Programme was the first development programme formulated by the post-apartheid national government. It was introduced in 1994. In 1996 the RDP was succeeded by a second four-year development programme, the Growth, Employment and Redistribution programme (Gear) that attempts to draw up an economic development framework for South Africa.

[5] Post-apartheid South Africa's re-entry into the international sphere has been marked by a set campaign of political and diplomatic promotion and leadership involvement in several multilateral fora such as the Non-Aligned Movement (NAM), the United Nations Conference on Trade and Development (UNCTAD) and the Commonwealth. A key feature of its foreign policy behaviour post-1994 has thus been its attempt to use multilateral organisations to profile itself as a global leader (see for instance Nel, Taylor and van der Westhuizen, 2001). The country's hosting of major diplomatic events such as the UN conferences can be viewed in the same light.

[6] The severe, negative effects of political instability on the tourist sectors of countries such as China in the wake of the Tiananmen Square incident, Egypt, Turkey and Israel, have been widely documented. In the 1990s the international tourism sector was also detrimentally influenced by the Gulf War (Seddighi et al., 2001; Pizam, 1999).

[7] Established in 1992 the SADC today consists of 14 member states: Angola, Botswana, Democratic Republic of Congo, Lesotho, Malawi, Mauritius, Mozambique, Namibia, Seychelles, South Africa, Swaziland, Tanzania, Zambia and Zimbabwe.

[8] In Southern Africa 'peace parks' has become popularly used to refer to the establishment of transborder conservation initiatives. In the context of this region, peace parks are seen as ways to foster greater levels of trust among groups who may have artificially been separated by colonially-imposed national borders, or to reduce political enmity between South Africa and neighbour countries who were affected by the country's military campaigns under its policy of destabilisation during the apartheid era.

[9] The Lubombo Transfrontier Conservation Area is unique in that it comprises five, smaller TFCAs. These are the Ndumu-Tembe-Futi TFCA between South Africa and Mozambique; the Nsubane-Pongola TFCA between SA and Swaziland; the Lubombo Conservancy-Goba TFCA between Mozambique and Swaziland; the Ponto do Ouro-Kosi Bay Marine and Coastal TFCA between Mozambique and SA; and the Songimvelo-Malolotja TFCA between Swaziland and SA.

[10] Statistical differentiation between African and overseas arrivals are confounded by the fact that Statistics South Africa, the national agency responsible for gathering data on, *inter alia*, tourism and migration patterns, 'overestimates' the number of African arrivals by including 'unspecified' arrivals (those foreign arrivals who do not obviously fit into either of the two main categories, or who do not report their origin country) under the Africa category. The purpose of this is to deliberately underestimate the number of overseas visitors. The problem with this means of segmentation is that the volume of African arrivals tends to be over-inflated and misleading.

[11] As a concept travel propensity refers to the inclination or potential of a given group of people to undertake tourist trips, and is the ratio of people who went on a holiday trip within a given time (usually a year) to the total population. The larger the percentage of the population that travels, the higher is the travel propensity of this population. Travel intensity is a brute measure of the total number of holiday trips undertaken in a year.

[12] A recent survey (*Geo Saison*, 1999) locates the average age of Germans travelling to South Africa at 43,5. The two largest groups of Germans tourists to South Africa are between the ages of 30 and 39 and 50 and 59.

[13] The South African Rand has been on a steady course of depreciation for most of the post-apartheid era. One of the main factors accounting for this is unfavourable global economic conditions. The apartheid era was however also characterised by the enforcement of protectionist monetary policies that artificially shielded and bolstered the Rand. It is thus widely believed that the adoption of a less protectionist stance by the post-apartheid government has enabled the currency to level out to market conditions. Nonetheless, in December 2001 the Rand experienced a major shock when within two weeks it lost approximately 20 per cent of its value against major currencies. A commission of inquiry appointed to investigate whether this severe depreciation was contrived, found little evidence of this. Since then, the Rand had steadily strengthened, at some points reaching the same values against the US dollar it had maintained shortly after the end of apartheid. The high degree of currency fluctuation, and in some instances, currency strength is however severely detrimental to the South African economy.

[14] Tourism Satellite Account (TSA) methodology was developed by the World Tourism Organisation and the World Travel and Tourism Council. It aims at providing a comprehensive delineation of all the economic activities related to, or influenced by travel and tourism in a given economy, by anticipating and depicting the flow-through effects of tourism-specific and tourism-related activities. Towards this end TSA methodology makes a distinction between the *travel and tourism industry*, those economic activities which directly are *related* to tourism, and the sum total of which can be designated a separate economic sector (included in this are transportation, accommodation, catering, recreation and travel services), and the *travel and tourism economy*, those activities that are directly and indirectly *affected* by tourism (WTTC, 1998; S. Smith, 2000).

[15] Criticism against affirmative action policies adopted by the post-apartheid government, and against black economic empowerment more broadly, has arisen in several different quarters over the past number of years. One of the main claims by critics of the BEE programme, is that self-enrichment, rather than widespread upliftment has characterised the programme and that as it has unfolded up to now, it has only succeeded in its goals of transformation to a very limited degree. The debate regarding the extent and effectiveness of the BEE programme reached a peak at the end of 2004 when one of the most respected anti-apartheid leaders, Archbishop Desmond Tutu, a former cleric and one of the chairpersons of the Truth and Reconciliation Commission publicly criticised the programme for only benefiting a few wealthy individuals. The dispute that followed between him and the African National Congress underscored the politically sensitive nature of the programme.

Chapter 4

The Dynamics of the Global Tourism Production System

Introduction

This chapter focuses on the structure, nature and dynamics of the global tourism production system. The previous chapter had indicated a certain degree of tenuousness regarding South Africa's placing in global tourism. The country's tourism sector is part of a larger global arrangement of production, consumption and regulation. It is interlocked into a system that sees multiple exchanges between producers and consumers, and in terms of production, is subject to a certain hierarchy of influence where larger, generally transnational or multinational producers shape global production and, often to a significant degree, determine tourism outcomes. In addition, forms of commercial engagement, collaboration and competition among local producers can have both positive and negative impacts on the national tourist sector. This chapter examines the various modes whereby production occurs in the global system, the types of interaction that exist among different kinds of producers and how processes of globalisation affect producer-producer relations. The purpose is two-fold. First, it denotes loci of influence and leverage in the global production system. Second, through an analysis of its functioning it demonstrates the dynamics involved in tourism production and how this is related to features such as tourism growth, distribution and development in a destination such as South Africa.

The first part of the chapter provides an overview of the structure and components of the global tourism production system. The various elements of this system are detailed. The second part discusses forms of organisation and exchange in this system. Processes of consolidation, horizontal mergers and alliance networks have become more intensified in global tourism production over the past number of years and have impacted on different producer spheres in important ways. Producer sectors in the South African system such as tour operators had been particularly characterised by industrial concentration. This had affected tour operators' relationship with other South African producer sectors. The third part of the chapter discusses the dynamic functioning of production, showing how South African producers interrelate with the global system through various commercial and transactional processes, and how local and international networks of collaboration and competition shape the South African sector.

The Structure and Nature of the Global Tourism Production System

As highlighted in Chapter 1 international tourism is a highly distinct economic sector. First, it has both a production and consumption component, and can usefully be seen as the nexus between systems of international production and consumption. Second, rather than constituting a single industry, it is most appropriately viewed as a collection of industries that share similar functions and produce similar products. This creates very interesting dynamics that are perhaps unique to tourism. As a form of production, tourism has a broad scope. It spans several economic sectors and is, as a whole, a relatively fluid system.

In Chapter 1 an outline of the various elements of global tourism was given. Britton's (1991) concept of the tourism production system – composed of the array of economic activities aimed at producing and selling tourist products, the tourist product itself (and the various physical and other features and attractions of which it is constituted) and the institutions that regulate the system – encapsulates the diverse and loosely networked arrangement of international tourism production.

As illustrated in Figure 1.1 the creation of the final tourist product, its marketing and distribution is a complex process that involves a range of different producers and suppliers. Indeed, production is a key component of the global tourism system, where interface between various kinds of producers, but also consumers, is established.

Tourism producers are firms engaged in the production of tourist goods and services and/or are involved in the establishment of the infrastructure that enable people to undertake tourist trips to destination countries. Since the state performs these activities, either deliberately or as a contingent of other activities, the state also qualifies as a tourism producer. The state however is also a regulatory institution (as is discussed below).

A distinction may be drawn between core tourism producers and non-core tourism producers (or what S. Smith (1989) refers to as tier one and tier two firms). Core tourism producers (tier one firms) are those that produce for economic sectors that would not exist without tourism and travel (S. Smith, 1989), i.e. the core tourism sectors. These include:

- accommodation;
- transport providers (airlines, wheels operators, cruise ships);
- travel intermediaries (tour operators and travel agencies);
- contractors, suppliers, and service providers that only produce goods and services for the above three sectors.

Non-core tourism producers (tier two firms) are firms whose activities are not solely geared towards tourism and travel and would exist in the absence of tourism (S. Smith, 1989). These include:

- transport (such as taxis, public transport facilities, car rental companies);
- restaurants;
- retailers;

- attractions and events;
- contractors, suppliers and service providers who produce for these, and other non-tourism sectors.

Travel intermediaries in turn are comprised of tour operators and travel agencies. Tour operators are firms that organise and sell tours and trips usually in a packaged form, i.e. all or most of the components of the trip are arranged by the firm and sold as a unit to the consumer. To do this, they usually establish a network of contacts with corporations across the broad spectrum of the tourism sector, such as car rental companies, hotels, guest houses, lodges, bus companies, and so on. Travel agencies are also travel and tour retailers, but they usually do not arrange or organise their own tours or sell trips as a company-specific (brand) product in the way that operators do.

The tour operator sector comprises operators whose sole function is to act as brokers in the tourism production system, by putting together travel products from other producers, and selling these to consumers. Such operators are known in the industry as 'consolidators'. Distinct from them are tour operators who themselves provide a service or produce a product. These are commonly known as 'wheels operators'. The latter usually operate standard tours in destinations for which they utilise their own vehicle fleets. Tour operators can further be distinguished by size: wholesale tour operators are producers who capture a very large part of the organised travel and tour market through their sheer size, their ownership of a range of tourism modalities (i.e. accommodation, travel and leisure facilities) and the annual turnover they generate as a consequence.

While tourism producers fulfil an important intermediary function in the tourism system, they only absorb or represent a portion of the total tourism market. Tourists can bypass the tourist producer sector when they go to tourist destinations or consume tourist products, by not utilising established producer channels, e.g. not making use of tour operator services or not making use of accommodation facilities. Such consumers Leiper (1990) typifies as having a 'low index of industrial dependency'. An example is travellers whose main purpose is to visit friends and/or relatives.

Regulatory bodies. The tourism system is monitored and regulated by several overarching bodies. These bodies provide the larger script against which tourism production takes place. Two types of organisations play a key role in setting the parameters within which the tourism system operates – states and producer associations. State legislation controls to what degree travel producers may operate into and out of national boundaries; secondly all states exercise some degree of border controls at ports of entry (Pearce, 1995). The registration of travel and tourism operators also has to occur through state conduits. National and sub-national state agents lay down rules that govern tourism production – these bodies grant licences to enable establishments to operate as restaurants, hotels or guesthouses.

The second type of organisation that has an important influence on the tourism production system, are industry-based interest and lobby groups, here termed 'producer associations'. A producer association is an organisation whose membership is drawn from a specific part of the travel and tourism sector, and which acts as a forum through which members' interests can be represented in exchanges with other actors (e.g. the state). Examples of producer associations include tour operator, travel agency and hospitality associations.

Tourism consumers display certain socio-economic and socio-cultural features. Demand for tourist products are determined by a number of factors: the income levels of tourists (Uysal, 1998); physiological and psychological needs to recuperate (Krippendorf, 1987), embark on leisure activities, or to explore or discover new places or societies (Cohen, 1979; MacCannell, 1976); and psychosocial needs to be accorded a certain social status or recognition or to be accepted within certain social groupings (Urry, 1990). As discussed in Chapter 2 there have been significant changes in tourism demand patterns over the past number of years, with consumer preferences often manifesting what may be termed post-modern values (i.e. focused on individual and shifting means of self-expression, in which tourism consumption is just one form) and with greater emphasis placed on post- or neo-Fordist practices.

The tourist product is diverse. It includes accommodation facilities, restaurants, retail goods and transport. It involves a wide range of producers who are responsible for the production of only part of the final tourist product. Because of this multiplicity some (e.g. Leiper, 1990; Tremblay, 1998) argue that there is a plurality of 'tourist products' linked to tourism. However, because of the nature of tourism and the peculiarities of what is produced – it is a highly perishable good (Mathieson and Wall, 1982) and the quality of service and experience form an important part of the product – it is analytically useful to regard the tourist product as a singular concept, recognising that it is made up of both tangible and intangible elements.

On a global level, the tourism production system may be outlined as made up of four core producer spheres: transport (consisting of airlines, car rental); serviced and non-serviced accommodation (hotels and other accommodation types); tour and travel intermediaries (tour operators and travel agencies); and ground or wheels operators (Figure 1.1). Each producer sphere has several primary or ancillary tourism suppliers and contractors attached to it. As can be seen in Figure 1.1 producer spheres crosscut at the international and the domestic levels.

Global tourism production is a compound course of negotiation, contest and collaboration between producers. Producers, themselves are acting towards projected sets of preferences by consumers who in turn, are shaped by what is offered to them by producers. The producer-consumer nexus, in other words is fluid and dynamic: there is a constant interchange and feedback between producers and consumers (Ateljevic, 2000). The result – the tourist product – is an amalgam of negotiation and compromise. The complexity of the 'producer over consumer' debate has been highlighted in Chapter 1. The analyses in this book indicate that rather than there being a one-way direction of influence, there is a mutually affective relationship between producers and consumers, the nature and consequence of which vary according to the type of product element that binds them. Consumer choice is limited with respect to aspects such as transport (e.g. flights or car rental), but consumer preferences do affect how tour operator packages are structured.

Organisation and Interaction in Global Tourism Production

Given the highly distinctive features of international tourism production – the interdependence of different producer sectors, amorphous markets (Pearce, 1992) and the 'spatial fixity' (Urry, 1990) of the tourist product (i.e. that tourists have to travel some distance to consume their product) – it is by nature, a more complex economic sector.

Tourism's economic organisation has been analysed from several different vantage points (e.g. Milne and Pohlman, 1998; Go and Pine, 1995; Iaonnides and Debbage, 1998; Shaw and Williams, 2004). With respect to the hotel industry, for instance, Dunning and McQueen (1982) and Go and Pine (1995) investigate the way that firms orient themselves internationally and how factors such as ownership, location and market internalisation determine the position of firms (Dunning and McQueen, 1982).

Clancy (1998; 2002a) applies a global commodity chains (GCC) approach to tourism production. Through this approach he investigates the life cycle of tourism – a service commodity – and the series of linkages that exist among producers and consumers across different national and international locales in the creation and use of the commodity. According to this framework international production is characterised by a division of labour between different locales, and different agents. By tracing the production sequence of a certain product from extraction or inception to completion, and the geographical areas where different phases of production occur, GCC analysis tries to uncover economic and social relations that exist in the world, the forces and actors that cause them, and the commensurate effects of these on local development. One of the key premises of the GCC framework, therefore, is that there is an intimate connection between the international and national economic systems, and that (changing) events in the international economic milieu play a key role in local development (Clancy, 1998). In this frame tourism is an economic process that is based on the intersection of activities between different actors and across different spatial locations. The commodity – the tourist product – emerges from different waves of interaction between a wide set of producers. In a similar vein Ateljevic (2000: 371) characterises tourism as a 'nexus of circuits operating within production-consumption dialectics enabled by the processes of negotiated (re)production'.

What is common to the different analyses is that global tourism production involves an overlay of different types of industries and economic activities. The forms of exchanges that occur, and differential power among producers as an aspect of this, are highly significant in determining outcomes, such as what is produced, how it is produced, and for what purposes. For a country such as South

Africa, its location in this system is an important element of what economic and broader developmental benefits can arise from tourism.

Tremblay (1998) presents a conceptual model for studying the industrial organisation of and the nature of producer interplay in tourism. Tourism, he argues is a highly dynamic and highly fragmented system of production constituted of many diverse firms that both compete, but also co-operate in a number of ways to produce certain products. Co-operation in the tourism system takes place 'through a web of cooperative and competitive linkages fashioned by the nature of the capabilities they possess and the available complementary inputs in the market' (Tremblay, 1998: 854). Producer relations are organised into, and shaped by loosely structured networks of interaction that straddle different firms and tourism sectors. Second, firms that have more economic or other resources hold greater sway in the tourism system.

Globalisation and Changes in Tourism's Industrial Patterning

Increased mobility, technological advances and the general thrust of globalisation have significantly impacted on tourism production and producer interaction over the past number of years. This occurs at two levels. First, the interface between different types of producers has increased and degrees of interaction are more intense. This is concomitant with changed production activities and methods. Second, and related to this intensified engagement, is a heightened level of competition among producers.

Changes in production activities are generally associated with broad shifts in the modes of production, encapsulated in literature on neo- and post-Fordism. As discussed in Chapter 2, this includes the adoption of flexible production methods and schedules, specialisation, the establishment of economies of scope and the expansive use of technologies such as CRS and GDS. The increased significance of 'place' (such as cities) as sites of consumption and 'culture' as commodities that have started to occupy central positions in tourism production, can also be seen as part of this (Ioannides and Debbage, 1998).

The industrial organisation of tourism's various producer sectors has also been influenced by globalisation. The two most significant trends have been the establishment of strategic alliance networks among different producers and that of industrial concentration (or consolidation).

Strategic alliance networks Alliance formation takes several forms in global tourism production. Given the great level of fragmentation within tourism and other constraints such as demand for rapid delivery, often narrow margins and the ephemeral and ethereal nature of the tourist experience, the establishment of cooperative relationships among producers is generally regarded as essential (Medina-Muñoz and García-Falcón, 2000). The increased move towards post-Fordist production techniques such as the use of subcontractors and outsourcing has accelerated the creation of closer supportive relationships among producers. Generally this involves the sharing of resources, particularly information, or the collaborative use of technologies such as CRS. The airline industry has been a central role player in the emergence and growth of strategic partnerships, with the establishment of major marketing and code-sharing alliances. Lufthansa's Star Alliance, which sees it cooperating with other big, international aviation firms such as Singapore Airlines, United Airlines of the USA, and smaller, regional carriers such as SAS Scandinavian Airlines, British Midland, Air Mauritius and South African Airways, is the world's largest airline alliance. It is followed by Skyteam, which is led by Air France-KLM and the American-based Delta Airlines and whose membership is made up of other smaller firms such as Korean Air. One World, a partnership between *inter alia,* British Airways, American Airlines and Australian airline, Qantas and Hong Kong-based Cathay Pacific, is the third major, international alliance.

The marked expansion of airline alliances over the past number of years has been prompted both by a desire by aviation firms to extend their market shares and by more stringent competitive conditions in a more hostile business environment. Excessive shocks to the global airline industry following the September 11th attacks had harsh impacts on most airlines, leading in some instances to extensive reshuffling or withdrawal. The consequences of 9/11 on the European market were seen in the dramatic liquidation of Swissair, and its subsequent transformation into Swiss International Air Lines. Smaller national carriers such as Sabena also had to undergo restructuring. Some of the larger European airlines have been able to capitalise on this and to consolidate their positions in the European market by acquiring other struggling carriers. In 2004 Air France's acquisition of KLM heralded what was regarded by many commentators as a new wave of consolidation. Lufthansa's announcement of a phased acquisition of Swiss International Air Lines in early 2005 seems to be part of this. To date, however, the constricting impacts of the global aviation regulatory regime, built as it is around bilateral agreements (this is discussed at length in Chapter 6) which govern airlines' rights and may change as ownership changes, have caused most airlines to be reluctant to follow the route of outright acquisitions (Done, 2005).

Collaboration and alliance formation also takes place across different producer sectors. Many destinations, for example have seen the establishment of national or regional reservation management systems that draw in national and other airlines, tour operators and hotel establishments. Generally, the largest international tour operators are all part of extensive strategic alliance networks and have been able to increase their influence on global tourism in this way. Nonetheless, Medina-Muñoz and García-Falcón (2000) note that to date, widespread and successful relationships between hotels and travel intermediaries have not emerged.

A further important example of cooperation relationships is the establishment of destination marketing alliances. Interdependence and the pursuit of common objectives often see state/public organisations and firms pool resources to produce promotional material, or invest in tourism and other infrastructure. Within the private sphere firms from various producer sectors may financially or organisationally collaborate to market a single tourist product or destination. Following Terpstra and Simonin (1993) marketing alliances can be distinguished by their geographical or functional extent (coverage), form, mode and motivation.

The maturity – and ultimately success – of marketing relationships is significantly influenced by the depth of cooperation, enthusiasm and commitment shown by partners and how tightly organised it is, although the political and economic environment within which contracting partners operate also greatly mould the nature and effect of alliances (Palmer and Bejou, 1995).

Consolidation Consolidation and integration have become particularly significant trends in the global tour operator sector, with very large firms merging, or buying up smaller operators. This feature is particularly marked in Western Europe. For instance, seven mega-companies[1] dominate the German market. These companies are also of the largest in Western Europe. Over the past number of years the West European market has become increasingly integrated as wholesale operators started to move in to markets traditionally served by national firms. This was most visible in Preussag's acquisition of the Thomson Group in 2000, which had consolidated Tui's position in Western Europe. To gain a perspective of the magnitude and impact of wholesalers in the traveller market, it is useful to consider that in 1999 the Tui Group had more than 12 million passengers.

Growing global consolidation among wholesale tour operators carries some implications for smaller, medium and micro (SMM) operators, who generally lose foothold in the organised travel and tour market as cheaper products from wholesalers threaten their competitiveness.[2] As a consequence many smaller operators have either liquidated or have been bought up by wholesalers. In the German market, for instance the proportion of independent operators and travel agents had shrunk from close to 60 per cent in 1996 to 37 per cent in 1999 (*FVW International*). Concurrent to this, the proportion of operator franchises and cooperatives has steeply risen.

The German case provides an interesting example of how tourism production and consumption processes interrelate and mutually affect one another. The organised tour operator sector is gaining in importance in Germany, reflected in the robust growth of this sector. Historically, tour and travel operators, independent of their size, did not occupy a central role in the travel and tourism market in Germany. For a long time this market was mainly comprised of the Free, Independent Travel (FIT) segment – travellers who do not utilise operator and travel agency services, but make their own travel arrangements. Since the beginning of the 1990s this has changed significantly, as the number of travellers who avail themselves of the services of operators rose, and additionally, the market base substantially grew after the German unification in 1990. Today, it is estimated that more than 50 per cent of all outbound trips is organised or sold by German tour operators. This represents a significant increase from the beginning of the 1990s when only one-third of all trips undertaken by Germans were organised through tour operators and travel agencies (DRV *Fakten und Zahlen zum deutschen Reisemarkt*, 2000). One reason for this growth is consumers' greater awareness of the legal obligation under which tour operators have to function, and the legal protection afforded to consumers under German travel legislation. This rise in the operator segment has had an important homogenising effect on the overall travel and leisure patterns of Germans, as they relate to particular destinations. It is highly significant in this regard that tour and travel operators' relative gain in market share in recent years has been accompanied by an increase in the sale of packaged tours, in particular all-inclusive package tours by wholesalers.

The net consequence of such developments in the travel and tour producer sector in Germany, and related changes in the consumption of travel and tourism products on the part of German travellers, is that destinations have become retailed in distinctly different fashions.

The political changes in Germany, and the unification of former East and West Germany in 1990 had a profound effect on German travel and tourism patterns. Prior to the unification the Federal Republic of Germany (FRG) and the German Democratic Republic (GDR) had very dissimilar travel preferences and trends. This difference was mainly due to the diverse economic systems both countries had in place, and in the case of the GDR, the restrictions placed on the movement of its citizens. In the former West Germany the travel and tourism market rapidly grew during the 1950s, fuelled on by rising income levels and generally improving standards of living (Hallerbach, 2000). In the 1970s, 1980s and the beginning of the 1990s this growth was further stimulated by easier access to other member states of the European Community, concomitant growth in the travel and tourism producer market throughout Western Europe, and the consequent broader travel opportunities afforded to FRG citizens.[3] With the fall of the Berlin Wall in 1989 and the unification of East and West Germany, significant changes occurred particularly in the travel behaviour of the citizens of the former GDR, with East Germans shifting their preferred travel destinations increasingly westward.

The shifts in the German travel and tour operator market over the past number of years have significantly impacted on the travel industry in two ways: the growth in the operator market was accompanied by increases in the travel industry as a whole. In addition, the expansion of the operations of many wholesalers saw a concomitant increase in charter flight operations. The six largest charter airlines in Germany (LTU, Condor, Hapag-Lloyd, Aero Lloyd, Air Berlin, Germania) for instance, all registered substantive growth rates in the latter half of the 1990s. This was mainly due to the rise in the number of Germans buying the products and destinations sold by charter companies, which mainly include destinations in the southern Mediterranean, and North Africa. The charter airlines, many of whom are owned by other wholesale operators, primarily operate as holiday and leisure transport providers, selling flights as part of all-inclusive or holiday packages. Undertaking group or individual bus tours is another important niche market in Germany.

South African Producer Spheres

The South African travel intermediary market has been significantly affected by global trends. The number of travel consortiums – conglomerates of tour operators and travel agencies who operate under one marketing brand – has grown in South Africa over the past five years. In 1999, for instance, the country had 460 inbound tour operators, with 15 major wholesalers. Tourism expansion – although international tourist arrivals have more or less stabilised since the rapid growth after 1994, tourism supply has seen significant development – has led to the growth of local inbound tour operators to more than 800 by 2004. At the same time, however, six firms dominate the market, accounting for 60 to 70 per cent of revenue generated. Figure 4.1 identifies the main South African operators.

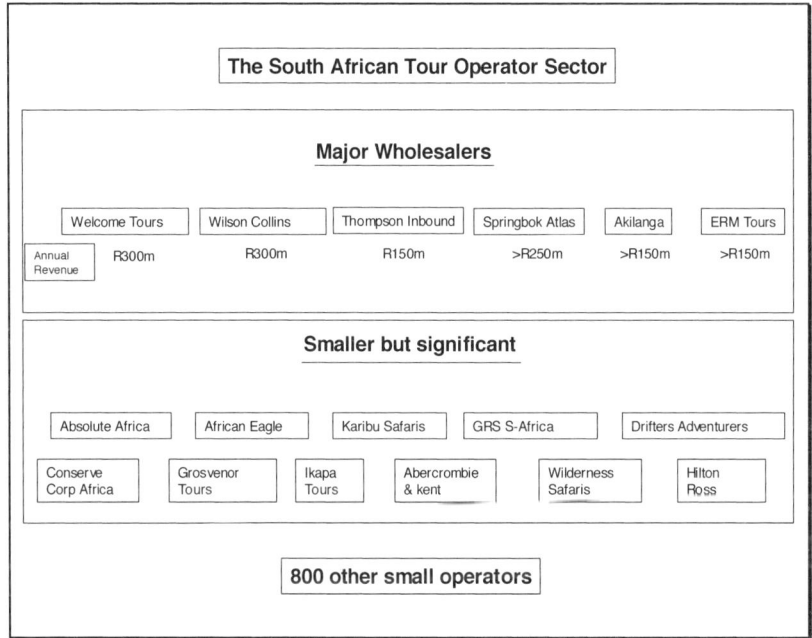

Figure 4.1 The structure of the South African tour operator sector
Source: Nedlac (1999); SA Tourism (2004)

Globally, expansive consolidation has significantly affected competition among tour operators, with the very large (or mega-) wholesalers generally crowding out smaller players. Market characteristics and consumer preferences have however also had a mediating influence, as typically, wholesalers aim for volume. SMM operators in contrast focus on specialised market segments and the creation of niche markets. It is thus common to describe SMM operators as the 'boutiques' of the travel and leisure industry, while the wholesalers are the 'supermarkets'. While wholesalers do have a better leverage in the tourism system, SMM operators are able to cater for selective markets. In addition to this SMM operators can also be players in the wholesale market by imitating the products offered by wholesalers (in the parlance of tourism and travel known as 'me-too' products).

Thus far the global trend towards greater coalescence among wholesalers has not had very many negative consequences for the South African tourism system, which given the country's main international product appeal has traditionally been the domain of specialist operators. Nonetheless, the basis of competition among producers has significantly been moulded by the increased formation of travel consortiums with, characteristically, large tour operators gaining greater leverage over other producers such as hotels. This has led to some degree of tension within the national tourism production system and in some instances price wars. As will be discussed below, such factors impact on the entire system.

Overall, the South African production system is interlocked with a global structure of production where exchange is both fluid and significantly framed by larger producers. The steady penetration into the country's sector since the end of the international sanctions era by multinational tourism firms means that many global players shape domestic production and tourism outcomes. As is shown in Tables 4.1 and 4.2 it is particularly in the transport sector where multinational firms have a significant representation in the South African tourism production system.

In air transportation this is due to the consolidated nature of the global air travel industry, the dominance of this industry by a few major airlines and the relatively small size of the country's national carrier. The car rental sector is closely aligned with the country's motor industry, itself a highly monolithic industry, dominated by only a few large motor corporations. Typically motor corporations use car rentals as a mechanism to absorb new motor vehicles introduced into the market and to eventually circulate these to the extensive domestic used car market. Franchise agreements between South African motor corporations and multinationals provide a presence to these multinationals in the South African market.

In contrast, as shown in Table 4.3 incursion by multinational firms into the South African hotel sector has been much slower. As such, only a few global brands have become established in the South African market. Multinational firms typically direct themselves to the international leisure sector that yields lower volumes but higher returns. Most of the global groups are therefore active in the four- and five-star sectors. With the exception of boutique hotels in South Africa, few South African firms specialise in the five-star sector. The two major South African hotel groups, Southern Sun and Protea Hotels are distinct in that they have positioned themselves across the entire spectrum of the sector, having developed brands that focus on different facets of the market. Protea Hotels' ownership and management structure, for instance, is typically neo-Fordist where through franchising agreements the hotel group acquires sub-brands that cater for both the higher and lower ends of the hotel market. In this way it has gained a considerable portion of the domestic leisure, tourism and business markets in South Africa.

Table 4.1 International air traffic to and from Johannesburg and Cape Town International Airports

Air traffic movement – 2001-2002			
Total no. of passengers departing (millions)		Total no. of landings	
Johannesburg	Cape Town	Johannesburg	Cape Town
5.7	2.4	80 343	41 969

International airlines operating to and from Johannesburg and Cape Town	
International	**Regional (Intra-continental)**
Air France	Air Botswana
British Airways	Air Gabon
Cameroon Airlines	Air Madagascar
Cathay Pacific Airways	Air Malawi
El-Al	Air Mauritius
Emirates	Air Namibia
LTU International Airways	Air Seychelles
Lufthansa	Air Tanzania
Malaysia Airlines	Air Zimbabwe
Olympic Airways	Congo Airlines
Qantas Airways	Egypt Air
Singapore Airlines	Ethiopian Airways
South African Airways	Ghana Airways Ltd
Swiss International Air Lines	Kenya Airways
TAP Air Portugal	
Varig Brazilian Airlines	
Virgin Atlantic Airways	

Source: Airports Company of South Africa

Table 4.2 Car rental franchises dominant in the market for international tourists to South Africa

Rental Franchise	Ownership	Approximate Market Share (%)
Avis Southern Africa	Barlow Holdings	33
Europcar	Imperial Holdings	25
Budget	McCarthy Motor Holdings	25
Hertz	Unitrans Motor Holdings	6

Source: Various

Table 4.3 Major hotel chains operating in South Africa

Group	Number of hotels	Number of rooms
South African-owned hotels		
Southern Sun	74	12 295
Protea Hotels	74	5 135
City Lodge	35	3 791
Three Cities	27	1 413
Don Group	9	411
Stocks Hotels and Resorts	9	1 119
Gooderson	9	480
Fortes King	6	505
Relais Hotels	3	221
Multinational subsidiary or franchise		
Best Western	7	683
Radisson SAS	1	182
Hyatt	1	244
Arabella Sheraton	1	483
Hilton Group	2	656
NH Hotels	2	*

* Unknown

Source: Various

The Dynamics of the Tourism Production System

Chains of Commercial Interaction and Transactional Processes and Linkages

The international production, marketing and selling of the South African tourist product is an interwoven process that involves a series of transactions among international and domestic (local) producers. It draws together a range of producers from various producer spheres that collaborate to produce tourist goods. A sequential flow of business characterises tourism, and a chain of actors is engaged in the sale of tourism attractions and destinations. This chain flows from international clients to local producers, such as hotels, via international travel agents and wholesalers and local ground operators.

The final tourist product is hence the outcome of the serial interaction and exchange among a diverse range of producers. As discussed in Chapter 3, given the nature of the South African tourist product and its main consumer segments, producer activities are geared towards the production and selling of the country as an explorer destination. This means that transport in the form of flights, car rental or guided tours, is a particularly significant component of the tourist product. International consumers characteristically purchase travel packages to South Africa, varyingly consisting of flights, accommodation, car rental and day trips or excursions to local sites.

Five commercial relationships between international and domestic producers and between producers and consumers may be delineated. This is depicted in Figure 4.2.

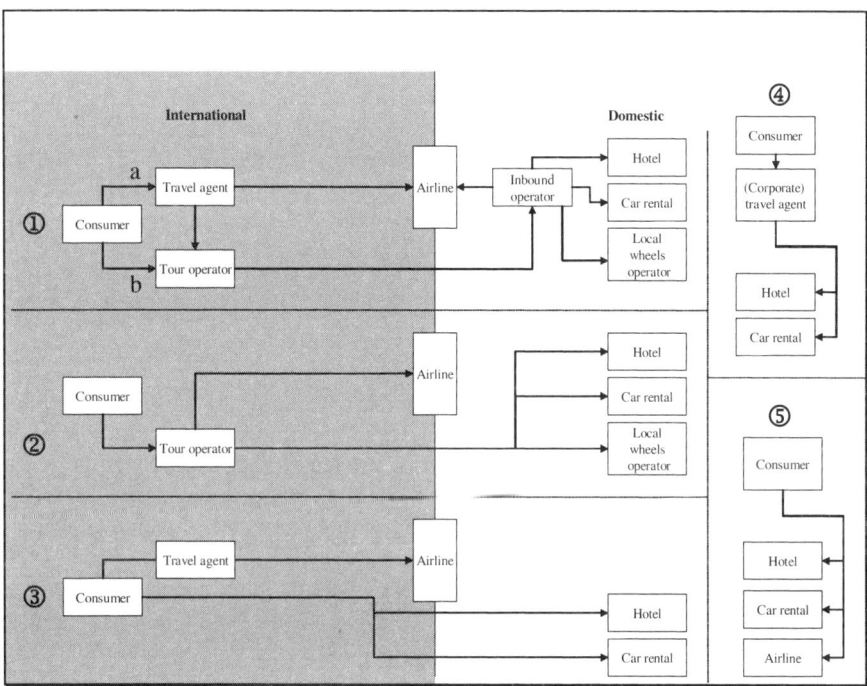

Figure 4.2 Commercial interaction in the global tourism production system
Source: Author's own design; based on interview data

The first commercial relationship involves an international tourist (based for example in Germany or the United Kingdom) purchasing a comprehensive travel package that includes an international flight to South Africa, domestic flights between different locations in South Africa, hotel (or other) accommodation in various locations, car rental, and day trips or excursions. The consumer may purchase the travel package from a local travel agent (a) or directly from an international tour operator (b). The international tour operator has in turn bought the various components of the travel package (flights, accommodation, etc) from a South African tour operator. This domestic inbound operator has negotiated and bought products from airlines, South African hotels, local wheels operators, and South African car rental companies. On the basis of this a travel package has been collated that involves a range of travel modalities and a number of South African destinations and locations.

In the second relationship an international tourist once again purchases a comprehensive travel package from an international tour operator. This time the tour operator has not made use of an inbound operator in South Africa, but has directly interacted and negotiated with different international and South African producers to compile a travel package.

In the third relationship the international tourist does not make use of the services of a tour operator, but directly purchases travel and accommodation components from the respective producers. The tourist may purchase the flight through a travel agent.

Fourthly, on the domestic side domestic tour operators and travel agencies act as conduits for domestic leisure and business tourism. These intermediaries interact with hotel and other accommodation establishments, car rental companies, domestic airlines and other transport producers to provide tourist products to domestic consumers. Corporate tour operators and travel agencies specialise in procuring and channelling business to domestic tourism producers.

Finally, domestic consumers can bypass tour and travel intermediary services and directly purchase tourist and travel components from producers in South Africa.

As is clear from Figure 4.2, the number of producers and the depth of commercial exchange involved in the tourist product that is eventually purchased by a consumer depend on the content of this product. Three aspects can however be highlighted. First, as far as international tourism is concerned, some producers occupy positions of centrality in the tourism production system. Given that airlines provide infrastructure and constitute the primary means of access between South Africa and its international source markets, they may be said to be salient actors in the production process (Britton, 1991).

Second, it is also apparent that as far as the travel components related to the tourist product is concerned, tourism consumers have limited manoeuvrability in their interaction with producers: producers offer a contained set of travel products (flights, excursions, or car hire) and restrict consumers to certain choices. In this instance consumers do not shape the product offer; the tourist product, as far as it is centred on travel elements, is generally fixed. Producers do however differentiate themselves on the type, price and quality of product they produce and offer to consumers. In an extensive series of interviews with a wide range of South African and international producers, regulators and consumers,[4] a representative of a car rental company for instance stated:

> (In the car rental sector), we all have the same product, we've got the same vehicles, the same systems. The only thing we can use to distinguish ourselves from the rest is through service, and periodically by lowering prices. But service is our priority.

Third, tour operators and travel agencies constitute a key link in the series of interactions that take place. There is a distinct division of labour between tour operators and travel agencies. Tour operators are producers, consumers and retailers in the production system. They purchase tour product components from other producers, which they on-sell. Travel agencies on the other hand only fulfil a retail function. Tour operators and travel agencies however share the function of brokerage.

Networks of Interaction: Size, Penetration and Proximity

Established networks of interaction exist between international and domestic producers. This is firstly based on size. Commercial interaction is built around larger, rather than smaller firms. This is due to the greater market reach that larger firms proffer versus the smaller ones. A representative of a car rental company for instance argued:

> Somebody like Dertour, the German tour operator,[5] would give us a huge amount of rental days, it's a very lucrative client. Dertour in November and December last year flew in about 3000 travel agents and tour operators and brought them into Cape Town to show them the market. So obviously it's to our advantage to have Dertour as a client, and to be their preferred car rental company.

Transactional networks or links secondly are based on the kind of penetration that firms have in overseas source markets. The manager of a foreign-owned hotel for instance argued:

> We are a global brand, and we have a strong presence in Europe. This places us in a very good competitive position in South Africa, because the feeder market for South Africa's international tourism is Europe.

Similarly, the representative of a car rental company in South Africa attributed the company's leading market share in the car rental sector to:

> the company's presence in the source markets. In order to capture those source markets you really need to have a presence in those markets, that's our advantage, no matter what country you go to, we operate there.

Britton (1991) attributes particular power to airlines (specifically the national airline in a tourist-receiving country) and tour operators to shape the tourism production system. He argues:

> Because of the enormous sunk costs which must be recouped, and their substantial carrying capacity, airlines have both the financial imperative and commercial clout to extract advantageous terms ... The competitive advantage of the tour wholesaler lies in their doubly strategic position between all principal suppliers and between suppliers and consumers. Their power derives from the enormous volumes they can command, their pivotal familiarity with diverse market segments, and the capacity to shift tourist flows

from one destination to another or one supplier to another through the travel products (tour packages) they construct and promote. In other words, those sectors of the tourism system which intersect between the tourist in the home market and tourist destinations wield considerable influence over interindustry transactions and the geography of tourist flows (Britton, 1991: 457-458).

However, a producer's proximity to both consumers and destinations provides a good vantage point from which to exercise influence over interactions in the tourism production system and producers such as hotels or car rental companies can also accrue competitive advantage over others in the production system if they are more proximate to target markets. In the South African case some producers by virtue of providing both size and access to source markets are more influential in the national tourism production system than others. In the hotel sector these include both the largest national groups such as Southern Sun and Protea Hotels, who by their sheer size constitute a dominant presence in the domestic market, and some of the smaller, boutique domestic hotel groups (such as Stocks Hotels and Resorts who operate some of the main luxury hotels) who consciously concentrate on the upper segment of the international market (Table 4.3). Similarly, established global hotel groups such as Hyatt or Radisson SAS benefit from a brand that is tied to a global marketing and distribution network. This dominance can also be seen in the car rental sector where the market for international tourists is led by only four large firms (Table 4.2) who together hold approximately 91 per cent of the market.

The airline sector is shaped by several industry-specific and wider environmental factors (the focus of Chapter 6) that affect all of the airlines operating to South Africa. Nonetheless, a few airlines are powerful players in the South African market due to the market share they command. This in turn comes from their proximity to key overseas source markets such as the United Kingdom and Germany. Thus large airlines such as British Airways, Virgin Atlantic and Lufthansa (and to some extent, KLM) and smaller carriers such as LTU are important actors. Although internationally a small airline, the home carrier, South African Airways plays a pivotal role, influencing the nature and extent of all air travel to the country.

Collaboration in the Tourism Production System

Co-operation is a key feature of producer interaction in the tourism production system. Tremblay (1998) contends that networks of collaboration draw together producers from different producer spheres. Such co-operation is strongly influenced by producers with more capabilities. The South African case is typical of wider international production, where a set of commercial agreements and rules governs the interaction between the various tourism producers. These rules and agreements stem from the regulatory organisations and institutions discussed in Chapter 6, but are also commonly contracted among producers themselves. One hotel operator described the transactional process between hotels and tour operators as follows:

There is a standard tour operators' (STO) fee. This is a special, lowered hotel rate that is given to tour operators. Usually this rate is 20-25 per cent off the standard advertised or what we call rack rate for rooms. Tour operators can then put their own mark-up to the price they offer to the end client. On top of that tour operators can also get commission from hotels for making bookings. This commission varies. Now if there is a two-step booking process where a travel agent is involved, you pay commission to each partner in each step. When a travel agent books directly with a hotel they only charge ten per cent commission. But when a travel agent books through a tour operator, you have to pay ten per cent commission to each. That means you pay 20 per cent commission in total.

In the airline industry a similar structure prevails. According to an airline representative:

We apply a standard commission as laid down by IATA, which is nine per cent. So we'd give tour operators and travel agencies nine per cent commission for international flights bookings, although depending on how you want to incentivise different markets, commissions can vary between seven per cent and 12 per cent of a flight ticket price.

Similar procedures are followed in the car rental sector, whereby tour operators and travel agents are paid commission for business sourced.

Commissions therefore constitute the primary mechanisms whereby the commercial exchange between international and domestic producers is directed, and is one of the important forms of co-operation among producers. A second means of cooperation is through the provision of price discounts. This may involve collaboration among several producer spheres to incentivise source markets in the short-term offer of travel packages incorporating international and domestic flights, accommodation and car hire at much reduced prices. This could also entail the introduction of charter flights. International examples of similar projects based on wide-ranging price cuts indicate that this significantly stimulated tourist demand in long-haul destinations such as Southeast Asia or Kenya.

In recent years state organisations have become more concretely involved in marketing alliances with key South African producers and over the past four years South African Tourism, the statutory national marketing body has cooperated with South African Airways and five-star hotels to launch a price scheme in the UK market aimed at raising tourist numbers the country's traditional low season (May to September). This entailed flight-and-accommodation packages at much reduced prices. In key South African destinations such as Cape Town tourism seasonality has proven to be a major problem. Marketing initiatives such as these are important to ensure financial viability in the sector, although, as is discussed below destructive forms of competition among local producers have damaging effects on the wider sector.

Producer Competition and Effects on the Production System

Although cross-sector collaboration is a common feature of the tourism production system, rivalry among different producer sectors is also pervasive. Intra-sectoral competition (for example among different airlines within the airline industry) is an essential element of global tourism. Often however, competition arises between different producer spheres (e.g. between airlines and hotels) that affects, often negatively, the general production system. In the South African system, despite the fact that the governing commission structure regulates commercial exchange and facilitates co-operation among producers, tensions exist. This centres on two aspects – the higher operational costs it brings to producers, and the greater advantage that some producers enjoy over others in the levying of commissions. The role and position of tour operators is one that is particularly criticised. A common position within the hotel sector, for instance is that the increased formation of consortiums in the tour operator and travel agent sectors afforded these bodies increased leverage in their exchange with hotels. One hotel manager argued:

> At present there are significant shifts in the tour operator sector. Because of the consolidation of tour operator companies local operators are becoming larger and larger. They are now gaining more power, and are starting to demand more and more commission. At the moment there is a big conflict between hoteliers and tour operators about commission levels, tour operators are now demanding up to 30 per cent commission.

Another manager claimed,

> Tour operators are putting the squeeze on us, they continually squeeze for lower rates and sell it at a higher price.

Over the past half-decade the hotel sector in important international tourist cities such as Cape Town has seen sharp increases in supply (particularly in the luxury, or four- and five-star sectors). A sustained period of low growth in demand and occupancies, coupled with rising competition has led hotels to depress their room rates in order to draw business (Cornelissen, 2005). However, declining hotel revenues and yields are also attributed to the system of rate discounts and commissions operating between hotels and tour operators, where in a less favourable environment for the hotels, tour and travel operators have gained significant leverage. The commission structure, in other words, held negative financial consequences for the hotel sector. In an attempt to assuage both the costs and increased pressures from tour operators, hotel producers advocated a change in the broader transactional structure, which entailed phasing out operator and travel agency commissions. With this, hoteliers were following an emergent international trend where there has been increased pressure on travel agents to professionalise. Rather than receiving commissions from other producers, travel agents and tour operators were expected to levy charges on consumers. In early 2005 this extended into the domestic airline sector when SAA announced that it will cancel all commission payments to travel agents. This has meant a major transformation in the way that trading between tourism producers has been contracted and regulated.

A second example of cross-sector rivalry in the South African production system concerns price levels, and how prices for tourism products are determined. Despite rising international prominence since 1994 South Africa has started to gain a reputation as an expensive destination in several key source markets. Tourist surveys conducted by the South African Tourism offices in Germany and the United Kingdom indicate that South Africa is widely regarded as a high-priced destination by the general population. In the United Kingdom, South Africa is known as the second-most expensive long-haul destination to visit (*Business Day*, 4 March 2002). A similar perception pertains in the German market (personal communication, head of South African Tourism, Germany, 14 August 2000). This is significant since South Africa is competing against several cheaper long-haul destinations such as Vietnam or, up until the tsunami disaster at the end of 2004, Thailand.

In a prime international tourist region such as the Western Cape, price levels have emerged as a central point of contention among local producers. While it is one of the most important tourist locales in South Africa, the Western Cape is generally regarded as a high-priced destination for international tourists. Surveys on tourist prices consistently place this region as one of the most expensive in the country (*Business Day*, 5 September 2001). Discord has arisen among local producers over who is responsible for the state of affairs. Interviews with representatives from different producer sectors yielded conflicting viewpoints. For instance, several tour operators maintained that high accommodation prices raised the overall price for tourist packages. A tour operator argued:

> The Western Cape is an expensive destination, because the hotel accommodation is very highly priced, it's ridiculous, it's out of most man's pocket.

In contrast, the manager of a hotel group argued:

> People say that hotels in the Western Cape are expensive. Impossible, it's simply impossible. It is essentially a factor of tour operators trying to squeeze hotels for more money. What is also a problem, are airline prices. What makes South Africa expensive in a package sense is that it's dollar-based airline fees.

The argument about higher airfares raising the overall cost of travelling to South Africa was made by a number of other producers. According to a British tour operator,

> The airfares make South Africa an expensive destination. It is cheaper for us to send our clients, and we do send a lot more to Australia, the airfare is cheaper for us to get to Australia than it is to South Africa.

Another argued:

What is an issue, particularly for the UK and German market, is aviation policy. Aviation policy is getting more relaxed since 1994, but it's still restricted. The policy aims to protect the South African airline's market share. What that does is it artificially limits supply. As a result of this, possibly, prices are being kept artificially high.

A common position in the airline sector, however, was that international airfares to South Africa from source markets such as Europe 'are too low', an aspect that was affecting the profitability and yield of airlines operating to the country.

This is not without basis. The South African airline market was particularly hard hit by the disturbances in the global airline industry following the September 11th attacks. In early 2002 Swissair, a major shareholder in South African Airways at that time, withdrew its 20 per cent equity in the airline after suffering financial difficulties from the disaster. Shortly thereafter it temporarily terminated flight operations to the country. Even before 9/11, however, several other key airlines had withdrawn from South Africa due to unfavourable market conditions. In early 2001 three of the larger European carriers who had entered the South African market after 1994 – Austrian Airlines, Alitalia and Sabena – ceased operations. Industry role players attributed this to these airlines' lack of access to the prime British and German source markets and relatively small demand in their home countries.

The strong impact that such factors play in shaping the South African tourism system can be seen in the fact that while there has been a flurry of new entrants into the South African market during the period of excessive growth in the early 1990s with 74 airlines operating in the country in 1997, by 2001 this had decreased to 52. For a sustained period after the start of the new millennium decreased flight availability from European source markets and a volatile South African currency had given rise to high airline prices which were partly responsible for the contraction in international tourist arrivals. Chapter 6 discusses South Africa's aviation policy and the debates around it. By 2002 South Africa had started to benefit from a destination substitution effect as many, mainly European travellers, changed their leisure destination from the Americas to amongst others, South Africa, although as discussed in Chapter 3, this has been unstable.

Notwithstanding, conflict over tourism prices remains an important feature of producer interaction. In certain producer sectors such as accommodation or car rental this has taken the form of price wars. This has been particularly damaging to those sectors over the past number of years. A Cape Town based hotel operator for instance stated:

> Many five-star hotels in Cape Town are charging the same rates as three-star hotels during the winter period, with the effect that they're squeezing the three-star hotels out of the market. I know of a three-star hotel which had only 8% occupancy this past May.

From a producer perspective the price debacle is problematic: it is reflective of a sector where the pursuit of producer interests is leading to conflict rather than collaboration. Furthermore, it points to a very fragmented tourism sector where the articulation of common objectives may be difficult to achieve. More importantly, it stems from an attempt by local producers to gain a stake in the growing international market after 1994 and the higher yields attached to this market. This has been to the detriment of the wider sector since it has given rise to price wars within specific producer spheres, and has led to South Africa developing a reputation as an expensive destination in international source markets.

Conclusion

The production process is multifaceted and is constituted of various means of exchange, competition, collaboration and self-regulation between different producer spheres. The manner in which producers engage with each other (shaped as it is by processes of globalisation) affects aspects such as the prices that are levied for tourist products (such as accommodation or car rental) and the economic benefits that flow from tourism. A key attribute of the global tourism system is that some producers have more leverage in the production process than others. This leverage is based on the size of the producer and relatedly, market access and penetration, but also in the case of airlines and tour operators, the positioning and function of the producer in the wider system. Local producers in the South African sector interact with global counterparts and through networks of cooperation 'produce' the destination. Intense and often negative competition among local producers however can be harmful to the national sector. Overall, the nature and dynamics of producer producer relationships are significant elements of the parameters of the global tourism production system.

Notes

[1] These are: the Tui Group, the LTU Group, Otto Freizeit- und Touristik GmbH, Kuoni Reise AG, the conglomeration of NUR, C&N, Deutsche Lufthansa and Condor (the so-called 'yellow group'), the Rewe Group, FTI Touristik, and the Deutsche Reise- und Touristik owned by the Deutsche Bahn. The particular ownership structures of these various wholesalers have led some to proclaim the German wholesale operator market as monopolistic.

[2] Numerically, a distinction can be drawn between large medium-sized operators who can be defined as travel and tour operators who have more than 200 000 passengers annually, but less than 700 000, while small medium-sized operators have between 200 000 and 10 000 passengers per year. A micro tour operator is defined as one which has less than 10 000 passengers per year (e.g. Kirstges and Schusdziara, 1999).

[3] Tourism in the former East German state initially saw an escalation concurrent to tourism and travel levels in the FRG. This was a consequence of East German legislation enacted in 1949 that entrenched the right of its citizens to enjoy state-sanctioned periods of recreation and leisure, and to take annual vacation. To this purpose the *Freien Deutschen Gewerkschaftsbund* (FDGB) was set up as the organ that

administered the 'state organised social tourism', through its regulation of the tourism infrastructure and supply in East Germany (Hallerbach, 2000). The resultantly cheaper leisure and vacation opportunities in the GDR meant that the travel intensity and travel propensity of its citizens surpassed that of former West Germany. This trend reversed by the 1970s and 1980s as East Germans' scope of travel destinations became more limited in comparison with that of their West German neighbours. While West Germans were able to travel more extensively, and inexpensively to other West European destinations, it was becoming increasingly unaffordable for East Germans to travel to traditional vacation destinations in the GDR and the former Communist bloc (e.g. Poland and Hungary) (Hallerbach, 2000).

[4] This was part of a wider study on the dynamics and impact of tourism in South Africa. A total of 125 interviews were conducted over a nine-month period during 2000 and 2001.

[5] Dertour is the fifth largest tour operator company in Germany. It holds approximately seven per cent of the total German market.

Chapter 5

The Political Economy of Destination Marketing: Producing and Imaging 'Place' and 'People'

Introduction

In recent years there has been a surge in interest in the economic significance of destination imaging and place promotion, and its role in tourism growth. Many authors have noted the increased use of tourism-linked competitiveness strategies such as the hosting of hallmark events (e.g. large-scale sporting festivals such as the Olympic or Commonwealth Games (e.g. Hall, 1992; Hiller, 2000; Roche, 2000), increasing a country or city's capacity for international business and conference tourism (Fainstein and Gladstone, 1999; Jessop and Sum, 2000) and the redevelopment of derelict urban areas (particularly harbours) into tourist theme parks (Beauregard, 1998; Pow, 2002). Destination imaging – the development of a particular 'image' with which a region can be associated – is an integral component of such strategies (Holcomb, 1999; Rogerson, 1999). In the striving for enhanced competitiveness, it is aimed at fostering a specific place identity that dually renders a region distinct, and more alluring to potential investors and visitors vis-à-vis other destinations.

What is often overlooked, however, is that destination image is one aspect of the wider tourism production system. As with other types of tourist products, discussed in Chapter 4, place image is the result of competition and collaboration among different sets of economic sectors and producers with diverging and converging interests. Analysing tourist imaging more closely as the result of interaction among a cluster of producers yields important insights into various collections of interests linked to a tourist destination.

Second, tourist imaging is also fundamentally a social and political issue. It is the contrivance of a particular representation of a destination by agents/officials/marketers; it draws on existing social and cultural elements within the destination to develop a place identity, but, importantly, much of it also depends on the fashioning of new image(s) and narratives and the use of desire-instilling myth(s) to attract people to a destination. Such a procedure has social and political corollaries. Like other processes of identity construction it is dialogical, with the image of a destination shaped by the cultural milieu from which it stems, but also affecting the very culture(s) it seeks to represent (S. Hall, 1997). An increasing amount of research is being carried out on the social dimensions of destination imaging (e.g. Waitt, 2003). It is much less recognised that such imaging carries political consequences for host populations, often with economic spin-offs. The effect of tourist imaging is summed up powerfully by Pritchard and Morgan (2001: 168) who contend that

> repressive and liberating discourses are reflected in the marketing of tourism destinations. ... the way in which landscapes and destinations are imaged do have significant implications for how those places and their peoples are perceived.

Taken together, the analysis of the production of destination image – and the political and social components of it – provides useful insights into the economic and developmental impacts that tourism is likely to have in a given destination. As yet too little is known about how a destination's image relates to growth and development.

This chapter examines these aspects in the South African tourism production system. There is a concerted attempt by the government to use tourism as a means to achieve economic goals such as drawing in foreign investment. Developing an attractive image and reputation is therefore regarded as crucial. The chapter examines to what degree the content of South Africa's present image, and the production process whereby this occurs, permits this.

The central argument is that the way that 'place' and 'people' is produced and couched in tourist image(s) has an important effect on how they are consumed. Certain producers hold key positions of influence in the tourism production system and their activities have fundamental consequences for a given destination. The attempt by the South African government to develop a tourist image that transcends the sector's former exclusiveness, is counter to the image that actors such as international tour operators predominantly project about the country – based on the country's natural, rather than cultural characteristics and as such an extension of the prevailing tourist image of apartheid South Africa. Much of the existing tourist image also derives from widespread stereotypical portrayals of the African continent. In its attempt to reframe South Africa's image, the government paradoxically both uses (and in the exercise, reinforces) broad representations of Africa, and at the same time tries to distance the country from its wider geographical location.

As discussed in Chapter 1, the debate on the relationship between producers and consumers is intricate. A large body of tourism literature follows the neo-classical economics approach and propose that tourism consumers and their preferences shape production. With regard to destination imaging, some analyses show that tourists exercise some discretion in how they internalise, accept or modify visual, cultural and political messages about destinations (e.g. Norton, 1996). By arguing that producers such as tour operators play an influential role in shaping tourists' knowledge about a destination, this chapter reflects the position in tourism political economy literature (e.g. Cheong and Miller, 2000; Hollinshead, 1999) that asserts the primacy of producers over consumers. The relationship is nonetheless one of mutual affect where, for instance with respect to the content of tour itineraries and the inclusion or exclusion of specific locales, demand impulses do impinge on what producers offer.

The Construction, Production and Consumption of Place

The visual consumption of place has long been recognised as a key aspect of tourism (Markwick, 2001). Urry (1990) most lucidly articulated this in his formulation of the 'tourist gaze'. According to Urry the way in which people travel through a destination is highly structured. More importantly, the 'tourist gaze', the way in which people view the places and people they visit is 'socially organised and systematised'.[1] 'The gaze is constructed through signs, and tourism involves the collection of signs' (Urry, 1990: 1, 3). These signs, in essence are ways of understanding tourist destinations. They constitute tacit rules for conduct that are used by tourists. They guide people in the 'appropriate' observance of and behaviour towards visited locales, objects and people.

The tourist gaze, however, also has an important power dimension: sociologically, the manner in which tourists engage with the places, objects and societies they visit, is imbued with certain values and based on power discrepancies between hosts and visitors (Urry, 1990). As originally formulated this was seen to pertain to the travel of Westerners to developing countries. In the 1970s many authors have noted the adverse social and cultural impact of Western tourism on developing societies. V. Smith (1978) for instance noted how apathy towards and ignorance about the values and cultural practices of host societies could lead to hostility and social alienation on the part of hosts, and eventually conflict. MacCannell (1973) argued that the search for novel experiences and cultural 'authenticity' constitutes a key motivation for travel to developing countries. This reduces hosts to nothing less than objects of wonderment, but also means that, to satisfy tourists' demands, host culture is performed or 'staged'. Often, according to MacCannell (1973) this leads to a loss of identity.

While this is suited as a generic critique of tourist representations of the developing world, depictions of the African continent are of a singular nature. A well-established body of literature documents themes that predominate tourist portrayals of the African continent. These include aspects regarding landscape (wide spaces, open for discovery by the tourist; romanticised (Bruner, 2001; Pieterse, 1992)), sexuality (either a subordinate or feminine, or warrior representation (e.g. Bruner and Kirshenblatt-Gimblett, 1994)), primevalism and exoticism (inhabited by peoples with strange and interesting customs and habits (e.g. Buntman, 1996)). In all, as argued by Bruner (1991) Africa is generally represented as 'the archetypal other', a place where Western tourists can attempt to refashion lost bonds with nature and the environment.

Importantly, while the tourist gaze in Urry's formulation partly stem from tourists' own established norms, it also arises from the signification of place and the representations that are linked to destinations. One set of agents that collate and present signs and visual and verbal messages to tourists is tourism producers, place promoters and destination marketers. They do this by means of imagery, photography, and tourist brochures, their prime marketing tool. As such, tourism producers and place promoters are key conveyors, but also creators of destination image (Ioannides, 1998; MacKay and Fesenmaier, 1997; Waitt and Head, 2002), and in Urry's terms, active constructors of the tourist gaze.

In their analysis of the tourist branding of Wales, Pritchard and Morgan (2001) for instance found that it was firstly, based on a recasting of Welshness, and deriving from a re-conceptualisation of ethnic identification in contemporary Wales. In this, a promotion of 'Cymru' and the Welsh culture and language was a key focus of marketing attempts directed at overseas markets. At the same time, however, given the political sensitivities surrounding the Welsh identity in the United Kingdom, this aspect was downplayed in domestic promotional campaigns. Instead, the emphasis was on the country's natural attractions.

This example shows how tourist representation is a political process in which tourism producers (and other marketers) are influenced by dominant political trends in the destination, and how they both draw from existing, but also create new narratives and myths in their promotion of destinations.

Destination imaging, in other words, is a powerful force. Tourism producers lie at the cusp of tourist destinations and the people who visit these destinations. Politically and socially, this leaves them with a considerable degree of clout over, not only the tourists, but also over the destinations they promote. Destination imaging however also has a commercial effect as tourism producers select and filter through information to consumers. In this process, according to Hollinshead (1999: 9) 'some things/ideas/attractions are powerfully and/or commercially made dominant, while others are subjugated, silenced or ignored'.

Since travel and tourism intermediaries such as tour operators and travel agencies straddle different producer sectors, they can be argued to play a key coordinating role in the production system. They however also occupy distinct positions of influence (Britton, 1991: 457-458).

In essence destination image and the various media through which it is transmitted to tourism consumers (such as brochures or postcards) form an important component of a destination's overall product, and plays an important part in how destinations are consumed (e.g. Dann, 1996; Markwick, 2001; Waitt and Head, 2002).

South African Tourist Re-imaging

Over the past number of years, a key aspect of the South African government's efforts to transform the tourist sector has focused on redrafting and extending the country's tourist image to be more representative of the country's population. A common criticism of the tourism sector during the apartheid era was that, aside from the fact that it provided very little access to the black population as producers, it was based on an image that was highly exclusionary (DEAT, 1996; Koch and Massyn, 2001). Social representation in apartheid tourism, according to Goudie, Khan and Kilian (1999: 22) was of a nature where 'black cultures were ignored or repressed, at best they became stereotyped and trivialised commodities in the tourism economy'. In its efforts to transform tourism, and realise its potential as an economic catalyst, the South African government therefore is also keen to develop a more inclusive tourism brand (DEAT, 1996; DEAAT, 2001). On the one hand this may be seen as an element of the government's larger nation-building project, which has the objective of forging a strong sense of a common nation among South Africans while at the same time accentuating the diverse cultural and heritage origins of its citizenry (Bekker, 1997). On the other, this will allow South Africa to reposition itself internationally vis-à-vis other competitor destinations.

This dual-faceted use of tourism is reflected in the following two policy statements of South African National Parks (the statutory body that manages the country's wildlife assets) and South African Tourism:

> The transformation mission of the South African National Parks is to transform an established system for managing the natural environment to one which encompasses cultural resources, and which engage all sections of the community (South African National Parks, 2000).

South African Tourism has reformulated its position and objectives in post-apartheid South Africa in the following way:

> South Africa is a country undergoing transformation. The result is that we are exploring our image. In the process our country's unique selling points are becoming increasingly clearer. The old Satour (the former name of South African Tourism) slogan, A World in One Country, is more relevant now than ever (DEAT, 1999/2000).

By far the most significant signal of the government's attempt to re-image, re-brand and re-position South Africa internationally, is the government's major branding programme, 'Brand South Africa'. Launched in 2000 as a marketing cooperation arrangement between state departments and some of the country's largest corporations, the campaign sets out to promote a favourable image of the country, both to domestic and international audiences. Its slogan, 'South Africa....Alive with possibilities', seeks to triumphantly convey the geographical, historical and social distinctiveness of the country, the relative success of its recent political transition, and, as a consequence of this, the opportunities that derive for investors and others. The brand is summarised as:

> (South Africa), in global terms a middling nation at the foot of a maligned continent, has the ability to inspire the world to new ways of doing things. Our unique historical heritage and population make-up, our creative approach and boundless optimism, all come together and find expression in the essence of the brand, 'South Africa...Alive with possibilities' (International Marketing Council of South Africa, no date).

In essence, therefore, South Africa's tourist image is of keen instrumental interest to its authorities. Economically, the assumption is that a more inclusive tourist image will help bring about a more equitable sharing of the developmental benefits of tourism. Politically, a suitable tourist image can help meet key domestic objectives of transformation. Towards this objective the government has undertaken various strategies to revise the country's predominant international image. There is however, an incongruity between what the government wants to achieve, and how it sets about it, that paradoxically, rather than offset established stereotypes, may indeed reinforce it. Two reasons account for this, first, the wider political economy of the tourism system and the role that other producers such as tour operators play, and second, the broader complexities that surround representations of the African continent and the added difficulties this pose to the South African tourism authorities.

Contending Tourist Representations

Portrayals of South Africa by Overseas Tour Operators

As far as the economic and developmental aims for tourism by South Africa's authorities is concerned, it is important to remember that the government is only one set of agents in an interwoven international tourism production system. The nature and structure of the international tourism production system suggests that the South African authorities' objectives of forging a more inclusive tourist image, is to a large measure contingent upon the actions and directions of others involved in the production and promotion of South Africa as destination. While it is commonly asserted that South Africa's international destination image is misrepresentative and limited, very little systematic research has been conducted on the role of producers such as tour operators in imaging the country, and the consequences it has. One exception is a study that examines the tourist brochures of Dutch and British operators who promote South Africa as a destination. It was found that representation in these brochures both stemmed from colonial and neo-colonial discourses, and perpetuated neo-colonial relationships between South Africa and its former colonial powers. This was done through the use of various images of landscapes and peoples that expressed exoticism, excitement and exploration (Foster, 2001).

Foster's study provides a useful analysis of the nature and ideological context of South Africa's representation in foreign markets. A more comprehensive scrutiny of not only the visual content of South Africa's destination image, but also its relation to the larger product offer by tourism producers, and the process whereby this occurs – in other words examining more closely the workings of the international tourism production system, and South Africa's position in it – could however provide important insights into the political, social and economic impacts that destination imaging has on South Africa, and how the developmental objectives that the country's authorities hold for tourism, could be attained.

With this purpose, a study was conducted of the way that the country is represented in Germany and the United Kingdom, its two most important markets for overseas tourists, and very important sources of tourism revenue. It entailed two types of assessments: tour operator brochure analyses, and interviews, conducted with overseas tour operators and South African tourism authorities.[2]

The brochure analysis sought to serve two purposes: to determine the places, destinations and attractions that overseas operators mainly promote, and to evaluate the destination images and representations that these brochures conveyed. Towards this end brochures were content analysed.

Content analysis has been defined as a method 'for making inferences by objectively and systematically identifying specified characteristics of messages' (Carney, 1972: 25). It refers to a set of techniques to analyse the meaning(s) of texts and other forms of communication. Content analysis can be approached both quantitatively and qualitatively. In the former, a text or other communication is analysed in terms of the frequency with which a certain element or category (e.g. a word, phrase or picture) appears (Slater, 1998). In qualitative content analysis, more attention is paid to the process and social context within which communication takes place. According to May (2001: 193), the researcher aims at 'reading …the text in terms of its symbols…The text is approached through understanding the context of its production'.

The content analysis of the brochures consisted of both quantitative and qualitative investigations. This hybrid approach enables a more complete understanding of the specific role tour operators play in producing 'place': quantitatively in showing how certain locales are chosen and marketed above others by them, and qualitatively, by indicating the various messages attached to their brochures. With regard to the latter, other qualitative studies of tourism marketing materials focus on the intertextual context in which certain meanings are created and communicated through specific types of photographs or imagery (e.g. Norton, 1996, Waitt and Head, 2002). While it is here agreed that imagery are 'social constructions, or naturalised, commonsense views or "ways of seeing the world"', and important signals of differential power relations between viewer and viewed (Waitt and Head, 2002: 320), rather than showing out the various types of photographs used by the overseas tour operators, this analysis gives an itemised account of the imagery they use (see below).

First, an enumerative component assessed the specific locales, travel routes and itineraries promoted in the brochures. This was done through an analysis of four types of tours advertised in the brochures – fly-drive tour packages; self-drive (so-called free independent travel (FIT)) tours; bus (group) tours; and escorted or guided tours (operated by local wheels operators). A total of 98 such tours were analysed. The tours were grouped according to the main destinations and attractions that formed part of the tour, and importantly, included a stopover (i.e. entailed an accommodation element). Figure 5.1 presents the results of the analysis.

Second, representations of South Africa were analysed. Photographs were examined and arranged into three categories: the type of product sold; the type of activity depicted; and the type of place (rural or urban) that was depicted. The way in which product, places and people were depicted, was additionally analysed. Attention was given to the kinds of messages and meanings that were conveyed with photographs. In this regard it was looked at who were the main consumers (in terms of gender, 'race', ethnicity), and what type of product they were consuming or engaging in. How place/space was presented in relation to people was also looked at. Finally, the texts (captions) that accompanied photographs were reviewed. The results of this analysis are shown in Table 5.1.

A key feature of the tour itineraries was that they combined different destinations in different parts of South Africa and the Southern African region into single tour routes. Tour itineraries were thus made up of multiple locales. A second feature was that all of the tour operator brochures comprised a 'classical' tour of South Africa that formed the basis of their South African product. This tour ran from Johannesburg in the north of the country to Cape Town in the south, was usually of a fortnight's duration, and included at least one other Southern African country. An example of such a tour is presented below:

> Arrive Johannesburg airport → Mpumalanga (private game reserves) → Kruger National Park → Swaziland → Zululand (visit to a Zulu cultural village) → Durban → Port Elizabeth → the Garden Route → Oudtshoorn → Cape Town → depart from Cape Town (Kuoni Worldwide 1 January 2001 to 31 December 2001).

A great degree of product standardisation and convergence centred around a few key destinations is hence evident in overseas tour operators' itineraries. Interviews with tour operators established three reasons for this. The first relates to the infrastructure for air arrivals and departures, with only two airports, Cape Town and Johannesburg servicing international operations. This encourages the structuring of travel routes between the two cities. The second reason relates to the existence of key tourist attractions, which are widely known and promoted internationally, in certain locations. The third reason centres on the demand by consumers to visit these key attractions. One tour operator argued:

> There's prime sites that are really focus points that people want to see, that will stand out in world travel terms. They want to see the animals, so they want to go on safari. They want to go to Cape Town, they probably want to go to the Victoria Falls. They want to combine at least two of those three things for their itinerary.

Operators singled out Cape Town as the primary tourist attraction in South Africa. One tour operator for instance stated:

> You've got to sell Cape Town, you can't sell a tour that doesn't include Cape Town because Cape Town is your honey pot. You need something that instantly attracts them, and Cape Town instantly attracts people. If you don't have Cape Town in, it's much harder to sell an itinerary.

Destination	Frequency
Western Cape province	
Cape Town	●●●●●●●●●●●●●●●
Breede River Valley	
Worcester	●
Montagu	●
Overberg	
Hermanus	●●
Cape Agulhas	●
Arniston	●●
Swellendam	●
West Coast	●●●
Great Karoo	●
Klein Karoo	●
Oudtshoorn	●●●●●●●
Winelands	●●●●●●
Garden Route	●●●●●●●
Knysna	●●●●●●●
Plettenberg Bay	●●●
George	●●
Wilderness	●●●●
Tsitsikamma	●●●●●
Mossel Bay	●●
Rest of South Africa	
Eastern Cape	
Port Elizabeth	●●●●●●●●●●
Gauteng	
Johannesburg	●●●●●●●●●●●●●
Mpumalanga (**game parks**)	●●●●●●●●●
Kruger National Park	●●●●●●●●●●●●●●
Kwazulu-Natal	
Zululand	●●●●●
Durban	●●●●●●●
Drakensberg	●●●●
Hluhluwe national park	●●●●
Northwest Province	
Sun City	●●●
Northern Province	●●
Northern Cape	●●●
Rest of Southern Africa	
Zimbabwe (Victoria Falls)	●●●●●●
Botswana	●●
Namibia	●●●●
Swaziland	●●●●●●●
Lesotho	●
Mauritius and Seychelles	●●●

Figure 5.1 Main South African destinations sold by overseas tour operators
Source: Various tour operator brochures

The classical route, according to tour operators, is the most optimal way in which key attractions and locations can be combined and sold as a cohesive package that will enable consumers, 'to see as much as possible (of South Africa) in quite a short time'.

All of this suggests that there is a delicate interplay between tourist demand and preferences, and tourism production, and that consumer preferences do mediate upon producer activities and the destination choices that are offered by tour operators. This is different to the relationship that pertains between producers and consumers in the case of transport elements, where consumer choice is limited (Chapter 4).

From a production aspect (and this links to the impact of tourism) it is important that select destinations and locales are included and marketed in tour itineraries. Figure 5.1 illustrates the effect of this – a number of destinations tend to be promoted above others. In the Western Cape there is a strong focus on the Cape metropolis and the Garden Route. In the rest of South Africa cities such as Port Elizabeth, Durban and Johannesburg, national and private game parks and other physical attractions in Mpumalanga and Kwazulu-Natal, and cultural attractions such as Zululand feature strongly. Beyond that a few of South Africa's neighbouring countries – in particular Zimbabwe, Swaziland and Namibia – are also promoted, although at a lower level than South Africa. Tour operators noted that South Africa constitute the focal point of the Southern African international tourist circuit, with the country often forming an infrastructural base for travel into the rest of the region. This, importantly, indicates how South Africa is differentially treated in the wider African continent by tour operators. The significance of this for the government's re-imaging endeavours, and the contradictions this gives rise to, are discussed below.

Table 5.1 shows the outcome of the analysis of the main representations of South Africa in the brochures. It categorises and ranks those images that most consistently appeared by: the type of product, the type of activity, and the place of consumption.

In terms of the product offered all the brochures contained detailed layout of car rental, flights and accommodation (mainly hotel) offers. Often this formed the core of many brochures. These sections consisted of photographs of the different types of vehicles and hotels that were promoted by the particular tour operator, along with price lists.

Aside from this, all the brochures widely featured animals. A wide variety of animals was imaged, although the 'Big Five' (elephants, lions, buffalo, leopards and rhinoceros) were mainly shown. In the main, the outdoor theme was one that pervaded all of the brochures. This is firstly evident in the importance of animals. Secondly there was a strong focus on nature. In all of the brochures, images of landscape, nature, and to a lesser extent, countryside dominated. The most important type of activity that was depicted, and one that consistently featured in all brochures, was game driving or game viewing. Wildlife and safari was clearly the focus of the brochures.

Table 5.1 Tourist representation of South Africa

Ranking	Product
1	Hotels
	Guest houses
	Car rental
	Flights
	Luxury trains
2	Animals
3	Cultural villages
4	Culture (e.g. women/children dancing in traditional clothing)
5	Arts and crafts

Ranking	Activity
1	Game driving/viewing
2	Hiking
3	Golf
4	Casino/gambling/resorts
5	Bathing/swimming
6	Sky/hang gliding
7	Horse riding/ponytrekking
8	Abseiling
9	Helicopter ride around Cape Town

Ranking	Place	
	Rural	Urban
1	The African bush	The Waterfront
2	Table Mountain	Cape Town Central Business District
3	Cape Dutch architecture	Sun City/Lost City
4	The Cape Peninsula	Durban
5	Drakensberg Mountains	Cape Town Parliamentary buildings
6	Wine estates (Winelands)	Union buildings in Pretoria
7	Blyde River Canyon (Mpumalanga)	
8	Chapman's Peak	
9	Cedar Mountains	
10	Cango Caves (Oudtshoorn)	
11	Traditional huts in rural area	

Where urban environments were depicted, this was usually done through a few core locations. All of the brochures, for instance, showed photographs of Cape Town; with the exception of Durban, other South African cities featured much less.

People were much less prominent in the brochures. Photographs of people were mainly in relation to wildlife or nature consumption – i.e. people could be seen partaking in game viewing, hiking, or bathing. Significantly, the vast majority of these photographs portrayed white individuals or families; there was very little depiction of black people consuming, or engaging in leisure. Black, 'coloured' or Indian South Africans were generally portrayed as cultural products: Ndebele women displaying and selling arts and crafts; isiZulu dancers; a Bushman woman in the Kalahari; or 'coloured' Coon Carnival troops in Cape Town at New Year.

The tourist image that arose from the brochures was one that emphasised South Africa as a destination for nature and wildlife consumption. More importantly, the way in which landscape and territory/space was presented in brochures, conveyed messages of adventure, discovery and subliminality to tourists: 'place' and territory were represented through wide, open spaces, suggesting opportunity and exploration. This was reinforced in the captions that accompanied many photographs, examples of which were:

Unbegrentze möglichkeiten (unlimited possibilities);

Alles was man sieht, atmet Groβe und Freiheit und unvergleichbare vornemheit (Everything one sees embodies size, freedom and inimitable exceptionality);

We carry within us the wonders we seek without us; there is all Africa and her prodigies in us.

Finally, Virgin Holidays, the tour operator arm of Virgin Atlantic Airways, defined South Africa as 'Virgin Territory'.

This is consonant with general portrayals of Africa in international tourist imagery highlighted earlier, where marketing materials project a primal depiction of African nature and the continent is shown as a space where Westerners can rediscover a pre-industrial self.

Nonetheless, South African tourist representation differs from the principal way of presenting Africa in several important ways. While Africa as a tourist destination is often coloured by broader, more negative imagery of hardship, poverty, war, hunger and turmoil that prevails in the popular media,[3] a pervasive international representation of South Africa focuses on its relative political and economic stability. This filters into tourist representation of the country. As a tour operator argued,

South Africa's attraction is that it is Africa, but it's not that kind that you see in the news, for example Uganda where tourists were slaughtered, or West Africa where there's no infrastructure. It is an African destination where you have perfect infrastructure.

Aware of this discernment made by international operators, South African tourism authorities seek to set the country apart from other African destinations in their marketing activities. In an interview a representative of South African Tourism in the United Kingdom, for instance stated the importance of 'putting South Africa out there as *South* Africa and not as South *Africa*'.

This distinctiveness is also echoed in the 'Brand South Africa' campaign. At one level there is hence some concurrence between the imaging objectives of the South African government and overseas tour producers. There is an important disparity however, in the aims and objectives of these two sets of actors on other aspects, one of which is the way culture is represented.

In the tourist brochures, emphasis was laid upon the diversity of the cultural heritage of black South Africa, and cultural villages and arts and crafts were often depicted as specific products for consumption, 'culture' was a very small component of tour operators' focus. More importantly, operators' depictions of culture diverged strongly from the way that the South African government is seeking to develop cultural locales, as sites of South African heritage and pride. Instead portrayals of culture in the operators' brochures were confined to limited and staged contact between international tourists and local populations in cultural villages, or visits to the Victoria and Alfred Waterfront, the latter being often promoted as the embodiment of South African culture. In this regard, several authors have criticised the architecture of the Waterfront development, which varies from post-modern to neo-Victorian/neo-colonial (e.g. Marks and Bezzoli, 2001). Goudie et al. (1999) argue that the architectural form of the Waterfront represents mainly the white history of South Africa. They contend:

> This Victorian leisure-world... is far from being a true reflection of local cultures. What is presented is a sanitised and carefully reconstructed history; the lives of black dockworkers, slaves, convicts, beggars and others whom made up the social fabric of everyday life in early Cape Town, lie buried beneath these depthless and romanticized images (Goudie et al., 1999: 26).

Overall, therefore the image found in the brochures is akin to the general international tourist portrayals of the broader African continent, based on stereotypical messaging concerning nature, landscape and people/cultures, and the possibility for the tourist to explore, rediscover and fulfil a primordial self. A broad critique can be made of this given the complexities surrounding land ownership in South Africa and the wider African setting (Koch, 1994). The image found in the brochures is not representative, but rather a reinforcement of the older, more exclusionary image that the country's international tourism has been founded upon since the apartheid era. The significance of this for the South African government's efforts to promote a new tourist image is further explored below.

State Strategies to Redraft South Africa's Tourist Image

Several initiatives and programmes have been undertaken by the South African government over the past half-decade aimed at advancing a revised tourist image. The most important of these are discussed. First, under the broad framework of 'Brand South Africa', tourist expansion strategies have been reformulated to incorporate re-branding objectives. For example, South African Tourism has devised its most recent Tourism Growth Strategy to focus on four main international 'brand audiences' (SA Tourism, 2002a). These are: 'Luxury in Africa'; 'Africa as Hip'; 'South Africa for Entertainment and Business'; and 'Value for Money in Africa'. The attempt is to expand both the size and yield of traditional source markets deriving from Europe and to target potential growth markets, particularly from Africa (SA Tourism, 2002a). It is significant that the agency is placing much greater emphasis than before on framing South Africa as part of the African continent, although still seeking to single out the country on its infrastructural superiority vis-à-vis the remainder of Africa.

Second, in an effort to give shape to its developmental and empowerment aims, the government's tourism development policy has focused on using a more inclusive tourism image to spread the economic benefits of tourism. In this, it has followed two main approaches. The first has centred on the active encouragement of 'culture' as a key attraction and market segment. While such efforts are contingent with trends in international tourism, the South African government's prime motivation is to use cultural tourism as a vehicle for large-scale employment-creation, and as a means to attain greater equity in tourism ownership. This is premised on the relative ease with which communities can enter the tourism sector as producers of cultural products (DEAT, 1996). The government's involvement is primarily driven through the Department of Environmental Affairs and Tourism (DEAT), the body responsible for formulating and implementing national tourism policy. Its Poverty Relief Programme is a scheme set up to expand and fund tourism infrastructure and product development projects. The emphasis is on projects that are located in disadvantaged areas and/or areas that have the potential of developing into tourism growth points or corridors. To date the financing of new products has been focused on the development of cultural products in the form of cultural villages, museums, craft stall and art galleries (DEAT, 2002b). A successful programme, in theory, will enable particularly poorer South Africans to generate and sustain an own income.

A second approach has been to try and alter the travel patterns of international tourists in an attempt to geographically diffuse tourism's economic impact. In the main this entails the development and promotion of tourist products and areas that generally do not receive much exposure in tourist source markets. The policies and strategies implemented in the Western Cape are representative of this broad national aim. In this province a number of initiatives have been implemented where core physical, social and cultural attractions have been identified and packaged into suggested routes, themes and itineraries that are then marketed by provincial tourism authorities (DEAAT, 2001). The 'routes-and-themes' strategy seeks to disperse tourist flows throughout the province, away from key attractions to lesser visited areas in the hinterland where tourism impact is much lower. In this frame while the provincial marketing programme centres on its tourism icons, by drawing in less well known areas into and offering them as part of standardised itineraries, such areas are enabled to draw greater economic benefit from tourism.

Effectively, all of these state initiatives seek to tie processes of re-imaging with concurrent processes of re-creating South Africa's product offer, and eventually, its tourist market. They are highly ambitious attempts to merge two very different, often contending objectives – tourist growth and equity or empowerment. However, the political economy of the larger international tourism production system, and the particular course through which tourist markets are created and/or influenced, negates this. This analysis has shown that the image that is predominantly sold by international/overseas tour operators is very different to the one that the South African government is attempting to fashion. Essentially these two actors are engaged in two antagonistic processes. The significance of this is that it many of the potential developmental gains of tourism are obviated. The promotion of certain locales, attractions and key tourism icons (Figure 5.1), influences travel flows in a very specific way. Consumers' knowledge about South Africa, the dissemination of information, and linked to this, product offer and image are important in determining the nature and direction of tourism flows. In this regard tour operators play a central role in maintaining established travel and tourism patterns. They do this by the destinations, and the image(s) around that, that they predominantly sell. They display a degree of conservatism in their production and promotion activities, and thus play an important role in sustaining a less progressive tourist image of South Africa.

However, tour operators are one group in the broader tourism production system, and other producers sectors that are engaged in international marketing channels (such as hotels) are also responsible for projecting distinct images and influencing the tourist market in a given destination. In this regard Visser (2004) has noted that the external marketing activities of South African Tourism itself do little to distribute tourism impact in the country. The routes (and ultimately image) that this agency uses to promote the country centre on those locales that are also predominantly marketed by overseas tour operators. This is indicative of the challenging position South Africa finds itself in, seeking to distinguish itself from the wider African continent in significant ways, yet its status as an African country is its greatest international attraction.

Conclusion

Tourism imaging is the outcome of a chain of interactions among several different international producers whose intentions and deeds are often counteractive. Tourism imaging is increasingly being used as a means to bolster a destination's competitiveness. Yet the success and ability of governments to project a desired image is subject to the actions of several other role players.

There are a number of lessons to be learned from the analysis of South Africa. Developing tourism in South Africa is clearly one of the paths chosen by the government to engage with the globalising economy and to draw economic benefit from it. A significant component of the country's tourism development policy is aimed at enhancing the developmental opportunities for the population through a more inclusive tourist image, altered tourist flows and a geographically less confined tourism impact. At present, however, the way that South Africa is imaged and promoted by international tour operators – broadly paralleling set tourist projections of the wider African continent – largely precludes this. The mechanism whereby this takes place is related to the position of tour operators in the larger production system, and the dual functions of brokerage and production that they fulfil in this system.

Tour operators constitute an important (often first) point of contact between tourism consumers and destinations. They affect tourist behaviour in four ways: i) by sending out certain messages in the way that marketing brochures are constructed; ii) by, in the setting up of travel packages and itineraries, promoting certain destinations and locales above others, and limiting destination choice for consumers; iii) by acting as selectors and conduits of information (and knowledge) about destinations; and, relatedly, iv) in the manner in which destinations are represented. The dynamics of the international tourism production system is such that international tour operators occupy a central location and position of leverage in this system. Given this, the South African government should primarily target tour operators as strategic communicators of a modified tourist image.

More broadly, the case of South Africa's tourism sector is useful for illustrating the strategies used by developing countries to link into established and progressively expanding global systems of production and consumption, and the various methods they employ to mould it to their advantage.

The success of tourism development campaigns is generally seen to depend on the ability of place promoters to develop commercially successful place images (Sassen and Roost, 1999). For this reason place marketing is viewed as an important aspect of the development programmes of most city or country boosterists and tourism officials. In today's world this has become so pervasive that it is often forgotten that what underlies this is an important shift in discourse prompted by structural changes in the international political economy over the past three decades. This discourse places emphasis on entrepreneurship, mobility and flexibility where the prime function of governments is seen to have altered from managerialism to furthering economic growth (e.g. Harvey, 1989). In this constant strive towards competitiveness, and of particular significance for developing countries, however, existing inequities in the international system are built upon and amplified – the level of resources and investments required to undertake various developments or projects are lacking in many parts of the developing world.

Tourism is one of a confined number of sectors that are to a greater extent used by governments to increase their competitiveness. The particular power constellations within the international tourism production system, and developing countries' location in it, demonstrate the difficulties many developing countries encounter in their broader endeavours.

Notes

[1] Urry derives his notion of the tourist gaze from Foucault's concept of 'the gaze', broadly, the way in which people view upon reality, something which in turn is created by dominant forces of power in society.

[2] This was part of a wider analysis of the economic and developmental impact of tourism in South Africa. Aside from statistical analyses, a total of 125 interviews were conducted with tourists, tour operators, airlines, accommodation operators, policy makers and regulatory bodies. In total 33 tour operators – 18 in Germany and 15 in the United Kingdom – were interviewed, while 21 brochures were analysed.

[3] This view of Africa was most vividly portrayed in a recent editorial of *The Economist*, where the continent was decried as 'the hopeless continent' (*The Economist*, 13 May 2000).

Chapter 6

The Global Governance of Tourism

Introduction

The previous chapters had explored the ways in which producers interact among themselves and with consumers and how this shape outcomes in the tourism system. The way in which the tourism system is ordered, and through which mechanisms of governance and regulation occur, is a further important element of this system. To date, however, the governance of global tourism and in particular the political and institutional dimensions of tourism remain under explored (Clancy, 1999; Fayos-Solà, & Bueno, 2001; Hall, 1994; Pearce, 1992; Shaw and Williams, 2004). This is an important oversight for two main reasons. First, since tourism is multifaceted, spanning numerous different sectors, state and non-state institutions fulfil central functions of coordinating and regulating interaction in the tourism system. Second, such institutions also directly affect the production process, either by acting as producers themselves, or as representatives of firms, cohering and harmonising opinions within and across producer spheres. Institutions therefore help to set the boundaries within which tourism as an activity takes place, and as such have an influence on tourism's developmental outcomes.

It is the purpose of this chapter to provide a framework for understanding the role and effect of regulatory institutions – public and private – in tourism. The first part of the chapter sets out a conceptual outline for how the state and other tourism organisations, as producers, regulators, and agents of governance, have bearing on tourism development. The second part draws on examples from South Africa's tourism system to illustrate the role of institutions in the production and consumption processes. The focus falls on two structures of international governance: the aviation regime and the effect of increased tourism trade liberalisation under the GATS. Regulation is an essential part of tourism activities. International regulatory institutions have an important function to fulfil in providing stability to what is generally a fractious system. Such institutions can have both positive and negative impacts on tourism growth and development in a country.

Governance and Global Tourism

As a concept, 'governance' has gained a great deal of currency over the past decade and is today widely seen as an important component of international political engagement. 'Global governance', which had been defined as 'the sum of the many ways in which individuals and institutions, public and private, manage their common affairs ... through which conflicting or diverse interests may be accommodated and cooperative action ... taken' (Commission on Global Governance, 1995: 2), is commonly used to refer to the multitude means in which the world's governments, firms, people and institutions interact, contract and cooperate. This may take the form of both formal arrangements, laws and organisations, or informal agreements, structures and practices (e.g. Rosenau, 1992; Karns and Mingst, 2004: 5). International regimes, which, following Krasner (1983) are composed of tacit or explicit values, rules and principles upon which structures of decision making are based, are widespread means of governing or regulating international areas of common interest (such as trade, transport, migration or development) or concern (such as HIV/Aids or poverty).

Tourism, as a key form of international migration, or today, one of the fastest growing global economic activities, is a sector whose governance has gained increased significance in recent years. Most visibly tourism regulation occurs through the control of cross-border flow that states exercise at ports of entry and exit, the granting of travel visas and the various channels of state diplomacy tied to this, and governments' management of domestic transport sectors. Air transport is a highly regulated activity that is closely connected to the larger international economy, and as will be shown later, can significantly influence the size of countries' tourism economies.

Less apparent is that tourism is fundamentally a form of international trade, in which currencies, revenue, goods, equity and of course people are exchanged on a very large scale between different countries and different economic sectors across the globe. International trade liberalisation, which had gained significant momentum since the establishment of the World Trade Organisation (WTO), had also started to impact in a more formal sense on global tourism with the contracting of the GATS. The GATS, one of the major focus areas of the WTO, came into existence in 1995. It aims to liberalise international trade in services. Core principles of the GATS include non-discriminatory service trade practices and equal access to foreign firms to operate in domestic markets. States, once committed to the provision of the GATS, should not engage in protective practices that exclude or limit foreign competition. Tourism is one of the service activities covered by the GATS. Series of negotiating rounds have produced a schedule of commitments by which global tourism has to be progressively liberalised. Indeed, by 2001 'tourism and related services' had received the largest number of commitments (Fayed and Fletcher, 2002). This can be ascribed to the amorphous nature of tourism production activities with many of the sectors and services covered by the non-tourism schedules of the GATS (such as construction and engineering or property management) also impacting on tourism (Hoad, 2003).

In recent years multilateral negotiations on the extent of tourism trade liberalisation under GATS have become highly divisive, with one group of supporters keen to deepen liberalisation and another opposing it. On the argument that tourism is a major global economic sector, several states have proposed the drafting and adoption of a GATS Tourism Annex. This Annex covers four specific tourist activities or sectors: hotels and catering; travel agency and tour operator services; tour guide services; and 'other services'. Major institutional role players such as the International Air Transport Association (IATA), the world's premier airline body, have resisted the expansion of the Annex to cover air transportation. International environmental groups, non-governmental organisations (NGOs) and many developing countries have also opposed tourism liberalisation for its projected negative economic, developmental and environmental consequences and the damaging effects it may have on sustainable tourism (Bendell and Font, 2004).

International and national regulatory institutions aside, a further less visible form of governance in tourism includes the many different kinds of commercial contracts and arrangements between producers, such as commissions and other types of discount mechanisms (Chapter 4) and the bodies of rules that regulate the exchange between producers and consumers. The latter, which generally entail forms of quality control and consumer protection, can be both formalised in the shape of state-promulgated laws, or can be sector-specific agreements on codes of conduct. Germany is an example of the first where strict legislation regulates the tour operator sector. For instance, a business may only function as a travel and tour operator if it has at least one tour operator licence, and one transportation licence. Usually this means a firm has to be licensed as an IATA and Deutsche Bahn (the German national railway corporation) agent. Extensive legal protection is also provided to tourism consumers. Examples of sectoral codes of conduct include rules laid down by producer (e.g. hotel or tour operator) associations about members' commercial behaviour. The manner in which producer associations regulate commercial exchange in the tourism production system is discussed below. In recent years many international tourism charters have also arisen where producers for instance undertake to engage in fair and sustainable tourism practices. *The International Network on Fair Trade in Tourism* is an example of an initiative that seeks to promote ethical practices. One of the aims of *Tourism Concern*, the UK-based body that set up the initiative, is to further sustainable tourism development and local participation.

Despite all these various forms of governance, in general little analysis is done of the role of institutions in regulating the tourism system. Given the complexity and intractable nature of tourism, the development of organisations and institutions to co-ordinate and order it is essential. According to Pearce (1992: 5):

> Tourism is characterized by the interdependence of its different sectors, by the generally small scale of its many operators, by the fragmentation of its markets and by the spatial separation of origins and destinations ... Interdependence, small size, market fragmentation and spatial separation are all factors which may lead to a desire for combined action, a willingness to unite to achieve common goals, a need to form tourist organizations.

Indeed, the tourism production system has a number of overarching organisations, structures and institutions that oversee commercial interaction between tourism producers (Britton, 1991).

A distinction can be drawn between private sector and public (state) regulatory organisations. The activities of the former are determined by their primary tourism motivations, i.e. profit maximisation. Co-operation, co-ordination and regulation are therefore geared towards the creation and maintenance of stable environments within which competition among producers can take place. Although state tourism organisations share this aim, they generally also collaborate towards certain developmental objectives, such as 'economic diversification, regional development and the stimulation of non-tourism investments' (Pearce, 1992: 6). They also monitor and regulate the social, economic and political effects that tourism production has (Britton, 1991: 455).

Regulatory bodies can themselves act as tourism producers, most notably by partaking in activities such as marketing. They may also be involved in tourism research and the development of statistical databases. Finally, most state organisations fulfil the function of tourism planning and development (Pearce, 1992).

In all, tourism regulatory bodies and institutions set, in a variety of ways, the parameters for the tourism production system. They can have a substantial impact on the tourism production process. This can operate in both an enhancing or restrictive fashion. Furthermore, as with many other structures of global governance, international tourism institutions and the way that they impact on destinations often reflect overarching imbalances in global power relationships, with developing countries often having less recourse to influence regulatory outcomes. This is particularly prominent in one of the most important components of global tourism – the air travel industry. In recent years, debates on the impacts of the GATS have also highlighted the differential effects this framework will have on poorer countries and their more developed counterparts. For developing countries, international regulatory institutions however also constitute important points of (inter)linkage with the larger global system. The next three sections explore these issues. The first investigates the role of tourism institutions in South Africa's tourism system. Analysis is done of how the South African system interrelates through several overarching regulatory and other institutions with the German and British tourist sectors, the two largest source markets for foreign tourist to South Africa. The second explores the dynamics and effects of one particular regulatory system, that of the international air transport regime and how it impacts on South African tourism. The third focuses on some of the impacts that the GATS could have on global tourism.

Structures of Governance

As is shown in Figure 6.1 a number of regulatory bodies and institutions exert influence on the South African tourism sector. Such bodies are present at different levels (international, sub-national, local), and are both public (i.e. constituted of states or governments) and private (consisting of firms).

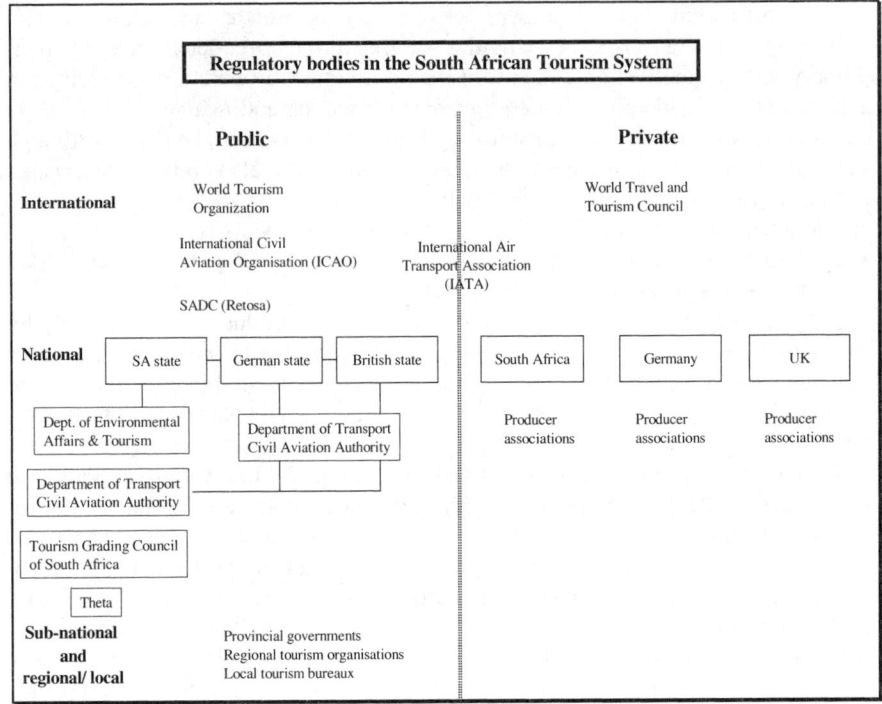

Figure 6.1 International and domestic regulatory bodies in the South African system

International Regulatory Bodies

The World Tourism Organisation and the World Travel and Tourism Council
With a membership of 139 states and territories, the World Tourism Organisation (WTO) is the largest public tourism body.[1] It is an intergovernmental organisation and forms part of the United Nations system. The WTO has the explicit objective of promoting and developing world tourism, and to foster economic and social development through tourism (WTO, 2002). Towards this end it provides guidelines to members on tourism development policies. It also has an important tourism education function. Structurally the organisation is made up of six regional commissions that formulate and implement tourism development objectives and programmes in six regions in the world – Africa, the Americas, East Asia and the Pacific, South Asia, Europe and the Middle East. Along with co-operating with individual member countries, these regional commissions also interact with regional tourism promotion organisations present in the respective regions. One of the most important functions of the organisation resides in its compilation and production of research on world tourism trends. The WTO is indeed regarded as the premier source of statistics on international tourist movements (Witt et al., 1995). The WTO also seeks to standardise

research and discourse on international tourism. It has for instance formulated definitions on what constitutes tourist activities. These definitions are widely applied in policy and academic spheres (Witt et al., 1995). One of the main focuses of the WTO is to articulate policies and practices that entrench sustainable tourism development internationally (WTO, 2002). As a member of the World Tourism Organisation South Africa is subject to the regulations, directives and policies drawn up by the organisation.

The World Travel and Tourism Council (WTTC) is the private sector equivalent of the World Tourism Organisation. Like the WTO the WTTC has the objective of developing and maximising the positive economic effects of international tourism. It also lays an emphasis on developing sustainable tourism bases. The WTTC is however a more closed organisation. Consisting of 105 full members, the membership of the WTTC is made up of individuals in executive positions in some of the world's largest tourism companies (e.g. airlines such as British Airways and Lufthansa, tour operator wholesalers such as Preussag and Thomas Cook, and hotel groups such Hilton International and Sun International). The majority of these companies are present in the South African market.

The WTTC represents the interests of tourism producers and businesses, and in this capacity engages with other tourism regulatory organisations and associations. Among the stated aims of the WTTC are the attainment of more liberalised travel and tourism regimes, and demonstrating the economic contribution of tourism (WTTC, 2002). Concerning the liberalisation of regimes, the WTTC lobbies national governments and intergovernmental organisations to lessen aviation regulation and to increase privatisation within the airline industry.

The International Civil Aviation Organisation The International Civil Aviation Organisation (ICAO) is an inter-governmental organisation consisting of 188 members. It is a United Nations agency. It has the objective of regulating, systematising and setting standards for international civil air transportation. It thus draws up rules on aviation safety, the licensing of aircraft and personnel, aircraft operation and aircraft noise and emission, that all contracting states have to comply with and enforce in their respective territories (ICAO, 2002). The ICAO also formulates guidelines for the functioning of national and international aviation systems, which include the provision of air traffic services, agreements on air transportation, and aspects such as air taxation. The ICAO was set up through the adoption of the *Convention on International Aviation* in 1944, commonly known as the Chicago Convention. This Convention constitutes the broad framework for the international provisions, rules and accords reached under the aegis of the ICAO.

The extension of commercial landing rights is an important facet of the international aviation regime, and an aspect that is particularly germane to international tourist volumes and the direction of international travel. One sub-component of the Chicago Convention, the *International Air Services Transit Agreement* seeks to provide a multilateral framework that governs the reciprocal extension of commercial landing and traffic rights between signatory countries on a world wide basis. To date, however, the granting of rights to operate commercial flights between different countries has generally been contracted on bilateral bases.

Such bilateral agreements however still need to be registered with the ICAO. The opening up and the multilateralisation of the international aviation regime is an important focus of attempts to increase international tourist movements and expand the tourist economies of different countries. This issue is further discussed below.

The International Air Transport Association   IATA represents the international airline industry. The association is made up of more than 270 airlines. IATA was set up in 1919 with the aim to cohere international civil aviation. In its present form the association has two components around which its functions are organised. On the first level IATA is a trade association that provides a forum for the co-ordination of airline activity. This entails the drafting of agreements on airline security and on technological aspects such as air navigation and requirements for airport structures. In addition, IATA sets the rules whereby inter-airline co-operation on route networking and interlining (the involvement of more than one airline on one journey) takes place. Finally, IATA is involved in providing aviation training and accreditation (IATA, 2002). The second component of IATA's activities centres around collaboration on and the co-ordination of air tariffs. By levying agreed prices and price increases for passenger travel, cargo movements, and for the commissions given to travel intermediaries (i.e. travel agents and tour operators), IATA is responsible for determining and maintaining the international air fare regime. IATA therefore regulates international airline activity and competition.

The Southern African Development Community   The SADC has been partly discussed in Chapter 3. It has the purpose of fostering technical, economic and political co-operation, and eventually economic and trade integration among its member states. Organisationally SADC consists of a number of directorates that oversee regional co-ordination in various technical, economic and political sectors. Tourism is one such sector.

Tourism co-operation takes place on a number of levels and through different fora. Tourism development policy is devised inter-governmentally on a ministerial basis. Regular meetings by the tourism ministers of the 14 member states are set up to cohere national policies with regional objectives. Thus far the inter-ministerial forum has produced agreements on a common visa regime that exempts tourists from certain countries from requiring visas to travel through SADC countries.

The promotion and marketing of the Southern African region takes place through an agency set up by SADC, the Regional Tourism Organisation of Southern Africa (Retosa). Retosa has the function of co-ordinating the tourism marketing undertaken by the respective tourism associations of the member countries, and to develop an independent regional tourism identity. Its activities mainly consist of producing promotional literature and material on Southern Africa and marketing the Southern African region as a tourist destination in international source markets.

National Regulatory Bodies

The South African state On a national level a number of public and private regulatory bodies affect tourism in South Africa. The most significant body at this level is the state, which provides the policy and legal framework for tourism. The national Department of Environmental Affairs and Tourism sets the policy and promulgates the legislation that direct tourism development and management in the provinces, although, under the South African Constitution, provincial governments have certain tourism powers.

The state has two other functions that are relevant to the discussion in this chapter. The first pertains to its role in setting and monitoring the legal boundaries whereby international travel into and out of the country is regulated, and conditions are applied. Its involvement in the drawing up of a common Southern African visa regime that is aimed at streamlining and increasing tourist movement in the region is an important example of attempts to impact on regional travel flows. The second function relates to the South African government's establishment of bilateral air transport regimes with other countries. In this regard the South African state, through its Department of Transport engages with transport departments in other countries (e.g. Germany and the United Kingdom) and draw up reciprocal air services agreements that control the frequency and volume of air traffic between the countries. This function, and the effect of air services agreements on the national tourism system is further discussed below.

The Tourism Grading Council of South Africa and Theta The South African state exercises a standards-setting and –monitoring function through two agencies – The Tourism Grading Council of South Africa, and the Tourism, Hospitality and Sport Education and Training Authority (Theta). The Tourism Grading Council of South Africa (TGCSA) was set up by the national Department of Environmental Affairs and Tourism in September 2000. It has the task of developing and implementing a national grading and classification system whereby tourism products and establishments are assessed and accredited according to agreed upon standards of quality and service. Towards this end a National Star Grading Scheme was launched in November 2001.[2] To date this scheme has only been applied to the accommodation sector. The national grading system is aimed at standardising tourism services and products in South Africa. This process has the dual function of converging standards on the supply side, and of creating expectations (for certain levels of quality) on the demand side. The grading system is however non-compulsory, and works on a voluntary application basis.[3]

In an attempt to standardise training and skills development in the tourism sector, another agency, the Tourism, Hospitality, and Sport Education and Training Authority (Theta) was created in April 2000. Theta forms part of a larger national skills development and qualifications frame set up under the Skills Development Act of 1998. This Act promulgates the establishment of a number of education and training authorities to oversee skills development and accredited training within different economic sectors (so-called Sector Education and Training Authorities (Seta's)). The purpose of the national legislative frame is to bolster the development of skills in industry through the creation of formal and non-formal channels of training, and the systematised certification of formally and informally acquired knowledge. The overall objective is to contribute to employment creation and economic development in South Africa.

As the tourism education and training authority Theta sets the criteria for skills development and training that tourism businesses in South Africa have to fulfil. These criteria are embodied in a tourism skills plan that is drawn up and annually reviewed by Theta (Theta, 2001). Theta also acts as the certifying body for acquired skills and competencies in the tourism sector, and relatedly, accredits employers or institutions as tourism trainers. Theta is thus responsible for the management of structured apprenticeships, or what is known as learnerships (i.e. practical and theoretical training within a work environment, which lead to a qualification) in tourism.[4] To finance skills development in tourism, a skills development levy, which ranges between 0.5 per cent and one per cent of total employee remuneration has to be paid by tourism employers. This skills levy is administered by Theta (Theta, 2001).

Together, these two agencies constitute two of the most important regulatory structures through which the South African state seeks to maintain tourism standards (the TGCSA) and to implement some of its economic and social development objectives (by means of the Theta).

Non-state bodies – national producer associations A number of South African tourism producer associations, and counterpart associations based in international source markets are of significance for the South African sector. Producer associations are collections of tourism producers that represent and interact on behalf of members' interests with other organisations and with the state.[5]

In South Africa's international source markets tourism producers responsible for bringing tourists to South Africa (i.e. tour and travel intermediaries) are subject to the rules and conditions applied by tourism producer associations in those countries. Internationally-based producer associations therefore have an effect, albeit less directly, on tourism in South Africa. These organisations represent and protect the interests of their members nationally and internationally.

Summary

From this description of tourism regulatory bodies a number of key features may be highlighted. These bodies perform several functions:

- they draw the perimeters for the activities of tourism producers;
- they set the rules of engagement and competition under which producers within their respective producer spheres have to interact, vie and do business;
- they formulate policies that guide producers' behaviour and inform producers' objectives;
- they levy standards and benchmarks that producers have to comply with, and they also monitor set standards and levels of quality in the various producer spheres;

- they represent the interests of producers in various fora; and
- they adjudicate in disputes.

These tourism regulatory bodies perform an important ordering function within the production system. Through their lobbying role they constitute conduits through which producer interests are articulated and represented. They also seek to standardise output in the various producer spheres and to act as industry watchdogs.

Beyond that tourism regulatory bodies fulfil a norms-setting role. They formulate and enshrine both explicit and tacit values and norms that on the first level provide the larger script for interaction, and secondly govern behaviour and expectations within the tourism production system. In this way, for example 'sustainable tourism development' is both a value and an objective that bodies such as the World Tourism Organisation and the World Travel and Tourism Council, through their size and position can promote as discourse and praxis.

Aside from this, however, tourism institutions can also very directly affect tourism production and development. The following section analyses the interaction between regulatory bodies and producers, the institutions and regimes that these bodies fashion and their consequences on the South African tourism system. It explores the balance of influence between regulatory bodies and producers. Analyses are made of the nature and effect of South Africa's air transport regime.

The International Air Transport Regime and its Tourism Consequences in South Africa

The Larger Structural Framework

The ICAO's International Air Transit Services Agreement, a sub-component of the 1944 Chicago Convention, provides the overall framework for the regulation of international air traffic. Specifically, the International Air Transit Services Agreement makes provision for the ceding of traffic rights between countries. It specifies five kinds of air traffic agreements (or what is entitled 'Freedoms of the Air') that countries could enter into. Each successive freedom entails a greater degree of depth:

- the First Freedom of the Air entitles the airline(s) of one country to fly over the territory of another without landing in that country;
- the Second Freedom entitles the airline(s) of one country to land in another country only for technical purposes (such as refuelling) but not to carry or drop off passengers or cargo in that country;
- the Third Freedom enables a country's airlines to carry passengers and/or cargo to a second country;
- the Fourth Freedom is the reciprocate of the Third Freedom and entitles the second country to carry passengers and/or cargo to the first country;

- the Fifth Freedom of the Air allows the carrier of one country to pick up or drop off passengers or cargo between three or more contracting foreign countries.

These agreements are contracted by states on behalf of their airlines. Depending on the size of an airline, its capacity and the routes and networks it services, the depth of such bilateral agreements may vary. A few very large international airlines (such as, in Europe, British Airways (BA), Lufthansa or Air France) command such extensive networks that their contractual requirements stretch beyond the five Freedoms. There are a further three supplementary Freedoms of the Air that are not officially recognised under the Chicago Convention, but which prevail in practice. These are:

- the Sixth Freedom of the Air. This entails the right imparted to a carrier to transport passengers or cargo from one country to a second via its own hub;
- the Seventh Freedom allows the carrier of a country to pick up and drop off revenue traffic between two other countries;
- the Eighth Freedom of the Air, or Cabotage involves the right imparted to a carrier to carry revenue traffic between two points *within* a foreign country (i.e. to operate domestic flights within another country).

While the International Air Transit Services Agreement provides for the multilateral extension of traffic rights among different countries, most countries use the agreement as a basis to draw up bilateral accords with partner countries. In the past, many bilaterals were aimed at protecting home carriers, which for a long time, were treated as the flagship of national economies and reflected national pride. In the context of prolonged international multilateral trade liberalisation, regional economic agglomeration and the formation of trade blocs such as the European Union (EU) and the Association of Southeast Asian Nations (ASEAN), international aviation has started to attain a less protectionist face over the past number of years. Developed countries characteristically lead the move towards aviation liberalisation. As part of closer economic integration, the EU created a multinational free trade aviation regime that in 1997 removed pricing, routing and capacity barriers to all airlines operating within the EU (Wheatcroft, 1998: 164). The United States has for many years prior been pursuing a more deregulated approach, both domestically and internationally.

The most comprehensive form of liberalisation in the civil aviation industry is by means of an 'open skies' policy, a regulatory regime driven mainly by market competition, and where governmental control is largely, or completely absent (ICAO, 2002). Rather than states determining airline routing or seat capacity, airlines conclude among themselves the nature of trade on particular routes. Some countries, such as Singapore had declared themselves open skies territory, effectively removing all state restraint on civil air travel to and from its borders. The US has for a long time been a strong campaigner for the widespread adoption of open skies, and stymied by a high degree of unwillingness by many countries to adopt a multilateral open skies regime, has contracted open skies agreements on bilateral bases. The decision by several EU member states to enter into open skies agreements with the US during the 1990s, has led some industry role players to predict an acceleration of global aviation liberalisation. Thus far however, using the argument that it may be anti-competitive, the European Commission has refused to allow a broad, EU-wide open skies accord with the US.

A further barrier to international aviation liberalisation is the reluctance by many developing countries to cede authority over what often are key economic industries. Since air transport is closely related to other sources of national revenue – such as the export of goods – it is generally accorded a great degree of strategic value (Clancy, 2002b). For developing countries, a more liberalised regime is often perceived as a threat to national sovereignty. In 1994 African member states of the ICAO vetoed the adoption of a multilateral accord on airline capacity and the reduction of tariffs (Wheaton, 1998). The ascendancy of IATA as, today one of the prime institutions that can set airline prices, and the desire by key airlines within IATA to shield their interests, have also served to slow down widespread liberalisation of air travel (Clancy, 2002b).

South Africa's Bilateral Air Regimes

Under this broad international frame South Africa has adopted a much more favourable stance towards liberalisation since 1994. As part of a wider national economic policy that emphasises greater international access to her markets and the encouragement of foreign direct investment, and keen to maximise on the high pace of tourism growth of the early 1990s, the South African government has undertaken to deregulate both domestic and international aviation. A discussion document released by the Department of Transport in 2001 for instance promised greater flexibility and choice to consumers and airlines. Domestically, aviation deregulation and liberalisation started in 1990, when competitors to SAA were allowed to operate in the country. Since then there has been a great deal of fluctuation in the domestic market with the closure of several new domestic operators. However, a few larger operators had emerged that rival SAA. This has partly come through the extension of licensing or franchise agreements to a number of foreign operators such as BA and Virgin Atlantic Airways.[6] The rise of low-cost airlines at the end of the 1990s has further opened up the South Africa domestic market.

But it has been particularly towards the international market that the South African government has assumed a more receptive stance, at least rhetorically. By 2001 South Africa had contracted bilateral agreements with more than 100 countries, although for lack of demand much it this has remained unused (Horwarth, 2001). From South Africa's perspective the most important accords are those made with source markets that offer both volume and high yield. Bilaterals with the United Kingdom and Germany thus have particular significance.

With both these countries third and fourth freedom traffic rights have been contracted. This means that South African airlines may carry passengers or cargo between South Africa and the UK, and between SA and Germany, but may not fly to any destination other than South Africa from, respectively, the UK or Germany. Conversely, German and British carriers may transport passengers from their own hubs to South Africa and back, but are not allowed to transport passengers from South Africa to any other international destination. Fifth, sixth, seventh or cabotage rights, in other words, do not exist between South Africa and these two source markets.

In addition to that South Africa has concluded bilateral air services agreements with Germany and the UK. These lay out the number of reciprocal flights that may take place between South Africa and its two source markets, the origin and destination airports that may be involved, and the type of aircraft that may be utilised in these flights. These agreements in other words, govern the frequency, the specific routing, and the volume of air traffic between South Africa, Germany and the United Kingdom.

Air services agreements are contracted between the national transport departments of each country. Under the agreements equal quotas of weekly flights are allotted to each country. This quota, which is subject to periodic review, is generally determined by actual and projected demand for flights on the routes. The quota of flights is in turn divided among each of the national carriers who operate to the other international destination and who all vie for their share of the available flight capacity on the route. Once the weekly quotas have been fixed by the national governments, the Civil Aviation Authorities within each country apportion landing slots to all the competing carriers.

The route between South Africa and the UK is serviced by three airlines – SAA, BA and Virgin Atlantic Airways. Under the current bilateral air services agreement a total of 64 weekly flights may take place between the two countries, i.e. 32 flights per week each for South African and British carriers. According to the agreement a further two flights per week in either direction may be added on an annual basis. The agreement makes provision for flights between Heathrow airport in London, and Johannesburg and Cape Town International Airports in South Africa. Table 6.1 illustrates how slots are allotted.

Table 6.1 Flight frequencies on the SA-UK route, 2001

	No. of flights per week between Johannesburg and Heathrow	No. of flights per week between Cape Town and Heathrow
South African Airways	14	7
British Airways	14	7
Virgin Atlantic	7	2

Three carriers are active on the route between South Africa and Germany – SAA, Lufthansa and LTU.[7] The bilateral air services agreement allows a set quota of flights per week between the two countries. On the German side the agreement provides for flights from two airports – Frankfurt and Düsseldorf/Munich – whilst from South Africa, flights may be operated from the Johannesburg, Cape Town and Durban airports. Table 6.2 indicates the flight frequencies.

Table 6.2 Flight frequencies on the SA-Germany route, 2001

	No. of flights per week between Johannesburg and Frankfurt	No. of flights per week between Cape Town and Frankfurt	No. of flights per week between Cape Town and Düsseldorf
South African Airways	7	7	
Lufthansa	7	7(i)	
LTU			3 (ii)

Notes: (i) Flight operated via Johannesburg
(ii) Via Munich.

Given that it services a comparatively larger market the SA-UK route is highly competitive. In contrast, SA pursues a more cooperative and more liberalised relationship with the large German carrier. This enables SAA to code-share flights with Lufthansa. The carriers therefore operate flights to and from South Africa that bear each other's marketing flight numbers. Second, through common agreement, SAA has in 2001 stopped offering direct flights between Frankfurt and Cape Town, but instead only flies to Johannesburg from Frankfurt and offers onward domestic shuttle flights to Cape Town. Direct flights to Cape Town from Germany are operated by Lufthansa. Through this co-operation the two carriers share markets and sell the capacity of the other.

On domestic routes within South Africa, Lufthansa works together with SAA. Through the sharing of marketing activities with the South African carrier and the operation of code-share flights, Lufthansa is hence able to offer connecting flights to seven other destinations in South Africa. Apart from the weekly passenger flights the Lufthansa Group also operates freight carrier flights to South Africa. These flights, for which the company has obtained separate rights, are done in conjunction with SAA and, via Nairobi, with Kenya Airways. For its part through code-share arrangements with Lufthansa, SAA is able to offer flights to 16 German destinations other than Frankfurt. Through the use of de-feeder services, SAA is also connected to passengers originating from other parts of Western Europe and other parts of the world.

In terms of the passenger composition and resultant profit yield on Lufthansa's flights to South Africa, Johannesburg – which draws more business travellers than Cape Town – is the most important destination for the carrier. This, along with the city's geographical proximity to other large cities in South Africa and the Southern African region, and the fact that its airport has the best absorption capacity for international air travel, has prompted Lufthansa to develop

Johannesburg into its transport hub for the Southern African region. Towards this end Lufthansa aims to expand its code-share network with SAA into Southern Africa. One of the more important developments in this regard had seen Lufthansa ceasing its tri-weekly direct flights to Windhoek and Harare at the end of 2000, opting to share operations with SAA on these two routes, and offering code-share flights via Johannesburg.[8]

Despite the primacy of Johannesburg International Airport for the German carrier's operations to SA, Cape Town has gained in importance as a destination. This was most concretely shown in the strong increase in the number of passengers to Cape Town from June 1999 onwards, when the Frankfurt-to-Cape Town route saw a 35 per cent increase in sales. This growth was in turn brought about by an increase in the passenger carrying capacities of the Boeing 747-400s used by Lufthansa in its South African routes. These changes, which entailed the re-fitting of all of Lufthansa's 747-400s to operate as passenger aircraft only (and not performing a dual function as passenger and cargo carrier) meant that the South African route had a 24 per cent increase in its passenger carrying capacity. Cape Town most benefited from the increased capacity. Notwithstanding the rise in the number of passenger sales to Cape Town, this destination remains a more costly one for Lufthansa to operate. There are two reasons for this: the majority of Lufthansa passengers to South Africa disembark in Johannesburg (this is to a large part determined by the routes that leisure travellers follow, with most overseas visitors starting their journeys in Johannesburg (Chapter 5)). Secondly, Cape Town draws more leisure (rather than business) travel. The profit yield from such passengers is not as high.

Future developments envisaged by the carrier for the South African route are mainly determined by Lufthansa's strategy to increase yield on the route, and are framed within the cooperation arrangement between itself and SAA. One focus is to streamline the activities of both carriers, mainly through the expansion of the code-share network. Another possible course of action might be to broaden the arrival and departure points between Germany and South Africa, either by the introduction of a flight from Munich, or by an additional direct flight to Durban. A third option for Lufthansa is the introduction of direct, non-stop turnaround flights from Frankfurt to Cape Town, where aeroplanes would have passengers disembark upon arrival in Cape Town, and after a short re-fuelling delay, would continue a new fully boarded flight to Frankfurt.

This option is however restricted because of the long flying times and its impact on the scheduling of flights (flights can only depart early morning or early evening in order to arrive at the other destination at a feasible time of the day) and due to the lack of available aircraft. Apart from the problems related to developing a flight schedule, other logistical problems hamper Lufthansa's further operational expansion into the South African market. The most significant of these concerns the geographical limitations of South Africa as a destination. Unlike other destinations in continental Western Europe, for instance, Lufthansa can not offer any more onward international flights beyond the two South African cities to which it is currently operating. The partnership with South African Airways is nonetheless an important one. It is one of the strategies of Lufthansa to co-ordinate its fleet development with SAA, and to decide in conjunction with SAA the frequency of flights in the future. An additional strategy is to try and develop the passenger volume and yield of SAA by channelling additional passengers on to the SAA flights to increase the load factor of the South African carrier.

In the British market, BA holds a much stronger position than its rival, Virgin Atlantic, in providing flights to and from South Africa. Overall, though, since it is the only South African airline offering flights on the route between London and South Africa, SAA is the only carrier that is able to expand its operations between the two destinations under the current regime.

Since only 32 flight opportunities are available from the United Kingdom, an intense competition exists between the two UK airlines. More flights are operated to Johannesburg than to Cape Town International Airport. This is due to the greater size and capacity of the Johannesburg airport, a stronger demand for flights to Johannesburg, the particular clientele mix on the route (with business travellers making up a significant component of the overall fare), and the proximity of Johannesburg to the national and game parks in the north of South Africa. In recent years, however, rising passenger demand for direct flights to Cape Town have made routing between London and Cape Town more lucrative, and attaining more slots at Cape Town International Airport increasingly became the focus of contention between the airlines.

In 1999, after three years of lobbying, Virgin Atlantic Airways was granted the right to operate one weekly flight to Cape Town,[9] alongside South African Airways (which at that time offered nine weekly flights) and British Airways (which offered six flights). In 2000 the British Civil Aviation Authority allocated an additional slot to Virgin Atlantic Airways, a decision against which BA appealed. The rivalry between the two UK carriers for greater access to Cape Town is part of a larger controversy surrounding the South African air regime.

The Air Regime, GATS and Impacts on Tourism Growth

The wider aero-political framework of South Africa and its source markets has a large impact. It not only sets flight capacity on the respective routes, but also, as is evident in the case of BA and Virgin Atlantic, directs competition among operating airlines. This serves to limit airlines' market manoeuvrability, and effectively restricts the mechanisms available to them to influence the market. As the case of the SA-UK route shows, the granting of slots and the conclusion of bilateral agreements are highly contentious. This is because the allocation of slots often takes place on an unequal basis, and often is determined by the market position and influence the airlines hold.

The context within which South Africa's air transport regime is fashioned is highly political. A common criticism is that the South African government operates a restrictive aviation regime. Some commentators contend that the way in which the government sets quotas in its air transport services agreements, and the manner in which landing slots are accorded to foreign airlines, limits foreign airline access into the South African market. In November 2000, for instance, the British Minister of Trade criticised the South African air regulatory regime, stating that 'foreign airlines (are) not allocated sufficient slots to fly to South Africa, to protect the market for South African Airways' (SAA news release, 23 November 2000).

Indeed, despite deregulation of its aviation regime since 1994, the government's reluctance to further open up the market to foreign competition has directly impacted on the South African tourism sector. For instance, one estimate is that demand for flights to South Africa from its major West European tourist source markets exceeds supply by 4 500 seats per week (*Hotel and Restaurant*, 2002). According to some producers in the South African system, the restriction of airline seats leads to higher travel costs and contributes to high tourism prices (Chapter 4). In terms of its effect on tourist volumes into the country, South Africa's aviation regime in other words holds negative consequences.

In recent years the government has come under increasing pressure to further liberalise aviation through the adoption of an open skies policy and the privatisation of SAA. Advocates of an open skies order in South Africa argue that the removal of entry barriers for foreign airlines into the South African market will improve competition, greatly stimulate international tourist flows into the country, and provide a boost to the country's tourism economy. Fluctuations in international tourist arrivals have made tourism stakeholders increasingly vocal about the need for greater capacity for South Africa's main source markets, and the availability of more flights.

On both measures, the government has however shown a great degree of unwillingness. The privatisation of the national carrier is part of the government's wider parastatal restructuring programme which, subject to an intense political standoff within the governing alliance, has progressed slowly. Prolonged opposition to privatisation by the government's alliance partners (the largest organised labour organisation, the Congress of South African Trade Unions (COSATU) and the South African Communist Party (SACP)) has slackened the pace of parastatal reform. The privatisation of the national carrier remains a difficult political issue for the government.

The same is true with respect to the adoption of an open skies policy. A strong self-view as a middle order nation that has limited recourse in a highly competitive global economy, underlies a defensive positioning with regard to the national airline. The comment below by a senior SAA representative reflects this:

> If the accusation is that SAA and the government co-operate to protect certain traffic rights, then I would agree that we're on the right track because we are doing what each intelligent country and national airline do together in order to protect jobs that are directly connected to the national airline. Because if the two partners, the country and the national airline would not do this, then the national airline would gradually be eaten up by other global players, and would eventually be reduced to a domestic little player, used by other global airlines to feed into their global network. And surely, this is not something the South African government would want to be co-responsible for.[10]

South Africa's position is similar to many other developing countries. The difficulty for these states, however, is that under the GATS tourism trade will increasingly have to be liberalised. While, to date, GATS covers largely the services provided by the hotel, tour operator and travel agency sectors, it also holds some import for air transport. Up until recently air transport was excluded from the Tourism Annex. Instead the regulation of air transport fell under the GATS Annex on Air Transport Services. Given the extent and complexity of the aviation regime and the existence of a great number of bilateral agreements, moreover, air transport – and specifically traffic rights and all services directly related to their operation – are excluded from the Annex on Transport Services. The latter covers only services such as the selling and marketing of air transport services, Computer Reservation Systems and aircraft repair and maintenance.

In recent years however, there have been increased pressure within the World Trade Organisation to incorporate air transport services in the Tourism Annex. The direct result of this is that air transport would be subject to a greater degree of liberalisation than had heretofore been the case. This has been opposed by very large players such as IATA, who contend that a sectoral approach (as exists through the bilateral system), rather than a comprehensive approach (as provided for under the GATS) is more beneficial for the airline industry (Smithies, 2001).

On the whole, however, smaller countries are less than equal players in the international airline market. Liberalisation and shifts in the airline sector through mergers and consolidation create different sources of pressure for smaller countries, while liberalisation of global marketing and distribution networks could hold latent benefits and costs for developing countries.

Further, the debate on open skies is compound. In the case of the UK source market where demand for air transport between South Africa and the United Kingdom exceeds current supply, the aviation regime does act in a restrictive fashion. On the other hand there is little empirical knowledge about what the effects of aviation liberalisation between countries with differential economies and markets would be, and specifically what indeed the impact on South Africa would be. More practically, the removal of air transport barriers in South Africa since the end of apartheid has not automatically produced a greater influx of carriers. In addition, as the market collaboration between Lufthansa and South African Airways on the South Africa-Germany route shows, producers can negotiate regulatory regimes.

As far as it limits competition, though, and limits tourist volumes to South Africa, the South African aviation regime is a constraint to tourism growth. In this context several stakeholders have lobbied the government to, rather than fully extract itself from the regulation of its skies by the implementation of 'open skies', practise the 'managed liberalisation' of its aviation policies or implement 'liberalised bilaterals'. For example South African Airways could make available its unused capacities to other foreign airlines. On the SA-UK route this will see SAA conferring part of its remaining nine flights to British Airways, Virgin Atlantic Airways, or any other carrier who wishes to enter the South African market. In addition, bilateral air traffic services agreements could expand origin and destination airports for international flights to some of South Africa's large regional airports.

A further market that has not been fully developed by the government is that of charter services. This will have the effect of increasing the supply of flights into the country, expanding international arrival points, and concomitantly providing greater physical access for other parts of South Africa to international source markets. A further consequence could be that patterns and routes of tourist travel through South Africa become more diffused and that tourism impact is spread. In sum some changes in air regulation and investments in airport development by the South African state could enhance international tourism growth not only in key access points, but in many other parts of the country.

On a broader level, whatever shape the GATS takes, it is likely to have an enduring impact on tourism development and growth in all countries. Debates on the motivations and consequences for GATS are at times acrimonious with opponents (such as international environmental lobby groups or NGOs) charging that it is a strategy by major corporations to remove barriers to profit maximisation and with little regard for the needs of local (poor) communities. In truth, however, it is fair to say that it is too early to draw conclusions on the impacts of GATS on the wider tourism system (Bendell and Font, 2004). Hoad (2003) makes a number of suggestions on GATS' likely consequences. These include the weakening of market access limitations, softened legal investment restrictions or requirements and the slackening of environmental protection measures. Given that many countries apply restrictions to protect fragile environmental resources, or as in the case of many developing countries, communal land ownership rights (e.g. the Bushmen in Southern Africa or the Maasai in East Africa) this could be to the detriment of national economies. This is worsened by the reciprocal mechanism whereby the GATS and the entire World Trade Organisation functions, through which preferential treatment of national producers and service providers has to apply equally to foreign counterparts. In this respect tourism development (or, as in South Africa's case, empowerment) programmes and policies can be affected.

Conclusion

Tourism governance is a vital component of the global tourism system. Governance takes place at various overlapping levels – subnational, national and global – and at various stages of the production process itself. Regulatory bodies and the rules they propound have both a direct and indirect effect on the tourism production system. These bodies proactively shape tourism production by laying down the rules of engagement and setting the parameters for production. Through its migration control function, the state plays a pivotal role in mediating tourism flows, although the state also lays down the regulatory and legal framework generally aimed at meeting specific developmental goals. In the private sphere producer associations oversee various aspects of the production process (such as standards maintenance) but also act as representatives or lobbying partners for members in their engagement with other tourism role players.

Air transport is one of the fundamental constituents of travel and tourism and as such, the international aviation regime has a formative impact on the global tourism system. Mainly composed of bilateral agreements contracted between states, the aviation regime has become part of a wider focus on tourism trade liberalisation through the GATS. As a regulatory structure, however, the international aviation regime – which governs direct international flight availability and tourism access – can have a constricting impact on tourism growth in many countries. With respect to South Africa a number of opportunities exist for promoting tourism growth through a more relaxed aviation regime. This includes a reformulation of South Africa's accords with other states to allow greater access to international airlines. Secondly, space could be created within South Africa's present bilateral aviation agreements for available slots to be shared between airlines. Finally, some of South Africa's larger airports could be upgraded and used as international arrival and departure points.

More widely, provisions for the relaxing of restrictions on tourism service trade by means of the GATS are likely to have major implications for global tourism. Liberalisation will carry generic benefits for global expansion, although it could affect national legislative or policy controls geared towards protecting environmental or other resources. Developing countries are likely to carry more of the costs of the GATS.

Notes

[1] Aside from state-membership, the WTO also consists of affiliate members from the private sphere.

[2] The National Star Grading Scheme is based on a classification system whereby tourism establishments and products are ranked from a level of one to five, with a ranking of five indicating the highest level of quality and service.

[3] Prior to the creation of the Tourism Grading Council the task of levying and supervising standards in the South African tourism industry was shared between South African Tourism, the South African Bureau of Standards, and the Automobile Association. Interviews with tourism stakeholders indicate that the old system was fragmented, haphazard and inconsistently applied.

[4] As part of its function to support learnerships in the tourism sector, Theta has been charged with implementing a learnership project financed by the national Department of Labour, and a collection of private companies, known as the Business Trust. The Tourism Learnership Project aims to provide training and qualifications to 15 000 unemployed and previously employed individuals within the span of four years, thus fast-tracking skills development in tourism (Theta, no date).

[5] In South Africa the largest and most important tourism associations are: i) the *Federated Hospitality Association of South Africa* (Fedhasa), a body that represents the national hospitality sphere, and whose membership is made up of hotels, guest houses, bed and breakfast, backpackers, and camping and caravan and self-catering establishments; restaurants; gaming and gambling establishments (its core membership) and tourism suppliers and service providers (allied membership); ii) the *South African Tourism Services Association* (Satsa). This is an organisation of tourism producers who promote inbound tourism to South Africa (i.e. international tourism). Members are drawn from the accommodation, tour and travel intermediary and transport spheres and consist of accommodation establishments, tour operators, airlines, attractions and marketing

bodies. The main function of Satsa is to ensure that its members maintain set standards of service and quality; it also lobbies and interacts with the national state, other public and private organisations, and producers; iii) the *Association of Southern African Travel Agents and Tour Operators* (Asata). Asata fulfils a similar function as Satsa, but its main constituency is travel agents and tour operators who produce and sell outbound tour products from South Africa (i.e. international tourism by South Africans); iv) the *Tourism Business Council of South Africa* (TBCSA) is an umbrella organisation whose membership draws together a number of tourism associations (such as Satsa and Fedhasa), individual businesses, and producer groups. The main focus of the organisation is to provide a conduit through which the objectives of tourism producers are represented and communicated to the South African state. The organisation also co-ordinates marketing initiatives to promote South Africa as an international tourist destination. Towards this end it has set up and administers a voluntary marketing funding scheme, entitled Tourism Marketing South Africa (TOMSA) which involves consumers paying a one percent accommodation levy. The levy is collected through participating producers and is used to finance international marketing undertaken by South African Tourism (TBCSA, 2002); v) the *Guest House Association of South Africa* (Ghasa) and the *Bed and Breakfast Association of South Africa* (Babasa). Ghasa and Babasa are the two largest officially recognised national associations representing, respectively, the guesthouse and the bed and breakfast sectors in South Africa. The two organisations share the objectives of setting and assuring certain standards in these sectors, and of negotiating with the state and other producers on behalf of their members.

[6] In 1996 BA gained a foothold in the South African market when it entered into a franchise agreement with small, independent South African operator, Comair. Virgin Atlantic Airways, for its part entered into a partnership agreement with domestic operator, Nationwide Airlines.

[7] LTU Airways is one of the largest charter airlines in Germany. It is owned by LTU Touristik, the third largest tour operator group in Germany, which makes LTU one of the more important charter companies in the German market. LTU commenced its operations to South Africa in 1992. All of its flights to South Africa are scheduled, not chartered.

[8] Given the historical and social connection between Namibia and Germany (with the African country having been a former colony, and with many people of German descent residing in Namibia), the decision to terminate direct flights from Germany to Namibia was significant. This was prompted by the negative operational results, and the relatively greater costs, which Namibia and Harare bore for Lufthansa.

[9] Virgin Atlantic Airways first entered the South African market in October 1996, when it operated three flights a week between London and Johannesburg.

[10] Personal communication, Manager, Central Europe, SAA, 26 April 2001, Frankfurt.

Chapter 7

New Global Niches: Tourism, Sport and Mega-Events

Introduction

One of the most noteworthy developments in tourism studies over the past decade or so is that the spectrum of activities incorporated into analyses of tourism economies has significantly broadened. Specifically, events and sport are two spheres that traditionally have been viewed as quite separate from tourism. Today growing bodies of literature explore the links between tourism and events, on the one hand, and tourism and sport, on the other. A rising international MICE sector has prompted new scholarship on how travel related to the attendance or organising of events feeds into the tourism sector and how it stimulates the development of new tourism infrastructure (e.g. Dwyer and Forsyth, 1997; Dwyer, Mellor, Mistilis and Mules, 2001; Fainstein and Gladstone, 1999; Weber and Chon, 2002). In a lucid analysis of tourist hallmark events, C. Hall's (1992) overview of the various array of commercial, cultural, religious and political events that increasingly is playing an important role in the international system bridged contributions by academics from several disciplines who progressively were arguing the economic and other values of events. His work also made an important contribution to understanding the motivations and impacts of sport events, which increasingly has been realised as a major economic and political factor.

In recent years more and more attention has been paid to sport events of a particular extent – the large-scale sporting festivals or sport mega-events such as the Olympic Games, the Commonwealth Games and rugby and soccer world cups. This can be attributed to the economic benefits these events are thought to have (Hall, 1992; Rooney, 1988), the positive tourism and political spin-offs hosts can derive from heightened international exposure (Horne and Manzenreiter, 2002) and the broad developmental opportunities such events could create. It is significant, for instance, that there has arisen a global sports mega-events industry characterised by intense competition among countries to host such events. An increasing number of countries have also started to integrate sport mega-events into national and urban planning programmes.

Despite the increased significance of sport events and the growing body of literature it has given rise to (e.g. Hiller, 2000; Ley and Olds, 1992; Waitt, 2001), with the exception of a few contributions (e.g. Fainstein and Gladstone, 1999; Sassen and Roost, 1999) little comprehensive analysis has been done thus far of how sport events link up to tourism. This is also in spite of the progress that has been made with the development of sport tourism as an academic field (see for example Gibson, 2003; Standeven and De Knop, 1999). It can be said that there is an intuitive link between sport and tourism with, in a socio-anthropological sense, both involving an element of performance or staging that attracts spectatorship. Practically, participation in or observation of sport activities often involve travel and can contribute to further demand for tourism infrastructure. An increasing volume of research is emerging on the relationship between tourism and sport, although some deficiencies, for example on sport tourism policy (e.g. Weed, 2003) still exist.

This chapter explores the nexus between events, sport and tourism by analysing how these three spheres, both separately and in interrelated fashion, have taken shape in South Africa. The country has the distinction of being one of the few African countries that has actively promoted itself as a host for major international (or mega-) sport events. A range of economic, political and ideological motivations underlies this (Cornelissen, 2004b). In the context of its wider internationally-focused tourism development goals and programme, South Africa's ambitions around sport mega-events carry a particular significance.

This chapter investigates the trends around South Africa's involvement in sport mega-events and how these relate to the development of tourism in the country. The first part of the chapter provides a conceptual background to the newfound significance of sport and events in today's world. The second reviews South Africa's experience in hosting or attempting to host a few major international sport events. Analysis is done of the country's involvement in three recent bidding processes or events – the competition for the FIFA 2006 and 2010 Wold Cups, the 2003 Cricket World Cup and the 2003 Presidents Cup. A common element in all of these is that a strong ideological impulse both motivates and influences South Africa's involvement in the global sport mega-events business. This sets the scene – and parameters – for other aspects related to events and tourism: how tourism and other economic benefits are derived from sport events; what sorts of objectives predominate in the planning and organisation of events, and how policy-making is affected or constrained by such wider objectives. As developing country confronted with the task of efficiently utilising limited resources to compete against more affluent countries for the capital tied to tourism and sport, the experience of South Africa can offer a few lessons in the priorities and challenges facing poorer states. The third part of the chapter thus investigates the broader issues tied to sport events and sport tourism development particularly as they pertain to the developing world.

The Contemporary Significance of Sport and Mega-Events

Sport events have become an increasingly important component of global tourism economies. This is partly related to the expansive growth of the wider MICE sector internationally, and the industrialisation of activities linked to the hosting, organising and publicising of events. But sport also has a particular dynamic and allure that as an element of the MICE sector makes it a highly distinctive. More broadly, it has long been acknowledged that close linkages exist between sport and tourism: both are activities of which leisure is an inherent part. More recently, sport tourism, i.e. the combination of the participation in physical activity for enjoyment (sport) and travelling outside of one's usual environment to partake in such activities (tourism), has become understood as a sector in its own right (see for instance De Knop, 1990, C. Hall, 1992; Kurtzman and Zauhar, 1995; Standeven and Tomlinson, 1994; Turco, Riley and Swart, 2002).

Sport tourism may broadly be defined as a particular form of leisure engagement that involves, either for competitive or non-competitive purposes, the partaking in, display or consumption of physical activities. That is, it could entail both an active and a passive component (Standeven and De Knop, 1999). Gibson (1998) suggests three types of sport tourism activities – active sport tourism where persons travel to participate in sports; event sport tourism where persons travel to observe sport; and nostalgia sport tourism where participants visit sport-related attractions such as stadia or sports museums. It is today widely understood that travel related to sport has become a major competitive sector and that the political economy of sport tourism is characterised by the intense pursuit of the growing capital tied to the consumption of sports. On both a national level in many industrialised countries, but increasingly on an international scale, the striving for the commercial spin-offs from sport tourism manifests in new economies being established around the construction of sport infrastructure such as stadia or sports halls (Eucher, 1999) or regeneration programmes being centred around the sport sector. This means that sport organisations or leagues have emerged as important political and economic actors in a growing sector within the wider events industry.

This is no more visible than in a particular segment of the global events sector – sport mega-events, i.e. sports events of a very large scale and bearing. In recent years such kinds of events have grown in intensity and significance.

Sport mega-events are quite specific in form and objective. It refers to major, short-term sporting festivals of worldwide status that are held on a regular basis (C. Hall, 1992; Hiller, 2000). It is widely recognised that they serve a particular function in modern-day societies. This is captured in the delineation provided by Roche (2000: 1) who characterises mega-events as 'large-scale ... (with) dramatic character, mass popular appeal and international significance'.

Mega-events can be differentiated by their size, scope, and appeal. First-order events have the widest reach in terms of prestige, attendance, interest, and particularly, publicity. The two prime examples are the Olympic Games and the FIFA Football World Cup. In terms of participation and spectatorship the football World Cup is the largest sporting tournament in the world. The 1998 football finals in France, for instance, had a cumulative global television audience of 40 billion, while that of the most recent finals held in 2002 in Korea and Japan was estimated to be even larger, despite the time difference between Asia and other football regions such as Europe (Manzenreiter and Horne, 2002).

Although also international in scale, the extent and level of participation in second-order events is less. Examples include the Commonwealth Games and Rugby and Cricket World Cups. Third-order events involve several countries, but are much more limited in scope. These include regional or continental tournaments such as the Africa Cup of Nations, the biennial, continent-wide football meeting or the Asia Games. Alternatively it includes sport meetings of which the participation, and media coverage is much smaller, e.g. the Hockey World Cup.

A further distinction can be drawn between multi-site and single-site events. The former refers to sport gatherings that involve more than one location in a country, or a number of countries. Events such as the Rugby and Football World Cups are of this sort. The Olympic Games is an example of a single-site event, which is usually linked to one city or urban region.

Conceptually, the rise and importance of mega-events are commonly framed and understood in terms of globalisation. Roche (2000: 7) for instance states that:

> Substantively, mega-events have been and remain important elements in the orientation of national societies to international and global society ... .(T)hey have been important points of reference for processes of change and modernisation within and between nation-states, and for globalisation processes more generally. Mega-events ... and their networks remain of considerable importance in terms of the exchange, transfer and diffusion of information, values and technologies.

Within this frame the values attached to mega-events are numerous. Mega-events firstly are high profile; they typically involve extensive media coverage and impart a significant degree of international exposure to hosts. This is usually seen to be contingent with a number of benefits and opportunities. Economically, mega-events are generally viewed to carry significant short-term, as well as long-term benefits for hosts. Advocates emphasise the immediate revenue associated with these events, stemming from public and private sector investments, and particularly, advertising and media revenue (Alegi, 2001; Crompton, 1995; Horne and Manzenreiter, 2002; Roche, 1992). Events are often used by governments to mobilise domestic corporate interests, and to encourage infrastructural developments and improvements (Hiller, 2000), and as such are sources of capital injections, and relatedly, employment creation (Mules and Faulkner, 1996). In addition, mega-events are usually linked to a visitor influx and related benefits to a destination's tourism industry (Fainstein and Gladstone, 1999; Teigland, 1999; Owen, 2002). Given this, particularly within an urban development frame, mega-events are therefore often used as part of regeneration strategies. The economic and tourism spin-offs that the hosting of mega-events are perceived to hold for a city, makes bidding for it a common activity of the entrepreneurial city and urban boosterism strategies (Jessop, 1997; Waitt, 2001). Post-event, associated economic benefits include the longer-term effects of the prominence and publicity that the host received, in terms of increasing a region's ability to draw foreign investments and international tourist flows. As such hosting a mega-event is generally seen as an effective means of place marketing and destination positioning (Hiller, 2000; Holcomb, 1999; Kearns and Philo, 1993; Rogerson, 1999).

In a broader sense, globalisation also leads to a more extensive and deepened international flow of finance, technology, capital and humans. According to Appadurai (1996) global flows impact fundamentally on the landscape of societies.

He identifies five categories whereby this occurs. In each category different actors are predominant: ethnoscapes (comprised of tourists, immigrants, refugees, guest workers); technoscapes (characterised by the mobility of technology); financescapes (indicating the role of global capital); mediascapes (broadly referring to the role of the media in fashioning imagined worlds through narratives and images); and ideoscapes (which refer to the role of political symbols and ideologies) (Appadurai, 1996: 33-36).

Appadurai's 'scapes' are useful to analyse the intensified internationalisation of sport over the past decades, the increased sports and tourism migrancy this has given rise to, and in particular the heightened commercialisation and commodification of sport, of which the rising importance of mega-events is exemplary (Horton, 1996). In this way international sport, and mega-events more specifically, are dimensions of civilisational changes related to globalisation (Maguire, 1999). Alternatively, Appadurai's depiction encapsulates the ascent of large corporations in international sport, and the global complex of media, financial, and technological networks and other commercial conglomerates that have come to play a dominating role in mega-events (Euchner, 1999; Maguire, 1999). As argued by Manzenreiter and Wolfe (2002: 5), 'sport has become inextricably linked to agents, structures and processes of global capitalism'. This is related to the increased industrialisation of sport as more than a mere activity of leisure, but like tourism, as an economic sector.

What the above illustrate is that the economic and political (and relatedly, social) dimensions of mega-events can be very significant (Waitt, 2002). The hosting of sport mega-events has become an important feature of many countries' development and other aims, and increasingly such events are recognised and analysed for their use by political and economic/corporate agents to attain certain objectives (Alegi, 2001; Maguire, 1999). Hiller (2000) argues that bidding contests for mega-events are usually accompanied by a process of legitimation, whereby the key promoters or agents of a bid, in an attempt to bolster both domestic and international patronage, engage in external, and in particular internal 'marketing' drives. He states:

> Since hosting mega-events are ideas promoted by elite segments, which ultimately become political initiatives, a rationale must be developed to mobilize public support (Hiller, 2000: 440).

A number of developing countries have hosted hallmark sport events. However, very little research has been conducted on the specific nature and dynamics of large-scale sport events in developing contexts, and little attention has been given to the recent increase in efforts by several developing countries to host such events and the motivations that inform such efforts. This is particularly the case in Africa where over the past number of years numerous countries have been involved in international competitions to host major events. For instance, since the end of apartheid in the early 1990s, South Africa has robustly attempted to position itself in the international arena. Actively engaging in the international mega-events 'market' has been a key aspect of this more outward focused foreign policy. The country has either hosted, or attempted to host a range of first, second and third order events. In 1995 it hosted the Rugby World Cup and in 1996 the Africa Cup of Nations. South Africa also made failed bids to host the 2004 Olympic Games and the 2006 FIFA Football World Cup. The bid for the latter has been followed up by a successful bid to hold the 2010 World Cup finals. Most recently it hosted the 2003 Cricket World Cup and in the same year the prestigious international golf tournament, the Presidents Cup.

South Africa has been one of the more active African countries with respect to sport mega-events, although several other African countries have also sought to host such events. Continentally, the Africa Cup of Nations is the largest and most widely publicised international event; it has been hosted by 16 African states in its close to 50-year history. Over the past number of years, however, some countries have made bid attempts for a number of first order events, most notably the Football World Cup. For instance, during the 1990s Ghana, Egypt, Morocco and Nigeria all put in initial bids for the 2006 World Cup along with South Africa. For the 2010 Cup bids have been made by six African countries. African countries' increased focus on particularly first-order events is striking, for the following reason: although not yet cogently articulated in literature on mega-events, there seems to be a tacit understanding among scholars that given many of the socio-economic challenges that developing countries face, and the costs and infrastructural requirements generally related to both bidding for and hosting mega-events, developing countries adopt a gradualist approach to such events, whereby they usually aim for second-order or lower ranked events first, and progressively 'build up' to larger events. This view is encapsulated in Hiller (2000: 440) who, with regard to South Africa's failed bid for the 2004 Summer Olympics states:

> (I)n a society plagued by the continuing ravages of inequality where sheer survival is a reality of daily life for many, the idea of another project of such a colossal nature as the Olympics appeared virtually overwhelming (to most South Africans) – if not misplaced and inappropriate.

Ostensibly, increased importance is being attached to sport mega-events by African governments, yet very little research has been done about this. Given the purported economic value and, specifically, the political instrumentality of mega-events, this is an important oversight. As illustrated above, much can be learned about governmental/elite agents' political objectives and directions by looking at their stated aims and rationales for hosting mega-events.

In a broader frame, common understandings of the African continent regard it as playing a marginal role in the global economy, and that the continent is largely de-linked from the main capitalist structures. Because of the commanding influence that global financial, commercial and other corporations have on mega-events, such events are progressively becoming an important component of the global capitalist system. Mega-events provide an entry point specifically for developing countries to be drawn into, and extract from, a global configuration of production, finances and commerce, and tourism is an important aspect of this. It is important to evaluate the aims of African state élites within the context of the predominant economic milieu and the opportunities and drawbacks that the larger environment poses. It is however also important to consider what the negative aspects of such strategies may be. Recent work by a number of authors (e.g. Coates and Humphreys 1999; Ley and Olds, 1992; Owen, 2002) has highlighted the manifold negative effects of such events. Some African countries' attempts to host the larger (and more costly) events raise the question of whether these countries are 'punching above their weight', and what the implications of this could be. At the same time, given the rising significance of sport tourism, however, it also has to be acknowledged that few opportunities remain for countries not to attempt to partake in an increasingly important subcomponent of the global tourism sector.

In the following section three recent sports or bidding events in which South Africa was involved are investigated. The analysis of the first, the bidding processes for the 2006 and 2010 FIFA finals, centre on the rivalry between South Africa and Morocco, both strong contenders to host the finals. It is striking that a strong political and ideological motivation underlay both countries' bids and that they based their campaigns on their status as African countries. South Africa's hosting of the two other events that are investigated, the 2003 Cricket World Cup and the Presidents Cup had similar characteristics. This feature had both positive and negative effects on the overall impacts and aftermath of all three events. More broadly, in terms of size and scope, the three cases span the entire mega-events spectrum, with differing degrees and levels of impact. As such they are useful for investigating how a country's participation in differentially ordered mega-events relates to tourism and policy development.

Bidding for Africa's Turn

The 2006 and 2010 FIFA World Cup Bidding Processes

In 1998, four years after South Africa's first democratic, general elections, the country signalled its intention to bid for the 2006 FIFA Soccer World Cup. It was joined in the bidding process by, initially four other African countries: Morocco, Ghana, Egypt, and Nigeria. The latter three later withdrew their candidacy in order to put forth a single, fortified African bid (*Mail and Guardian*, 6 July 2000). However neither Morocco nor South Africa extracted themselves from the competition. Both proceeded to the final round of the competition against Germany, England and Brazil. Eventually, Germany was selected to host the event in 2006.

It is generally agreed that mega-events have a significant ideological dimension. Sport is often an important basis for nationalism and identity (Houlihan, 1994), and international sport meetings are often used to showcase national prowess and achievements (Jarvie, 1993). Alternatively, as the vigorous promotion of a Catalan identity during the 1992 Barcelona Olympic Games attest, mega-events are also used to foster, advance or legitimise identities (Jarvie, 1993). Similarly, events can be used to influence or change the image or branding of a city or state (Hiller, 2000; Waitt, 2002). For example, one of the main objectives of the city of Atlanta's bid for the 1996 Olympics was to promote an image of Atlanta as the 'capital of the New South' (Holcomb, 1999), a city that in the context of racial difficulties of southern America, has been successful in achieving racial harmony, a city of progress and development, and one where achievements have been made in curbing crime. The new imaging of Atlanta was as much aimed at an international audience (and a related tourist market), as it was an attempt to consolidate the city's economic and political position in the state of Georgia (Holcomb, 1999). More importantly, it was an attempt by Atlanta's authorities to increase their political legitimacy among the citizenry of Atlanta.

Similar factors underlay South Africa's bid for the soccer world cup. The first few years after the end of apartheid were marked by attempts by the post-apartheid government to forge a common national identity and sense of loyalty towards the new political entity, and sport was an important mechanism. This was evident in the manner in which the 1995 Rugby World Cup, which South Africa hosted and subsequently won, was promoted by state élites, most significantly by former president Nelson Mandela, as a key national moment[1] (Black and Nauright, 1998; Booth, 1999). This momentum was maintained in South Africa's victory in the Africa Cup of Nations in the following year. It was in the same spirit that the country announced its objective to bid for the 2006 Soccer World Cup during the finals of the 1998 African Cup of Nations in Burkino Faso. The bid for 2006 firstly had a clear political intent: it was aimed at building upon the success of the 1995 Rugby World Cup, and in particular, the reconciliation and nation-building that that event sought. Externally, the bid was an attempt to showcase South Africa's peaceful democratic transition, and to appease rising international concerns over possible political instability in a post-Mandela era.[2] The 2006 World Cup would hence be a vehicle for consolidating both South Africa's international position, and its domestic transformation.

Economic and developmental objectives were the other principal components of the South African bid. It was estimated that the hosting of the World Cup would generate an additional tax income of approximately US$550m, contribute two per cent to the Gross Domestic Product, and create 129 000 jobs, 60 per cent of which would be permanent (*Beeld*, 11 August 1999; *The Star*, 27 June 2000). Overall, it was expected that the event would make a valuable contribution to the country's tourism sector, which had seen an initial rapid period of growth after 1994, and was boosted by the 1995 Rugby World Cup campaign. The government's international tourism development strategy rested, in part, on the promotion of key tourism icons and brands (built on natural and cultural attractions), and in part, on the development of the Meetings, Incentive, Conferences and Exhibitions market (Satour, 1997; South African Tourism 2002b). Being awarded the event, it was assumed, would reinforce these attempts and would help position South Africa in the international tourism market. Publicity and prominence afforded by the event was also expected to contribute to the country's tourism sector in the longer term (*Beeld*, 11 August 1999).

A number of infrastructural developments, mainly consisting of the construction of new stadia were linked to the bid. In its entirety, the bid proposed to involve nine South African cities in the tournament. Some possessed completed football stadia, while in others, existing rugby stadia would be utilised. Of the new infrastructural developments that would take place, the biggest was the projected refurbishment of the FNB Stadium near to Soweto, the largest football stadium in South Africa. The refurbishment would have increased capacity from 85 000 to 110 000 (*Die Burger*, 02 November 2000). The prospect of securing lucrative state tenders for such developments, and of accruing commercial prominence, gained the South African Football Association (SAFA) Bid Committee, the body that led the bid process, a high level of corporate sponsorship. Seven of South Africa's largest companies acted as financial supporters or suppliers to the bid.[3] For the Bid Committee this type of financial underwriting by the private sector was evidence of the feasibility of the bid project. Moreover, the Committee often used it as justificatory argument against criticisms of the costs that the bid project would incur (*Beeld*, 11 August 1999).

The third goal of the South African bid was to enhance the country's international status by promoting the country's recent democratisation. The South African bid made an emotive argument that the football World Cup had never been hosted in Africa, and that if the international community were to act upon their promises of furthering the 'African Renaissance', the World Cup would be the most apt vehicle. This was encapsulated in the initial slogan of the South African bid: 'It's Africa's Turn.' The Pan-African focus also had the strategic aim of mobilising African votes within CAF, the African football governing agency, in favour of South Africa (Alegi, 2001).

The bid of South Africa's other African opponent, Morocco, had a similar foundation. Morocco started its campaign for the 2006 World Cup at the end of the 1990s. It had made two previous unsuccessful attempts to host football World Cups in 1994 and 1998. The country's third bid was an attempt to substantially improve upon the previous two bids. It had, like South Africa, a strong economic focus and the potential of generating revenue and of stimulating infrastructure development was a key incentive for the Moroccans. Its 2006 bid proposed the construction of new stadia in eleven cities, including some of the larger metropolitan centres such as Marrakech, Casablanca, Rabat, Tangier, and Fez. The proposed flagship venue would have been the to-be-constructed Casablanca Grand Stadium with a capacity of 100 000 spectators (*Arabic News*, 11 October 1999). The financial investments needed for such constructions (for which the Moroccan government was willing to spend US$ 600m) and other developments, would have been secured from some of Morocco's largest parastals and private companies in the telecommunications, banking and oil sectors (*Arabic News*, 28 October 1999).

Morocco's bid was strongly informed by the desire to strengthen its tourism sector. The country is the third largest destination in Africa, after South Africa and Tunisia. As in South Africa, international tourist arrivals had substantially increased in Morocco since the mid-1990s (between 1995 and 2000 arrivals rose annually at an average of 11 per cent (WTO, 2000; 2002). Tourism is also a strategic sector in the Moroccan economy. In support of the 2006 bid, Moroccan authorities undertook to increase accommodation supply, and specifically that of hotel beds by 40 000. For this, the government announced a set of measures to stimulate investments in the hotel sector. These included the lowering of the prices of designated land, and the setting of reduced tariffs for imported equipment (*Arabic News*, 24 September 1999).

Like South Africa, the Moroccan bid had a strong emotive thrust and it strongly rested on the invocation of an African identity. Like the South African bid, the Moroccan bid also depended on the support of other African countries, and a considerable component of Morocco's legitimation campaign was directed at the vote-carrying African members of FIFA. However, given historical and cultural connections with the Middle East and Europe, and the fact that these regions presented additional voting blocs, a great deal of Morocco's lobbying focused on Arab and European countries. The contention between South Africa and Morocco therefore had an interesting ideological component. Both were vying to be the first African host of the largest prestige international sport event. Both presented themselves to different constituents as the 'gateway to Africa' and as 'true African representatives'.

The announcement of the winning bid was made by FIFA's executive committee on 6 July 2000. The months prior to this were characterised by robust lobbying and intense politicking on the part of the contending countries. Although, officially the executive committee's decision is made on only two sources – the official bid proposal submitted by the respective countries, and reports on the existing infrastructure and other conditions made by a FIFA technical committee who visits those countries – it is commonly recognised that a country's chances of success in the bidding process are largely determined by 'personal friendships, networking and back-room deals' (Alegi, 2001: 3) within the structures of FIFA and its individual confederations.

With regard to Morocco and South Africa, two factors played a pivotal role in the outcome of the bid process. The first was the tension that the dual African bid created within CAF, the African football confederation, and the body's refusal to support the candidacy of one over the other. The unwillingness of South Africa or Morocco to compromise, and their continued candidacies however presented difficulties to CAF. Indications were that there was division within the African football body over whom to support (*Mail and Guardian*, 6 June 2000; *The Citizen*, 20 August 1999). Ironically therefore, despite the African motivations and claims of both bids, it served to polarise the African vote. CAF did not announce which country it would vote for until the day of the award.

The second factor that had a crucial effect on the outcome of the bid processes, was the role played by individual personalities within FIFA. Joseph Blatter, president of the executive committee of FIFA, was an ardent advocate of an African host for the 2006 tournament. Indeed, in 1998 he was elected into that position largely on the vote of South Africa and a number of other African countries, on the promise that he would support an African bid. As president, and leader of the 24-person committee, Blatter would have the power to cast the deciding vote in the event of tied vote. Securing his patronage was therefore a key purpose of all the contending countries. To South Africa's advantage, it was widely known that Blatter supported the South African bid (*Arabic News*, 12 January 2000) and it was therefore assumed that South Africa shall be awarded the tournament (Alegi, 2001). On the day of the vote South Africa's chances were however thwarted when, in the final round of voting, with only Germany and South Africa in contention, one executive member from the Oceania confederation abstained. Instead of a tied ballot, which would have enabled Joseph Blatter to cast his vote, in all probability in favour of South Africa, therefore, Germany was awarded the World Cup tournament. There are some indications that the abstention was a personal act of reprisal against Blatter (Sugden and Tomlinson, 2002; *Sunday Times*, 9 July 2000).

The above is exemplary of how 'FIFA politics have become increasingly defined in terms of the interest of confederations, or of separate groupings within confederations, as well as rivalries between and alliances among confederations' (Sugden and Tomlinson, 1998: 3). The outcome reinforces how accessing key alliances and coalitions within international sport organisations is an important factor for success. But it is also indicative of how power blocs within international sport organisations, built around key personalities or distinct agglomerations of interests, very directly determine the conduct and outcome of bidding competitions.

An unfortunate element of the bid process was that its outcome was read by many African countries, South Africa included, as part of an overwhelmingly negative, patronising, and even racist, international stance towards the continent.[4] FIFA, like the game it represents, has a long tenuous history in much of developing world, but particularly in Africa. Darby (2000) notes how the early diffusion and ultimate internationalisation of soccer was closely tied to the imperialist penetration of European powers in Africa. A missionary doctrine characteristically underlay this process. FIFA's unwillingness to democratise its governance structures during the 1950s and 1960s, according to Darby (2000), was reminiscent of such a doctrine. The perception of FIFA as neo-colonial is still pervasive within the developing world.

In partial acknowledgement of the unequal structural position of developing countries within FIFA, and largely on the campaigning of Blatter, FIFA have adopted a directive in terms of which the hosting of the World Cup tournament takes place according to a system of rotation among the six regional confederations within FIFA.[5] On the basis of this Africa was designated as the region where the 2010 tournament will be held (*Arabic News*, 18 January 2002). By the end of 2002 six African countries had indicated their intention to bid for the 2010 event: South Africa and Morocco (both of whom have renewed their respective proposals for 2006), Libya, Nigeria, Egypt and Tunisia. In early 2003 Nigeria sought to extend its initial proposal into one that also involved Togo, Benin, Ghana and Cameroon. However, mainly due to the experience of the logistical complexities surrounding the co-hosted 2002 World Cup, FIFA had rejected the joint West African bid as 'not feasible' (*Mail and Guardian*, 18 March 2003). By the end of that year Nigeria completely withdrew its candidacy. At a later stage Libya and Tunisia also sought to combine their bid, but for similar reasons were compelled to withdraw shortly before the announcement of the successful bidder. On 15 May 2004 more than half of FIFA's executive committee (14 of the 24) voted in support of South Africa's bid. Morocco received the remaining 10 votes and to the surprise of many, Egypt received none.

The moves towards a joint bid on the part of Nigeria, and subsequently Libya and Tunisia, were aimed at pooling resources and to enhance capacity within the respective African regions to organise the event, and to reduce costs for any individual country. This alludes to an aspect that is of significance for all countries that seek to convene large-scale sport events, but, given the economic difficulties many African countries find themselves in, all the more so for the African region: that of whether the expected benefits outweigh the costs. The rationalism and developmental benefits of mega-events, and particularly, aspects such as the construction of stadia, are often queried. Sugden and Tomlinson (2002: 57) for instance note,

> There are many ... examples where any discussion of the projected benefits is, after the event, far from welcomed. Only one year after the climax of the Olympic Games in Sydney, there was much debate as to the usefulness of the Olympic Park, where Stadium Australia is host to very few large-scale capacity-drawing events.

As in all cases, the argument of the economic virtues of mega-events in Africa is one that needs to be qualified. For instance, were South Africa's bid to host the 2006 football tournament successful, while it was expected to generate US$2.3bn in revenue, it would have incurred an estimated cost of US$1.7bn (*Mail and Guardian*, 6 July 2000). There is much dispute over the purported economic consequences of mega-events. Overall, the link between sport events and tourism is empirically muddled (Crompton, 1995). State élites, however, have a political incentive to highlight (and often overstate (Sack and Johnson, 1996)) the economic impact of events. Given the perplexities and inaccuracies around the economic effects of mega-events, Chalip and Leyns (2002) note that over the past number of years researchers have shifted their focus away from aggregate impact to factors that led to successful outcomes, or prevented events from producing the anticipated results. Research points to problems with ineffective planning and management (e.g Bramwell, 1997), the disruptive rather than stimulating effect of events on regular business and the local population, who may choose to stay away from restaurants or retail areas (Chalip and Leyns, 2002), and inadequate market and cost-benefit analyses prior to events (Teigland, 1999). All in all, research underscores the importance of cogent management before, during and even after an event for there to be maximum positive impact.

In this regard it is significant that soon after the exhilaration surrounding South Africa's nomination as host of the 2010 FIFA finals subsided questions arose as to whether the country indeed has the ability to host an event of this magnitude. This was worsened by reports in July 2004 that the South African Football Association was experiencing severe financial difficulties and, at the end of that year, a discomforting rivalry within SAFA over the establishment of the local organising committee (LOC) responsible for managing 2010. It is an indication of the high expectations surrounding the 2010 finals, that early in 2005 a number of South African media establishments criticised the ostensible lack of progress that had been made thus far in planning for the event. The final part of the chapter discusses some of the challenges South Africa faces in preparing for the event and the implications of inadequate or inappropriate planning and management.

Given that mega-events produce varied, and often also negative economic outcomes, and that they are costly affairs, it needs to be asked whether the opportunity costs related to them are too high for developing countries. In the context of Africa, this question becomes all the more pertinent.

Evaluations of the success of mega-events also have to take into account a number of other, broader factors. An example is the most recent Cricket World Cup, which was hosted by South Africa in the first half of 2003. This event, the largest of its sort, was seen by many as a litmus test for the African continent's ability to successfully contribute to the growing mega-events enterprise. In its aftermath, the success of the Cricket World Cup was widely proclaimed as a major economic and publicity feat for the continent, yet the political entanglements that characterised the event carries some wider implications for African countries' access and participation in high profile international events. The next section explores this.

The 2003 Cricket World Cup

The eighth Cricket World Cup was to date the largest event to be hosted in Africa. Although it was mainly centred in South Africa, it had a regional focus; eight of the 54 matches of the tournament were scheduled to be played in Zimbabwe and Kenya. The three African countries' co-hosting of the tournament was the outcome of a lengthy historical build-up, but it had an explicit political aim. The fact that the event was co-hosted, moreover, also led to a number of unanticipated consequences.

The initial decision to hold the tournament in Africa was made in 1993 (Bacher, 2002). South Africa, a test playing nation, was the most favoured candidate for a number of reasons. The country was emerging from a lengthy period of international isolation, and faced the challenge of political and societal democratisation. For South Africa's political elites, hosting the Cricket World Cup would bolster the country's re-entry into the international arena, and contribute to national reconciliation and nation-building, two of the prime objectives of Mandela's presidency. The eminence that Mandela had come to occupy internationally, and the normative stature that South Africa had gained through its non-violent political transition, fed into efforts by the country's cricket administrators who lobbied heavily that it was time for the event to be held on the African continent (Bacher, 2002). Implicitly, the country projected itself as a model for the rest of Africa, and one that the international community should support. For the International Cricket Council (ICC), the world governing agency, awarding the event to South Africa posed a number of other benefits. In the main it would allow for cricket to be developed beyond its main traditional markets, particularly Asia, and to gain a foothold in the African market where cricket was largely overshadowed by the popularity of football. Second, because of cricket's close association with the Commonwealth, and the imperial connotations surrounding it (Malcolm, 2001), the ICC was keen to increase the legitimacy of the sport in Africa. By the latter part of the 1990s, in the spirit of efforts to bring about African economic and political revival (driven most forcefully by Nelson Mandela's successor, Thabo Mbeki) South Africa's cricket governing body, the United Cricket Board, undertook that Zimbabwe and Kenya would be co-hosts of the tournament.

Financially, the event was anticipated to be highly lucrative. Pre-event, it was predicted that the tournament would draw 25 000 foreign visitors (*African Business*, February 2003), and that ticket sales would generate approximately US$4.4m, all of which would translate into substantial revenue for South Africa and its co-hosts. The biggest benefit, however, lay in the revenue created from the sale of television broadcasting and sponsorship rights, of which South Africa retained approximately 40 percent (*Leadership SA*, 20 February 2003). The publicity opportunities provided to specifically South Africa, were also regarded as one of the most important impacts of the World Cup. The tournament had a worldwide television audience of approximately one billion, which was utilised by South Africa's tourism authorities and marketers as a means through which the international tourism image of the country could be improved. Overall, in terms of raising and altering the international profile of South Africa, the Cricket World Cup had a bolstering effect on the country's tourist sector.

As discussed in Chapter 3 the reason for this was that despite the rapid rate of tourist growth after the end of apartheid, the high level of violent crime in South Africa has led the country to be viewed as an unsafe destination in many of its key source markets, and has restricted further tourism growth. Statements about South Africa being the fastest growing global destination, made during the build-up to Cricket World Cup in early 2003, were misguided, given many of the other factors that impact on the country's tourist sector (Chapter 3) but played an important part in generating a positive image both within and outside South Africa and indeed shoring up its own claims. According to tourism authorities the Cricket World Cup has 'positioned the country in such a way that it can be seen to manage a big event in a safe and conducive manner' (*Business Day*, 10 February 2003), and provided the country with an important (re-)branding opportunity.

In contrast to South Africa's successful projection of itself as safe tournament venue, concerns around security in Zimbabwe and Kenya led to a political debacle that had far-reaching effects on the tournament itself. First, the England cricket team became embroiled in the political tensions between the British and Zimbabwean governments concerning broad political trends, and specifically, the issue of land reform in the African country. Prior to the tournament the England team was pressurised by the British government not to play in Zimbabwe, which would be seen as endorsement of Mugabe regime (*Time Atlantic*, 13 January 2003). Similar calls for a boycott of the scheduled Zimbabwe games by the Australian government, and threats made by certain groups in Zimbabwe that the safety of the English and Australian teams could not be guaranteed if they were to play in the country (*Business Day*, 7 January 2003), worsened the situation. In addition, following two terrorist-related attacks in Kenya shortly before the Cricket World Cup, the New Zealand team refused to take up fixtures in this country out of concern for its safety. Pressure by these teams on the UCB to shift the scheduled matches to South Africa, yielded little success since South African cricket authorities in turn faced pressure from the South African government not to disaffect Zimbabwe, whose support would be essential during the FIFA 2010 campaign (*Die Burger*, 17 February 2003). In the end it was only Australia who played its match in the co-hosting country.

The decisions by England and New Zealand had direct impacts on the outcome of the tournament itself. Both teams were penalised with the loss of points. For England this meant an early departure from the tournament. More importantly, however, the boycotts exposed and in many ways worsened the political rift that exists between the developed (Anglo-Saxon) and developing countries in the Commonwealth around Zimbabwe and many other issues. While the Africa-hosted Cricket World Cup therefore had the aim of ameliorating international cricket's neo-imperial image, it served to highlight it.

Despite the political and other entanglements that characterised the Cricket World Cup, it was widely held as a success. The inability of the South African team to qualify for the second round of the tournament did deflate the population's enthusiasm for the event, and initially raised concerns that this may lead to lower match attendance, and resultantly, reduced income. In the end, however, this did not translate into substantially lower revenue for South Africa (*Sunday Times*, 23 March 2003).

South Africa undoubtedly gained a great deal of legitimacy from the event. It has displayed itself as an African country that is able to hold a large-scale international sport event and has gone a long way in dispelling contentions, particularly popular during its 2004 Olympics campaign, that it was overextending itself in attempting to host an event of such magnitude. South Africa, however, is in many regards unique in the African context. It possesses a range of economic and other resources that place it in a better position than most other African countries to accommodate and provide for a large event.

The debacle that the English and New Zealand boycott of the fixtures in Zimbabwe and Kenya created raises a number of broader implications for African countries' prospects to be host to mega-events. First, it highlights how important a requirement the adequate provision of security has become in the present era. Aside from lacking the capacity to provide the infrastructure that is needed for large events, many African countries are also not able to ensure satisfactory levels of security. This does become an important obstacle to African countries' participation in such events. Second, the debacle focuses attention on the wider political context within which African countries vie for mega-events, and which determine their opportunities. As an outcome of the boycotts, a fair portion of the anticipated economic and tourism gains did not reach Zimbabwe and Kenya. In this sense, South Africa's attempt to use the Cricket World Cup as an instrument for the economic benefit of the wider African region, and simultaneously to promote its project of 'African Renaissance' to an international audience, badly backfired. Overall, the Cricket World Cup underscores how firmly political facets interweave with other factors in determining the direction and outcome of bidding processes or actual events.

The Presidents Cup 2003 and Golf Tourism Development

Eight months after hosting the Cricket World Cup, South Africa hosted the fifth Presidents Cup, a major golf tournament held under the aegis of the United States Professional Golfers' Association (PGA). It is a highly prestigious event on the international golf calendar, since participation is limited to the world's highest-ranked golfers. The event derives its name from patronage by political leaders who traditionally have been American presidents. The event generally is held with the purpose of raising revenue for donations to charity bodies, yet it is in the first instance an opportunity for some of the world's best golf players to compete against each other and is as such an important tournament. Given the prestige and high profile of the event, it was a particular feat for South Africa to host it.

Once again, there was a strong Africa undertone in how the event came to be held in South Africa and in the manner in which it was publicised and marketed internationally. Being of third-order magnitude, participation in the event is focused and limited – players' participation, for instance is by invitation – yet it is exactly such restrictions that afford the event its international eminence. The 2003 tournament was led by Jack Nicklaus, one of the founders of the President Cup, and Gary Player and saw the participation of golfers such as Tiger Woods and Ernie Els. As is the custom with the event, in 2003 South African president Mbeki acted as honorary chairman, although further distinction was lent with the attendance of former presidents Mandela, Frederik Willem de Klerk and Bill Clinton.

While spectatorship of the event is much less than in the other two, larger-scale sport tournaments discussed in this chapter, the event does receive widespread, international television coverage. This is primarily due to a concerted attempt by the world's golfing associations to extend the scope of golf and to exploit the growing global sports television economy. Indeed, there has been a distinct popularisation of the sport over the past number of years, with rapid growth in the levels of golf participation and consumption. Golf is increasingly shedding its image as being elitist. Similar to South Africa's successful bid for the FIFA World Cup, and its hosting of the Cricket World Cup, therefore, its hosting of the Presidents Cup had much to do with the efforts of an international sport organisation to capture a new market. The event was of particular significance for South Africa, however, since the country did experience several positive effects in the form of international publicity and other spin-offs (it for example hosted the Women's Golf World Cup in 2004). Nonetheless, in the aftermath of the event controversies surrounding golf tourism and developments related to this emerged, that made more overt many of the challenges that underlie sport tourism. This carries some lessons for developing countries more widely.

Planning for South Africa's hosting of the event started two years prior. Wider political factors and involvement of key individuals related significantly to the event eventually being held in South Africa (Capostagno and Neild, 2003). The

Presidents Cup has taken place on a two-yearly basis since 1994. It was created by the US PGA in response to the European Ryder Cup, the other major international tournament of high status. Since the Ryder Cup is a biennial event, golf authorities saw the need to address the time lag in the international golf calendar. The Presidents Cup was established to provide players of wider nationality the opportunity to compete in an event of similar status as the European tournament. The first four tournaments were held in the United States and Australia. South Africa was selected as venue for the fifth tournament in 2000, primarily through the advocacy and influence of golfers such as Ernie Els and Gary Player, both former world golf champions. Initially scheduled for 2002, the event was postponed in the aftermath of 9/11. It was eventually held in 2003 at one of the most prestigious and internationally well known golf estates in South Africa, Fancourt, in the Western Cape province.

Several factors underlay the selection of South Africa as venue. From the perspective of the event organisers, this involved attempts to increase the scope of golf as international sport, and to extend it to new markets. For a long time golf has had the image of being an exclusive sport, although it is increasingly losing that reputation. This is due to advances in widespread golf development programmes, changes in the organisation of sport at domestic levels in primary golf markets, with youth and women's golf for example becoming more common, and not an insignificant factor, the rising significance of golf as an international economic sector, with golf tourism becoming an increasingly important niche market. The latter is particularly visible in the prolific rise in the number of golf courses worldwide and strategic moves by several countries to develop themselves as primary golfing destinations (common to many regions, but highly marked in countries such as Saudi Arabia, Malaysia and Indonesia).

Data from the International Association of Golf Tour Operators indicate that in world terms the most important demand for golf tourism is from Europe (particularly the UK, Germany, and France), Japan and the United States. Key international golfing locations include European destinations such as Scotland, England, Spain, Portugal and Ireland and the Caribbean. Well-established golf tourism circuits exist in several regions, for example between Japan and Southeast Asian neighbours such as Malaysia and Indonesia, while North African destinations such as Tunisia and Morocco are capitalising on their locations as short-haul destination for German and French tourists. Over the years these two countries have positioned themselves as golf sites, particularly for German travellers.

In this context, South Africa was favourably regarded as location for the fifth Presidents Cup. As with other major events that were hosted by South Africa and are discussed in this chapter, a strong Africa-claim underlay decision to host the event in the country, with a tacit understanding that positive coverage would be beneficial for the wider continent. The existence of several prime international golf courses in the country, along with the involvement and promotion of eminent South African world golfers contributed to the selection of the country as host. For South Africa, who had hosted the Golf World Cup in 1998 the main significance of the event lay in its high stature.

As such the event aimed at stimulating a growing and very lucrative component of the country's tourism economy. Similar to many other developing countries, South Africa had seen significant rise in golf courses and golf tourism has developed into important and high-revenue tourism market. In world terms South Africa's share of the international golf tourism market is small (for instance being only the eight most visited destination for German golf tourists (DEADP, 2004)). Golf is however fast becoming an important motivation for travellers from South Africa's two prime overseas markets, the UK and Germany. At the same time, a significant producer sector has developed around specialist, niche tour operators focused on the promotion of golf tourism to the country. Golf clientele tend to be wealthier and their travel conduct is typically linked the higher-yielding segments of the tourism sector. In addition, as discussed at length below, attempts by public and private sectors to develop the golf niche market, very significant affect investment and infrastructure development patterns in key locations such as the Western Cape.

Indeed, the Presidents Cup had a number of impacts. Specific to the event, the tournament drew up to 23 000 tourists and spectators, most of whom resided in George, the town where the Fancourt golf course is located and where the tournament took place. The event was thought to have raised revenue of R110m for the local economy (*Cape Times*, 28 November 2003; *Weekend Post*, 8 November 2003). A further major by-product was the country's hosting of the Women's Golf World Cup one year later.

Despite these positive impacts of the Presidents Cup, the event was particularly significant for raising to prominence some of the challenges characterising golf tourism development. The Southern Cape, the region of the Western Cape province within which the event was held, has in recent years become mired in a rising dispute over the intense nature of golf estate developments. This region had seen a rapid increase in the number of golf courses and estates over the past number of years and golf estate developments have become the largest component of tourism investments in the province (Chapter 3). By the end of 2004 for instance, up to 83 golf courses have been developed or were approved for development in the province. Most of these were located in the Southern Cape region.

The prolific rise in such developments over a short period of time has given rise to growing conflict over the benefits and disbenefits of such developments. Increased polarisation over whether golf estates bring broad economic spin-offs in the region or whether they carry heavy ecological costs has led the provincial government to intervene by the end of that year, first by commissioning a consultancy report on the impact of polo and golf courses in the province, and subsequently, in line with a recommendation by the report, declaring a moratorium on further new golf developments. At the time 33 applications for new golf course development (20 of which were concentrated along a small coastal strip of the Southern Cape) were pending approval.

Golf developments have emerged as a highly political and divisive matter in the Western Cape. On one side of the dispute a large and influential body of private sector developers have pleaded the economic advantages of golf courses and estates. Arguments mainly centre on the impact that the construction of estates could have on local economies and temporary employment that can be created during the construction phase. Post-construction it is commonly emphasised that opportunities arise for people to be permanently employed both by maintaining the infrastructure of golf courses (for example as caddies or cleaners), or in servicing the residential and other components of golf estates (such as domestic workers, gardeners or in providing other support services). It is also argued that estates will stimulate tourism growth. These claims have resonated strongly with a significant sector of the region's population, of which more than three-quarters is constituted of 'coloured' and black groups. Even though the Southern Cape is a wealthy region and tends to draw higher-income tourists relative to the Western Cape's other tourism regions (Cornelissen, 2005), large disparities exist among the region's population, with blacks and 'coloureds' in the main having lower levels of education and standards of living than whites. One of the paradoxes of the region is that despite the ascent of new sources of economic growth (of which tourism is one of the most significant) in the recent past, unemployment has been a persistent problem, with up to forty percent of the region's population not employed.

In this context and given the rising centrality of golf tourism as a significant component of the region's overall tourism economy, the development of golf estates has become a focus for several community leaders who seek to draw investors' attention. Over the past number of years several prominent and politically influential individuals, moreover, have become involved in the development of new estates by entering into joint ventures with foreign investors, or as part of black economic empowerment (BEE) transactions. One example is of an extensive development near the region's major town, George, initiated and led by the former South Africa ambassador to the United States and that involves a number of other eminent individuals who occupy key positions in various spheres of influence such as the judiciary and the political domain. The promoters of the development proclaim it to be an attempt to stimulate growth of the local economy. In structure the development draws a consortium of private developers, the political figures and a range of community organisations into a flaky alliance. Despite projections of large inflows of revenue, the creation of employment opportunities and the promise of focused community tourism and development programmes, there has been a high level of division within the local community (*Mail and Guardian*, 4 March 2005). Lack of cooperation by community groups and an outright challenge by some have been some of the factors that prevented the development to progress very far over the past four years.

Nonetheless it is increasingly common for high profile political figures to promote golf estate developments as vehicles for local economic empowerment and transformation. This has contributed to such developments gaining a decided political hue, and in some spheres being regarded with scepticism. This partly stems from misgivings on the part of communities in the region as to what the motives of developers and some political leaders are. Cases where high-ranking provincial officials have been shown to have acted fraudulently with respect to such developments strengthen negative sentiments around these developments. One example is where in 2002 the then premier of the Western Cape and the provincial minister for environment affairs and development planning, were found to have taken bribes from a foreign firm to bypass official procedures and requirements to approve proposals to develop a major estate in the Southern Cape region. Although the two officials were relieved of their duties and subsequently prosecuted, the case had led to some wariness on the part of the province's residents.

A number of environmental groups have arisen as a highly vocal and influential lobby against golf estate developments. In the main their opposition centres on the impact that such developments purportedly have on the environment. Much criticism has been levelled against developers' ostensible lack of appreciation for the ecological sensitivity and uniqueness of the region. Three principal areas of concern are the removal of indigenous vegetation to construct estates, the reduction of the fynbos biome and the damage this brings to local ecosystems, and the high volumes of water needed to maintain golf courses. Arguments are that golf developments pose an inherent threat to environmental resources and as such, that they are not sustainable forms of tourism development. Many Southern Cape community groups have aligned themselves with environmental lobbyists.

For communities another major concern however is that the projected broad economic benefits seldom materialise and that only small segments, generally not the most impoverished, of the population seem to gain from such developments. The construction of golf estates is also said to have dramatically raised the value of property in the Southern Cape, making it unaffordable for the majority of the local community to acquire housing. One of the specific negative spin-offs of the 2003 Presidents Cup, for instance, is that the event prompted a surge in golf estate developments across the region, increasing property prices and local inflation levels. Further, some developments on the coastal parts of the region have been criticised for restricting the access of local communities to beaches or the coast. This, it is argued limits the ability of communities to fully utilise coastal areas for leisure or economic purposes.

Much opposition to golf developments also focuses on water consumption by golf courses and estates. One estimate is that on average, a golf course uses up to two million litres of water a day (DEAPD, 2004). Consumption by golf estates, which also have residential components, is likely to be even higher. In addition, it is argued that golf courses and estates place additional stress on service infrastructure such as sewage removal and increases the likelihood for pollution. Since 2002 the use of water resources has become a matter of key public and political interest when, due to changed climatic factors, erratic rainfall patterns and generally drier conditions, the Western Cape province started to face the rapid depletion of its surface water reserves. Since that year the government has enforced annual restrictions on domestic and industrial water usage in many parts of the province to limit pressures on the province's reserves.

It has been acknowledged that tourism activities, and golf developments in particular, can place severe stress on a particular region's water supply (Essex, Kent and Newnham, 2004; Gajraj, 1981; Holden, 2000). In emerging international golf tourism locations such as the Balearic Islands, for instance, the growth of golf estates has become an important issue as diversification of the tourist product has led to higher water consumption. Essex et al. (2004) note how water supply management policies in Mallorca have had to change in response to more water usage prompted by, amongst others, a quadrupling in the number of golf courses on the island over the past number of years. Attempts to implement a tourist 'eco-tax' to help finance environmental regeneration, and negative publicity on water shortages in key source markets such as Germany have adversely affected the island's tourism economy (Essex et al., 2004). Destinations in North Africa such as Egypt, which depend to a significant degree on medium-haul golf tourism from North Europe, have started attempts to impose environmental regulations on golf developments and to introduce methods of environmental protection. This involves, amongst others, redirecting and limiting irrigation, using desalinated water more efficiently, building golf courses to keep desert landscapes intact and implementing standards for water usage by which golf course operators are monitored and rewarded (Hassan, 2003).

As one of the regions in South Africa where a strong golf tourism sector is emerging, the Western Cape province is hence exhibiting many of the planning and regulatory difficulties experienced in other golf locations. In the Western Cape golf developments have the added political dimension in that they ostensibly place high levels of stress on already scarce environmental resources, and more significantly, raise to prominence profound economic contrasts between the consumers of golf developments, who domestic or foreign, tend to be white and affluent, and the wider local population who is not. In the context of South Africa's recent political past and the focus on transformation in the post-apartheid era, it is understandable that such a condition leads to political tension.

The government of the Western Cape thus faces the challenge to balance attempts to promote a growing and important niche in the provincial tourism sector, one that is significant for the wider economy, with transformation and redistribution goals. It has generally adopted a harsh stance towards unfettered development and seeks to maintain a strong regulatory role in golf developments. Two major motivations for the government is that developers' projections on employment opportunities seem to be gross overestimations, and that rising land prices through golf estate developments may threaten the government's land reform programme (Cabinet of the Western Cape, media statement, 10 December 2004). In line with national land reform objectives, this programme aims to through various restitution mechanisms effect a 30 per cent change in land ownership in the next ten years.

Golf development and the expansion of golf tourism more broadly, is thus a complex issue in the South African context. On the one hand this niche market has significant growth potential and the extension of this activity can yield important benefits both specifically for the growth of tourism, but also for the broader economy. On the other hand, however, it faces many challenges. Many of these are specific to golf tourism as a sector. Generically, however, the development of sport tourism into a coherent industry can be a difficult task for governments. The principal reason for this is that separately, in form and structure both sport and tourism are two inchoate economic sectors. Sport specifically is constituted of a range of diverse, often highly dissimilar codes and activities. Setting goals and making policy in this sort of environment can be very demanding. The final section of the chapter discusses challenges and opportunities for event and sport tourism development in South Africa.

Events, Sport and Tourism Policy-Making

Despite the inherent synergies between sport and tourism, few countries have made extensive progress with the development of cohesive sport tourism policies or institutions. Specifically, even though many countries have established government departments for sport and recreation whose task it is to coordinate agencies across different sporting codes and their development activities, there often is little interconnection between such agencies and those who are responsible for promoting or extending national tourism sectors. This is surprising given the growing acknowledgement by governments of the global significance both of sport and tourism, and with respect to tourism, an increased realisation that as an intermestic issue area (C. Hall, 2001) tourism policy-making spans across many levels of regulation and is enacted by different political actors (Chapter 2).

With regard to the United Kingdom, Weed (2003) suggests six causes for a long-established rift between sport and tourism actors: ideological differences over the visions and goals that should inform the respective spheres; differences in organisational culture; distinctions that arise from the various geographical regions that are covered by each sphere; the impact of national government policy, that sets the parameters for sport and tourism agencies and often account for non-transmutable divisions; related to the former, often vastly differing conceptions and definitions of sport and tourism; and finally, the influence of dominant individuals in each sphere and preferences and objectives set by them. These factors, along with the general structures of policy and decision have major implications for whether a 'sport-tourism policy network' (Weed, 2003) can arise that on a longer-tem basis can set formal and coherent development goals for sport tourism.

All of the factors identified by Weed (2003) are applicable to South Africa and are relevant to explain what can be termed a distinct lack of progress with respect to sport tourism development, although however, that country's political context also makes for unique obstacles. With the creation of the post-apartheid government, a ministry for sport and recreation was established with the task of managing sport activities. Given the ideological significance of sport and often very stark political tensions among the three main sporting codes in the country, i.e. soccer, rugby and cricket, the ministry faced the challenge of articulating a vision and goals that were acceptable to all the main sport role players.

This has been extremely difficult. One of the reasons is that the South African government has prioritised transformation as one of the main vehicles for sport development. This has specifically meant racial transformation in rugby and cricket, two sporting codes that historically have been played and supported by whites (while soccer has historically been more popular among the black population groups), and in the case of rugby in particular, have fulfilled a particular role in Afrikaner identity development during the apartheid era (Black and

Nauright, 1998; Grundlingh, 1998). Even though the government realised the value of sport in supporting its post-apartheid nation-building project, it set out on a precarious path of enforcing fundamental transformation of simultaneously the racial composition of rugby and cricket management boards and teams, and in the way that leagues are organised. This saw the government for instance introducing highly controversial race quotas for national rugby and cricket teams and for some of rugby's most lucrative domestic leagues. A lengthy battle over such provisions and a generally acrimonious relationship between the South African ministry of sport and the rugby and cricket establishments, have hampered progress in the setting of common sport development goals.

Rugby, cricket, and increasingly soccer are of the most well-organised and financially powerful sporting codes in the country. Other sports have not successfully mustered up the same level of support, spectatorship or revenue as these sporting disciplines. Another factor accounting for the slow advance in sport development has thus been the dominance of the three main sporting codes and significant institutional and financial deficiencies in other types of sports. In an attempt to improve the broad-based conditions of and participation in sport, the South African government established the National Sport Council (NSC) in 1994. After more than a decade, however, with low levels of resource allocation, the NSC has not been entirely successful.

As far as the development of sport tourism is concerned, the situation is even more dire. It is clear that there is a very stark separation between the respective government ministries and agencies for sport and tourism, with little attempt to coordinate activities. However, realisation of the economic and political value of events, sport and tourism, and attempts to develop the country's MICE sector, has prompted other, unrelated agencies to make some advance towards viewing the three spheres in combination with each other. One example is the various branding initiatives by the International Marketing Council and their international promotion campaign, Brand South Africa (Chapter 5). This campaign is based on the collation and publicising of various assets of allure in South Africa, of which advertising the country's goals around mega-events is an important element. The International Marketing Council is likely to be an important lobby for coordination among government sport and tourism departments. One area where this has started to emerge is in the events sector, where South African Tourism recently introduced a national events strategy (SA Tourism, 2002c) that aims to establish a framework for successfully developing an events economy in South Africa that interrelates with the national tourism sector. Although significant these are ad hoc institutional arrangements that are a far cry from the full alignment of the two spheres and their related policy-making structures that is needed for the development of a comprehensive sports tourism policy network.

This lack of progress holds particular negative implications for the organisation of the 2010 FIFA finals. Already SAFA, the national soccer management body and the institution responsible for organising the event, has become mired in controversy over its intents and targets. First, questions have been raised about the ability of SAFA to carry the responsibility for the event when soon after South Africa was announced as host for the 2010 finals, it emerged that the body has been experiencing financial difficulties for a number of years. Second, at the end of 2004 rivalry within SAFA over the composition of the local organising committee, the panel of persons responsible for coordinating, in collaboration with FIFA, all arrangements for the event, led to Joseph Blatter directly intervening and selecting the LOC members. Enmity among high-ranking SAFA officials for membership of the LOC was in the main negatively viewed by the South African public who regarded it as tasteless and irrelevant to the main affair of steering organisation towards the event (*Business Day*, 13 January 2005). Broad assessments of the LOC's progress seem to have become even harsher in recent times. During the first part of 2005 the media reported that weighed against Germany's early progress towards finalising arrangements for the 2006 finals, South Africa's preparation appears to lag far behind (*Mail and Guardian*, 25 April 2005). Other issues of dispute have centred on the LOC's decision to reduce the number of stadia participating in the 2010 event from 13, as initially proposed in the bid document, to ten. As is typical of the jostling and competition that takes place among cities aiming to be selected as venues for matches during major sport events, an intense contest has arisen among many, particularly smaller urban centres in the country.

Beyond sifting through the boosterist campaigns of urban authorities, major tasks of coordinating diverse public institutions of policy-making and service provision, such as the construction of infrastructure, planning around waste management and safety and security, await the LOC. Much of the burden of investment and infrastructural development will fall on the governments of the three main metropolises – broader Johannesburg, Cape Town and Durban. However, extensive and central direction needs to emanate from the national government, who would for instance be required to cohere national development goals and public works programmes with infrastructural requirements for the 2010 event. This requires in turn focused planning, with a central agency that steers a strategy for organising the event. As such it is disconcerting that to date, little advance has been made with the development of an approach towards institutionally combining the spheres of tourism, sport and events.

In all, despite the clear benefits tied to mega-events, they can also place excessive fiscal and management burdens on a country. For South Africa, the principal challenge lies in not only amassing the requisite economic and material resources, but in effectively managing those towards the arrangements for the event. However, long-term and broad-based development goals that extend far beyond the event should constitute the primary bases upon which planning and organisation take place. For this, it is imperative that much greater synergy – both in terms of policy organisation and institutionally – is established between the sport and tourism sectors.

Conclusion

Contest for sport mega-events may be said to be a developmental instrument and goal of an increasing number of developed and developing countries. In Africa, a select few states have also opted for mega-events as a policy course over the past number of years. African countries have had very little success in securing events of major significance. South Africa, which has aggressively solicited events as part of a larger external strategy, is the singular exception. Mega-events are geared to serve several functions in Africa. Although largely aimed at accomplishing set economic objectives, many governments attempt to use mega-events to fulfil larger political aims, such as consolidating national legitimacy or as a means of nation-building.

There are a number of factors that are of significance for the prospects of African countries to gainfully participate, and be successful in the mega-events enterprise. First, the example of the bids for the FIFA Soccer World Cup shows that the way in which international sport organisations such as FIFA are structured, and the way in which bidding contests are conducted and decided, pose significant impediments to smaller countries (and developing countries more generally). The basis on which the global competition for mega-events occurs, therefore, is unequal.

A second issue concerns the capacity of African states, and the availability of appropriate infrastructure to host mega-events. The African continent, perhaps more than any other developing region finds itself in a paradoxical situation where mega-events pose a means of entry to other structures of production, finances and technology that so configure the global economy, but it is largely lacking the resources to access it. Despite the cogency and parsimony of globalisation as explanatory framework for mega-events, therefore, a great deal of it is structured from a position that does not wholly account for the types of challenges faced by African countries.

Sports bids and events are highly political affairs and politics play a significant role in shaping events, bid processes and outcomes. Beyond that, however, factors related to the preparation and administration of bids and events are critical. Recent research on mega-events emphasise the importance of sound and effective management. While a number of role players are responsible for this, the state needs to fulfil the pivotal function of coordination. Aside from not having the requisite infrastructural and resource capability to host mega-events, a great number of African states are politically and also economically weakened, and not able to execute such tasks.

In such contexts, and given the costs usually involved in running for, or hosting large events, the question of whether seeking to host such events is an appropriate development strategy for developing countries, becomes all the more pertinent. In addition tourism spin-offs from major sport events, more than any other tourism segment, are tied to the character and related interests of the particular corporate and financial involvements in such events. This carries import for the type of tourism impacts that evolve out of mega-events. In light of this, core questions need to be asked about the economic and other costs that hosting mega-events can carry for African states and societies, and whether expected benefits do indeed outweigh the costs. The rising significance of both sport and events as global economic niches means that much greater attention needs to be given to investigating the links between these two spheres and that of tourism development.

Notes

1. Former president Mandela presented the victory trophy to the South African team dressed in a Springbok rugby jersey, which for a long time has been regarded as unrepresentative and an embodiment of apartheid South Africa. Later he told the (predominantly white) team that 'rugby, once the symbol of division and exclusion, had crossed the threshold into a new era of a united and reconciled nation' (*The Star*, 26 June 1995).
2. Personal communication, CEO of South African Football Association Bid Committee, 13 February.
3. These companies included First National Bank, a financial group, Vodacom, one of South Africa's cellular providers, South African Breweries, Telkom, South Africa's state-owned telecommunications provider, Southern Sun, a hotel group, ICL, an information technology company, and the Industrial Development Corporation, a parastatal (Alegi, 2001).
4. The South African president, Thabo Mbeki, for instance lamented: 'When will some in Europe be ready to accept that Africa is part of the global human family and not an irrelevant appendage whose marginalisation is, to some, in developed Europe, an acceptable outcome' (*Eastern Province Herald*, 19 July 2000).
5. These confederations represent different regions in the world. They are: CAF (Africa); UEFA (Europe); AFC (Asia); CONCACAF (North and Central America and the Caribbean); CONMEBOL (South America) and OFC (Oceania).

Chapter 8

Conclusion: Tourism Development in the Contemporary Era

Introduction

This book was an analysis of the political economy of tourism production, consumption and regulation and its developmental consequences in the era of globalisation. Through an investigation of how the South African tourist sector interrelates with and is shaped by the larger structural frame that is the global tourism system, the book has provided an example of how the dynamics of this system impact on national sectors, and how it brings differential gains and costs. For a country such as South Africa, many unique features and attractions, its position as an African destination and well-suited tourism infrastructure provided a good base to establish itself as a popular site over the past decade. Yet it has not been an easy path of growth as several external factors detrimentally affected the country's sector. The way that it is interlocked in global structures of production and governance, in particular, has directed aspects such as international marketing, imaging and tourism regulation and affected tourist flows. In this developmental and transformation goals have often been offset or weakened.

There are several lessons to be learned from the analysis of South Africa's participation in international tourism that are of use for developing and developed countries alike. Primarily, the book's delineation of the various elements of the global tourism system is valuable to understand the compound nature of an economic activity that involves many global industries and sectors, and engages many stakeholders at different levels. Making sense of the depth and complexity of the commercial, social and political relations that constitute global tourism is essential to understand the extent and dynamism of this sector.

This chapter provides an overview of the main arguments and themes arising from the analysis and outlines some of the major challenges and opportunities for international tourism development.

Global Tourism's Structural Components

Global tourism is best viewed as systems of production, consumption and regulation that separately, each has its own character and cadence and is formed by the dominance of specific actors, but also interrelate in dynamic fashions to produce an overarching global sector.

Production is one of the formative components of the tourism system. Globally, tourism production comprises of core sectors such as accommodation, air transportation and tour and travel intermediaries, although linkage to an expansive network of ancillary sectors means that tourism-specific and related activities have substantial impact in a wide range of other industries.

Tourism production follows its own momentum as core producer sectors interconnect through relations of collaboration and/or competition. The former may manifest in destination marketing alliances or in resource sharing such as in GDS, while horizontal mergers, market consolidation and integration constitute aggressive ways in which producers may compete within or across producer spheres. Intensive competitive interaction in the South African production system carried negative impacts for the wider national sector and attributed to the country gaining a reputation as an expensive location. Since the country vies for a share of global tourism with other, often cheaper long-haul destinations in *inter alia*, Southeast Asia, this is an example of how producer relations can have damaging consequences for a given destination. In general, however, mechanisms of self-regulation provide means whereby producer-producer relations are ordered. The establishment of producer institutions is also aimed at providing stable endogenous environments within which producer cooperation and competition can occur.

Networks of commercial and transactional linkages among international and domestic tour operators, travel agents, accommodation operators and transport providers constitute the foundation by which local and international sectors interlink. Globally, however, a logic of hierarchy exists, as characteristically larger (generally multinational) firms have greater sway and direct producer interaction. Some of the world's largest hotel chains, tour operator consortiums and airlines exercise commanding influence on the rest of the global tourism system. Such dominant producers have determining impacts on global travel flows, processes of international marketing and distribution.

Processes of *consumption* closely relate to production. The producer-consumer nexus is one of the important pillars of the global tourism system, with the engagement between producers and consumers giving form to the tourist product and determining in what manner consumption occurs. Yet tourism consumption is also a discrete social process that is shaped by separate sets of impulses. The cultural turn in tourism analysis has aptly led to greater emphasis being placed (again) on the socio-cultural sources of tourist motivation and preferences in the contemporary era. Lifestyle expression, individualisation and self-enhancement are important manifestations of changed forms of social orientation at this particular juncture of capitalist development. These types of changes reframe tourism in important ways, and go some way in explaining the rise of alternatives to mass tourism and the centrality of the so-called 'new tourist'. Nonetheless, the producer-consumer nexus is an essential analytical tool for understanding that there is a mutually affective interplay between consumers and producers. In the same way the 'consumer over producer' debate appropriately reminds us that both sets of actors influence tourism outcomes.

Regulation is an important mechanism in the global tourism system: to provide proper balance among producers in their engagement with each other; to offset some of the destructive consequences of intense rivalry; to protect standards and consumer rights; or through legislative and judiciary tools, prevent oligopolistic or anti-competitive practices from providing unfair advantage to some. More abstractly, regulation also plays a social protective role as it, either in concrete form or by being based on certain tacit values and norms, directs what sorts of social representations are acceptable in tourism production (such as in destination imaging) or what sorts of practices are deemed appropriate for sustainability or are socially just. Seen this way tourism regulation can be cast as fulfilling an essential corrective function in a particular global context within which tourism not only has an economic, but also socio-democratic purpose.

The state has an important intermediary role to play in this regard, setting the legislative parameters for producer interaction and consumer mobility and on a broader level, being constitutive units in regional and global institutions of governance. Such institutions very directly impact on the global tourism system, laying the boundaries and dictating the pace at which global expansion can occur. As the examination in this book of the two major regulatory regimes that also affect international tourism – i.e. aviation and trade liberalisation under the GATS – has shown, the very unequal structural make-up of the global political economy means that, in general, developing countries have less recourse to sway outcomes in global institutions of governance in their favour. Agreements concerning, for instance, flight frequency, capacity or the content and tempo of tourism trade liberalisation, generally reflect the economic dominance of multinational firms that are based in the North, or the negotiating weight of richer countries. Paradoxically, however, participation in global institutions of governance are essential forms of global representation and (self-)protection for developing countries.

Unequal means of exchange in global institutions of regulation aside, there is no overlooking the fact that the common pursuit for a share in world tourism and the lucrative economic gains contained in tourism expansion, and the unrelated encroachment upon the powers of the state through processes of globalisation, has meant that there has been a coherent logic in the way that developing and developed countries orient themselves towards the global tourism system. Homogeneity in policy objectives, institutional coagulation (such as the establishment of public-private partnerships or destination marketing organisations), branding endeavours, or even urban restructuring, as cities prepare themselves as sites of leisure and other consumption, have typified the activities and priorities of the governments of both developing and developed countries. In this tourism does have an odd equalising impact on the rich and poor states of the world.

The South African Case

For a number of historical reasons South Africa's political economy (including its tourism sector) reflects characteristics of both the developing and developed world.

As such, the country's experience in attempting to build out tourism as a basis for development within an overarching global tourism system and structures of governance is applicable to a broad spectrum of contexts. South Africa shares similarities with many other countries with respect to the tourism policy choices it has made over the past decade and many of the constraints and opportunities it faces. Further, a location as a country of low to medium global economic, political and diplomatic capacity places it in a league with many other developing countries for whom gaining more favourable placing in the international system is a priority. In this regard, South Africa's wider foreign policy and multilateral activism geared towards providing the country a more prominent international position, is characteristic of the global middle power role the country has increasingly adopted during the post-apartheid era (Nel, Taylor and van der Westhuizen, 2001). Its greater use of international bidding competitions to host sport and other mega-events, and the economic and political publicity afforded by such activities (Cornelissen, 2004a), and particular attempts concerning international tourist imaging (Chapter 5) can be seen as important elements of a developing country's endeavours to increase its global standing. Various resources, of which attractiveness as a tourist location is one, are put to use to attain larger domestic and foreign policy objectives.

South Africa however has many idiosyncracies and an own dynamic that sets it apart from other countries. This is shaped by the political history of apartheid, and the societal and institutional revolution that has taken place over the past 15 years. As an African location, it possesses many of the physical attributes of other African tourist destinations, but seems to fare economically better than its continental counterparts. This enables it to interrelate more cogently with the global tourism system. Yet the country has the distinction that it has the greatest number of HIV/Aids infections in the world, and projections are that this epidemic will have immense and enduring impacts on the country's economy and society in years to come. The lessons that can be learned from the South African case study have to be viewed within the context of the similarities the country shares with others, and the refractory influence of the factors that make it distinctive in the global setting.

Patterns of Expansion and Development

The swift pace of growth that South African tourism has seen since the end of apartheid demonstrates the vast potential that global tourism development holds for countries. However, the variability of this growth over the past decade also accentuates many of the externalities that go along with tourism expansion. On the basis of its political currency the country was able to develop a highly distinctive tourist product that offered a fresh appeal to an international market that itself was growing speedily. The country capitalised on its allure as an African location and its political and cultural novelty to draw in large numbers of international tourists and to build a large tourism economy.

Yet successes in establishing itself as tourist destination have also been counteracted by two main factors: a precarious balance between supply and demand; and events and forces in the exogenous environment, and their effect on destination image and tourists' perceptions.

Tourist demand rapidly increased after 1994. This was followed by a significant rise in tourism supply in all sectors of the tourism economy, particularly in accommodation. Demand has however been highly variable and shifts in demand have often been insufficient to sustain the growth in supply, leading to a tourist sector characterised by over-capacity. Seasonal swings in international demand constitute a further constraint.

Changeable demand is to a large degree the outcome of broader structural factors. Political events and wider global instability both positively and negatively affect South African tourism, tending to channel tourist flows to, or from the country. A reputation as a destination characterised by high levels of violent crime has also been a major constriction on inbound tourist volumes. Within this context, disparities between supply and demand levels can become larger.

In terms of product development, the government places a great deal of emphasis on cultural tourism as a growth market. 'Culture' is indeed an important element of the overall South African attraction and image. Yet, demand in the international market for alternative products such as cultural or township tourism, is still small. Infrastructural insufficiencies, tourist concerns for safety in the case of township or township-related tourism, and below standard products, offset demand. There is also a lack of knowledge and information about new/alternative products within source markets. Limitations to current product development, product promotion and policy also account for demand patterns. Indications are that the present product offer does not fulfil the preferences of the main target market(s), and that this is compounded by limited promotion campaigns in source markets.

All of these factors have led to many of the government's policy goals surrounding tourism transformation and empowerment to date not having had a large measure of success. Less than adequate impact distribution, partly contributed to by a lack of tourism capital investments in lower impact (and generally poorer) areas, has meant that many of the positive spin-offs of tourism growth have not filtered down to the broader population. As such furthering development through tourism has been one of the failures of government policy.

South Africa as African Leader? Opportunities and Challenges

Slow delivery on some of the social objectives of tourism development notwithstanding, South Africa has managed to distinguish itself in the African market. Indeed, by drawing the greatest volume of inbound international traffic, the country has established a principal position on the continent. This is also reflected in the country's participation in some of the international initiatives on sustainable tourism development, as one of the government's focuses has been to encourage sustainable practices on the African continent. South Africa has also made much of its touristic appeal as an African destination. With the various patterns of self- and wider continental promotion it is fair to say that the country has sought to entrench itself as an African leader.

This is perhaps no clearer than in the country's bid campaigns to host the FIFA football World Cups. While South Africa's bid for the 2006 event was unsuccessful, its campaign for both the 2006 and 2010 finals consisted of an emphatic projection of itself as custodian of the aspirations of the entire African continent for whom awarding the event to South Africa would see many of the developmental opportunities heretofore denied to the continent, to take root. The country also cast itself, nonetheless, as an African country that has gained moral stature through its relatively successful democratic transition that, as an act of reward by the international community, deserved to be awarded the finals (Cornelissen, 2004b). This latter projection South Africa used quite strongly in the competition for the 2010 finals when it sought to differentiate itself from other African contenders, and particularly Morocco, one of its closest rivals.

South Africa was correct in representing the 2010 World Cup as an opportunity for the African continent to participate in what today has developed as a sports mega-events industry, comprised as it is by a wider political economy of sponsorship agents, global media corporations, merchandise and investors. Recent years have seen increased attempts by several African states (such as Nigeria, Tunisia, Egypt) to partake in the economic, publicity and development spin-offs associated with sport mega-events. South Africa's successful co-hosting of a second-order event such as the 2003 Cricket World Cup (the political debacles around Zimbabwe that accompanied the event notwithstanding) legitimised African countries as viable hosts for events of large magnitude.

As a means to promote tourism to the country the 2010 FIFA World Cup, by virtue of its size, profile and scope would be an important stimulus for the South African economy, and arguably the wider Southern African region. The South African government needs however to devise a focused strategy that utilises the momentum of the event and spin-offs prior to and after the finals to establish the foundation for a longer-term events economy. As yet, there seems to be a decided lack of strategy. Planning towards the event has also been slow with in the recent past, some controversy surrounding the composition of the local organising committee and preferences for certain individuals leading to dispute. An aspect that South Africa needs to be wary of is that it does not develop an arrogant and complacent or paternalistic attitude towards Africa. A wider context of growing hostility by many African countries towards South Africa's has hampered this country's attempt to establish economic and political supremacy in the continent. With a looming event such as the 2010 World Cup, it would be severely detrimental if South Africa is unable to muster the requisite support from other African countries. In order to draw full benefit from the growing significance of global sport and events economies, further, it is imperative that the country develops a comprehensive, long-term national sport events strategy that feeds into and supports its tourism sector. Much also needs to be done to develop sport tourism as a self-standing industry.

More broadly, the focus on Africa and other developing contexts raises a number of implications for the type of research that is currently conducted on sport events and their effects, and highlights the shortcomings of this research. For instance, existing research on the link between sport events and tourism development tend to concentrate on total impact derived from aggregate statistics. Such a type of analysis is not appropriate in developing contexts, where, as has been shown in this chapter, numerous factors play in on the eventual outcome of events, and where economic sectors may significantly differ from those in industrialised countries. As an illustration, while tourism is by nature a highly dynamic and fragmented sector, it is of a distinct feature in developing, and in particular African countries, where less formalised tourist activities such as the production and sale of arts and crafts may be an important component of the overall tourism economy. Economic impact assessments of events need to incorporate analyses of how often large segments of the population who are not part of the formal economy, can be drawn into and accrue revenue from an event. While new directions in tourism and sport research are starting to factor in local economic and other conditions, a shortcoming is that tourism is still treated as an intransient sector, with the assumption that tourism sectors share similar characteristics in all contexts.

There are other distinctions between industrialised and developing countries that bear upon the way that the relationship between sport events and tourism is evaluated. One relates to the differential effect that locational factors may play in different contexts: while there is possibly a congruence between sport events and urban tourism in industrialised countries, the same may not be true in developing countries, where different tourism and spatial characteristics prevail. By the same token, an event (and planning and infrastructural development towards it) may have a dramatically dissimilar impact on the developmental landscape in developing countries. All in all, existing methodologies for local impact studies in the industrialised world – based as they are on assumptions and conditions particular to developed countries – are in the main not suitable for developing environments, given the often disparate structure of the economies, the disproportionate importance of informal producers, and the developmental exigencies governments often attempt to address through sport events.

Since developing countries more broadly, and Africa specifically, are becoming more active with regard to sport mega-events, the development of adequate methods of study are essential to gain proper understanding of the impacts of such events. This includes the use of methods that incorporate the economic and societal idiosyncracies of developing/African countries; is based on an understanding how tourism functions in these countries; and draws on innovative techniques, perhaps combining quantitative and qualitative instruments to assess impact. With regard to the latter, standard indicators of tourism impact – bed occupancy, sales or employment multipliers – may not be adequate to reflect the total effect of an event on a local economy. Much better would be the use of household surveys to measure household income multipliers during and after an event, with full consideration of the particular structure of local tourism economies in African contexts, and that are geared to capture the impact of an event on activities that are not formally integrated into the tourism system, but nonetheless affect income and employment.

With respect to South Africa's potential to establish itself as an African leader, it is important to note that there is a tenuous balance between South

Africa's accentuation of its African appeal and wider, Western concerns over security that the South African government does not always seem to realise. In terms of influencing tourist demand negative images and representations constitute major impediments. In this regard two related factors – South Africa's positioning in Africa, and the role of the media in shaping perceptions – are problematic. The international image of Africa is overwhelmingly negative, and the media, as conduits, but also selectors of information, occupies a powerful position in forming this image. As a way of obviating the effects of Africa's negative connotation South Africa's international marketing campaign seeks to extricate itself from Africa and emphasise its 'non-African' qualities (i.e. more developed, better infrastructure, facilities and hygiene). But there is an inherent tension in this approach, as a significant aspect of South Africa's attraction lies in it being an African destination, with all that Africa has to offer (such as wildlife, nature, the promise of a different experience).

A further problem is that up until recently, there has been little policy foresight with regard to South Africa becoming an African leader in the fuller sense of the term, i.e. becoming a leisure and business destination of choice for Africans through the promotion of regional and intra-continental tourism. Industry and societal biases have meant that there has not been adequate acknowledgement of the market potential of day, VFR visitors or shoppers from neighbouring states or other African countries. There is now greater realisation of the value of, in particular business tourism from Central and East Africa. Recently, some attempt was made to build out the African component in South Africa's tourism economy. The 2002 Tourism Growth Strategy by South African Tourism, among others, prioritises the African market as one where promotion resources will be concentrated. The focus is on increasing the value from African tourism by up-selling and cross-selling into other product areas (SA Tourism, 2002). Enduring constraints to intra-African tourism, however, are underdeveloped infrastructure, poor and expensive air connections, weak currencies and the lack of capital (Dieke, 1995). In the same way as African tourism has been underexploited, there has been a very slow realisation in South Africa of the value and necessity to nurture domestic tourism, which is the bedrock of the country's tourism economy. A lack of domestic promotion and skewed investment patterns have meant that the potential of domestic tourism – particularly in the stimulation of travel and tourism consumption by the black population – has not been fully developed.

Overall, South Africa enjoys a degree of prominence in international markets. There is great potential for fostering further tourism growth if the constraints that have been highlighted are addressed.

Wider Lessons

A number of general factors may be identified that have import for tourism development in a wider global context.

First, demand-stimulation through new product offer is an important policy course for many governments. Chapter 5 had demonstrated the power relations within the global tourism production system, how a destination is produced and imaged and what particular actors are predominant in this. In theoretical terms there is a mutually affective interplay between tourism producers and consumers. For policy-makers this means that they should exercise discretion in the targeting and fostering of markets. Given the centrality of tour operators in affecting travel flows, the marketing and promotion of tourism products to *producers* (specifically tour operators) should be the first focus of governments.

Second, interaction and commercial exchange among producers in the global system is closely related to the developmental outcomes of tourism in a given destination. Producer-producer interaction is highly dynamic and based on the establishment of mainly co-operative transactional linkages among producers. The case of the price debacle in the South African sector however shows that often producer interaction and competition can be unbeneficial to growth in a given destination. Conflict among producers concerning the levying of tourism prices does not bode well. Too stringent competition, resulting in the oft-occurring price wars that have characterised many producer sectors in South Africa over the past number of years, is to the detriment of the larger production system, and particularly for smaller producers. If the viability of small or medium-sized tourism firms is affected by price wars, the product variation and offer may similarly be affected. This could have an impact on tourism growth.

Growth opportunities are further impacted by the regulatory institution governing international aviation to and from South Africa. It is an important example of how state actions and policies restrain growth and development. In the context of a generally constricting external environment the effect of such constraints can be magnified.

Fourth, the tourism development policy of the South African government is in essence a combination of modernisation and alternative/sustainable/community tourism approaches: it is geared, on the one level towards achieving large-scale impact through absolute growth in tourist arrivals, and the trickle-down of this impact throughout the country; on another, the policy is promoting the establishment of smaller-scale tourism initiatives such as eco-tourism and encouraging the entrance of small and micro local producers into the sector. Some lessons could be learned from this approach. On the whole, such an approach could have desirable developmental outcomes, but it requires the existence of favourable growth conditions in the first instance (i.e. sustained demand, products that meet the preferences of tourists, and a favourable exogenous environment). In order to ensure a diffusion of growth opportunities within the destination it also requires targeted infrastructural developments, the establishment of strong institutions, and institutional co-ordination.

Overall, however, the goals of growth and distribution are difficult to balance. Tourism growth, greater distribution of impact, and sustainability are interrelated and mutually reinforcing. Growth is necessary to ensure greater impact and the diffusion of this impact. Sustainability, in turn, pertains when conditions of continued growth and distribution are in place. National policy is aiming to satisfy many of the requirements for sustainability. It is seeking to improve the nature and quality of the province's tourist product, to promote local ownership and economic linkages, and to have greater skills development. In terms of outcome, however, there are several shortcomings. Some government strategies are inadequate to fulfil the distribution objective and some government actions indeed have a stymieing effect.

Globalisation and Tourism Development

In the contemporary era, there is a close interplay between tourism and globalisation. As a process of economic, technological, social and cultural diffusion, globalisation has come to constitute the overarching framework whereby tourism growth, shifts in demand, adjustments in production and in policy goal-setting have come to encased. Further, global tourism development both embodies the multilayered expansion that typifies globalisation, but also provides further impetus to it.

Globalisation has affected the global tourism system in important ways. Greater variability in the way that capital is internationally dispersed has impacted on tourism production and enabled the large-scale growth of smaller and medium producers who have started to establish a strong position in certain global niche markets. At the same time, however, capital coagulation through intra- or trans-sectoral mergers has also increased, providing greater leverage over the production process to the large multinationals. Production techniques have also been influenced and while wider factors account for increased flexible specialisation and neo- or post-Fordism in tourism, globalisation provides a propelling momentum to the spread of different production forms.

A further important consequence of globalisation is that it has brought the producer-consumer nexus closer. Global tourism consumption follows its own dynamic and is affected by an own set of factors. Increased mobility through globalisation has however impacted both in a physical and attitudinal sense on geographical distance; greater physical and cognitive proximity between the tourist and locale have had important effects on the culture of travel and tourism consumption. Production, itself affected by globalisation processes, is an important contributory factor in this respect. Overall, globalisation is a principal enabling mechanism whereby systems of production and consumption interrelate and mutually (re)shape each other.

Globalisation has also had effects on the third component of the global tourism system, that of regulation. As international tourism continues to expand, governance of this sector at the global level becomes growingly important. Mechanisms and institutions of governance have become more extensive. A multiplicity of actors, state and non-state, interrelates, negotiates and reaches compromise through formal and informal arrangements of regulation. Such regulation in turn sets the contours by which production and consumption can take place.

At the level of policy-making, the quest for the developmental impacts of tourism has served to shape the priorities set by governmental agents. Globalisation has been a force that encouraged a large measure of policy homogeneity across various political spectrums and levels of economic development. The framing of national, urban and even industrial policy to capture tourism – and increasingly, global events and sport – markets and the capital tied to it characterises the policy-making processes in most countries in the world.

This is not to understate, however, the stark differential effects that global tourism have for developed and developing countries. Processes of globalisation have tended to accentuate the contrasts as economic and technological interaction, though it may have speeded up and intensified, still is rather concentrated in only some parts of the world. Since global tourism development is so integrally linked to globalisation, this does mean that many of the latent positive effects that globalisation can bring for tourism expansion, remain out of reach for many of the world's poor states.

This is due the political economy of the global tourism system where powerful role players – large multinational firms and, in the context of state-based governance institutions, developed, rather than developing countries – shape the system. The international aviation regime is most reflective of this, where the larger global airlines, through the various marketing and cooperation alliances they establish, have more leverage in determining the pace and extent at which civil air trafficking, and in effect, global tourism movement, occurs. Developed countries are better positioned to negotiate favourable agreements with airlines than their poorer counterparts, for whom the protection of small, national airlines importantly relates to the wellbeing of wider national economies.

The example of the political economy of destination imaging used in this book has also highlighted the role that large, international tour operators can play in determining how developing countries and its peoples are characterised, packaged and retailed. In a sense, despite shifts to flexibility in consumption and production, the strong growth of smaller producers, and an awareness of the need for social and culturally empowering tourism, there still exists a global division of leisure, where the power balance is tipped towards certain role players who set the production and consumption agenda.

As far as global governance is concerned, developing countries are also likely to be less able to influence the tempo and direction of tourism trade liberalisation. The easing of restrictions on certain global production dimensions may have positive effects for developing countries as greater access to international production structures could promote tourism growth. Other dimensions, particularly as they relate to national mechanisms for the protection of fragile environments or social or minority rights, may however be to countries' detriment, particularly as they will have consequences far beyond the local tourism sector. As yet, however, too little is known about the overall consequences of the GATS on global tourism development.

Overall, the case analysis of South Africa has shown that globalisation brings both prospects and challenges for tourism in developing countries. Provided that a requisite level of infrastructure development exists (both in the physical accommodation of tourist, and institutionally), and that the destination is able to promote unique or attractive products, by virtue of the expansionary drive to international tourism, the threshold for entering the global tourism market is relatively low. While tourism can bring immense gains, expansion also has internal and external costs. National policy-making should be an instance where consideration is given to when tourism costs outweigh its benefits and how such costs could be obviated.

In this regard, three broad elements may be identified that are of significance for increased growth, and a greater distribution of the economic spin-offs of tourism. The first relates to the nature of the tourism market itself, and in particular the processes through which tourist markets are created and/or influenced. Linked to this are aspects pertaining to product development, market enhancement, and value-creation. The significance of globalisation is that is has enabled the emergence of a vast array of tourist activities and markets. For developing countries this provides many opportunities to distinguish themselves in the global market, without compromising on developmental pursuits. The second element centres on the role of various tourism actors in the attainment of a greater spread of impact and the division of tasks towards this end. The multiplicity of actors and levels involved in determining tourism outcomes has intensified through globalisation. More fluid and varied flows of engagement bring both challenges, but also possibilities. For government actors priorities should always be to direct resources and forms of development so as to optimise impact distribution. The third element concerns the forces that negatively affect both tourist markets and actors, and how these could be managed or attenuated. Factors exogenous to the global tourism system have major impacts on this system. The precariousness and vulnerability of tourism is something that should also be addressed on a global level through cooperation in international governance institutions.

On the whole, the complex arrangement of which global tourism consists – comprised of networks of producers, consumers and regulators – provides a multitude of ways in which developing countries can interlink and affect the tourism system and harness the opportunities available for tourism growth.

Bibliography

Abercrombie, N. (1994). 'Authority and the consumer society', in R. Keat, N. Whiteley and N. Abercrombie (eds.) *The Authority of the Consumer*. London: Routledge, pp. 43-57.

Adorno, T. (1991). *The Culture Industry – Selected Essays on Mass Culture*. London: Routledge.

African Business (2003). 'Seize the Cricket World Cup opportunity', February.

Aleghi, P. (2004). *Laduma! Soccer, Politics and Society in South Africa*. Scottsville: University of Kwazulu-Natal Press.

Alegi, P. (2001). ' "Feel the Pull in Your Soul": Local agency and global trends in South Africa's 2006 World Cup Bid'. *Soccer and Society*, 2, 3: 1-21.

Appadurai, A. (1996). *Modernity At Large: Cultural Dimensions of Globalization*. Minneapolis: University of Minnesota Press.

Arabic News (2002). 'Football: 2010 world cup shall be held in Africa, FIFA chief', 18 January.

Arabic News (1999). 'African football confederation is embarrassed by Morocco, South Africa bids', 27 December.

Arabic News (1999). 'Casablanca water and power company backs Morocco's World Cup bid', 28 October 1999.

Arabic News (1999). 'King Mohammed VI will lay foundation stone of new Casablanca Grand Stadium', 11 October.

Arabic News (1999). 'Moroccan hotels to provide additional 40,000 beds for world cup-2006', 24 September 1999.

Archer, B.H. (1982). 'The value of multipliers and their policy implications', *Tourism Management*, 3, 4: 236-41.

Archer, B.H. (1977). *Tourism Multipliers: the state of the art*. Bangor Occasional Papers in Economics, no 11. Cardiff: University of Wales Press.

Archer, B.H. (1973). *The impact of domestic tourism*. Bangor Occasional papers in Economics, no. 2. Cardiff: University of Wales Press.

Archer, B.H. and Fletcher, J. (1996). 'The economic impact of tourism in the Seychelles', *Annals of Tourism Research*, 23, 1: 32-47.

Ashley, C. (1998). 'Tourism, communities and national policy: Namibia's experience', *Development Policy Review*, 16: 323-352.

Ashley, C. and Lafranchi, C. (1997). 'Livelihood strategies of rural households in Caprivi: Implications for conservancies and natural resource management', Directorate of Environmental Affairs Research Discussion Paper No. 20. Windhoek: DEA.

Ateljevic, I. (2000). 'Circuits of tourism: stepping beyond the "production-consumption" dichotomy', *Tourism Geographies*, 2, 4: 369-388.

Bacher, A. (2002). 'Mandela set the ball rolling', in C. Bryden (ed.) *SA Cricket Annual 2002*. Johannesburg: Mutual and Federal, pp. 45-47.

Baudrillard, J. (1998). *The Consumer Society: Myths and Structures*. London: Sage Publications.

Baudrillard, J. (1970). *La Société de Consommation*. Paris: Gallimard.

Bauman, A. (1992). *Intimations of Postmodernity*. London: Routledge.

Beauregard, R.A. (1998). 'Tourism and economic development policy in US urban areas', in D. Ioannides and K.G. Debbage (eds.) *The Economic Geography of the Tourist Industry: A Supply-Side Analysis*. London: Routledge, pp. 220-234.

Beeld (1999). 'Sokker 2006', 11 August.

Bekker, S. (1997). *Suid-Afrika se eksperiment met kulturele pluralisme*. Stellenbosch: University of Stellenbosch Annals.

Bendell, J. and Font, X. (2004). 'Which tourism rules? Green standards and the GATS', *Annals of Tourism Research*, 31, 1: 139-156.

Bernstein, J.M. (1991). 'Introduction', in T. Adorno, *The Culture Industry – Selected Essays on Mass Culture*. London: Routledge.

Black, D. and Nauright, J. (1998). *Rugby and the South African Nation: Sport, Cultures, Politics and Power in the Old and New South Africas*. Manchester: Manchester University Press.

Black, D. and van der Westhuizen, J. (2004). 'The allure of global games for "semi-peripheral" polities and spaces: a research agenda', *Third World Quarterly*, 25, 7: 1195-1214.

Blowers, A. and Pain, K. (1999). 'The Unsustainable City?' in S. Pile, C. Brooke and G. Mooney (eds.) *Unruly Cities*. London: Routledge, pp. 247-298.

Bonzaaier, E. (1996). 'Negotiating the development of tourism in the Richtersveld, South Africa', in M.F. Price (ed.) *People and tourism in fragile environments*. New York: John Wiley and Sons.

Booth, D. (1999). 'Recapturing the moment? Global rugby, economics and the politics of nation in post-apartheid South Africa', in T. Chandler and J. Nauright (eds.) *Making the Rugby World – Race, Gender, Commerce*. London: Frank Cass, pp.181-200.

Bramwell, B. (1997). 'Strategic planning before and after a mega-event', *Tourism Management*, 18, 3:167-176.

Brenner, N. (2004). *New State Spaces – Urban Governance and the Rescaling of Statehood*. Oxford: Oxford University Press.

Brenner, N., Jessop, B., Jones, M. and Macleod, G. (2003). *State/Space: A Reader*. Oxford: Blackwell Publishing.

Brenner, N. (1998). 'Global cities, glocal states: global city formation and state territorial restructuring in contemporary Europe', *Review of International Political Economy*, 15, 1: 1-37.

Britton, S.G. (1991). 'Tourism, capital, and place: towards a critical geography of tourism', *Environment and Planning D: Society and Space*, 9: 451-478.

Britton, S.G. (1989). 'Tourism, dependency and development – a mode of analysis', in T.V. Singh; H.L. Theuns; and F.M. Go (eds.) *Towards Appropriate Tourism: The Case of Developing Countries*. Frankfurt am Main: Verlag Peter Lang GmbH, pp. 93-116.

Britton, S.G. (1982). 'The political economy of tourism in the Third World', *Annals of Tourism Research*, 9, 3: 331-58.

Brohman, J. (1996). 'New directions in tourism for third world development', *Annals of Tourism Research*, 23, 1: 48-70.

Bruner, E. (2001). 'The Maasai and the Lion King: authenticity, nationalism, and globalization in African tourism', *American Ethnologist*, 28, 4: 881-908.

Bruner, E. (1991). 'Transformation of self in tourism', *Annals of Tourism Research*, 18: 238-250.

Bruner, E. and Kirshenblatt-Gimblett, B. (1994). 'Maasai on the Lawn: Tourist Realism in Africa, *Cultural Anthropology*, 9, 2: 435-470.

Bull, A. (1995). *The Economics of Travel and Tourism* (2nd ed.). Melbourne: Longman.

Buntman, B. (1996). 'Bushman images in South African tourist advertising: the case of Kagga Kamma', in P. Skotnes (ed). *Miscast: Negotiating the presence of the Bushmen*, Cape Town: University of Cape Town Press, pp. 271-280.

Business Day. (2005). 'Blatter reads riot act to SA soccer chiefs on 2010', 13 January.

Business Day. (2003). 'World Cricket Cup is advertising, tourism bonanza for sporty SA',10 February.

Business Day. (2003).'Murder adds weight to boycott call', 7 January.

Business Day (2002). 'Taking a fresh approach to the overseas market', 4 March.

Business Day (2001). 'Report shows all is not well in SA's tourism sector', 5 September.

Cape Times. (2003). 'Cape Town and George join up to develop golf tourism strategy', 28 November.

Capostagno, A. and Neild, D. (2003). *Fancourt: The Road to the Presidents Cup*. Johannesburg: Viking.

Carney, T.F. (1972). *Content Analysis – A Technique for Systematic Inference from Communications*. London: B.T. Batsford Ltd.

Castells, M. (1997). *The Power of Identity*. Oxford: Blackwell Publishers.

Cerny, P. (2003). 'What next for the state?' in E. Kofman and G. Youngs (eds.) *Globalization: Theory and Practice*. London: Continuum, pp. 207-221.

Cerny, P. (1990). *The Changing Architecture of Politics: Structure, Agency and the Future of the State*. London: Sage Publications.

Chalip, L and Leyns, A. (2002). 'Local business leveraging of a sport event: managing an event for economic benefit', *Journal of Sport Management*, 16: 132-158.

Cheong, S and Miller, M.L. (2000). 'Power and Tourism – A Foucauldian observation', *Annals of Tourism Research*, 27, 2: 371-390.

Clancy, M. (2002a). 'The globalization of sex tourism and Cuba: A commodity chains approach', *Studies in Comparative International Development*, 36, 4: 63-88.

Clancy, M. (2002b). 'Globalizing the skies: domestic and international sources of the liberalization of commercial air transport', Unpublished paper delivered at the 2002 International Studies Association Meeting, New Orleans, United States.

Clancy, M. (1999). 'Tourism and development – evidence from Mexico', *Annals of Tourism Research*, 26, 1: 1-20.

Clancy, M. (1998). 'Commodity chains, services and development: theory and preliminary evidence from the tourism industry', *Review of International Political Economy*, 5, 1: 122-148.

Clarke, A. (2001). 'Research and the policy-making process', in Nigel Gilbert (ed.) *Researching Social Life*. (2nd edition), London: Sage Publications, pp. 28-42.

Coates, D. and Humphreys, B. (1999). 'The growth effects of sport franchises, stadia and arenas', *Journal of Policy Analysis and Management* 16: 601-624.

Cohen, E. (1984).'The sociology of tourism: approaches, issues and findings', *Annual Review of Sociology*, 10: 373-92.

Cohen, E. (1979).'Rethinking the sociology of tourism', *Annals of Tourism Research*, 6: 18-35.

Cohen, E. (1974).'Who is a tourist? A conceptual clarification', *Sociological Review*, 22: 527-55.

Cohen, E. (1972). 'Towards a sociology of international tourism, *Social Research*, 39: 64-82.

Commission on Global Governance. (1995). *Our Global Neighbourhood: Report of the Commission on Global Governance*. Oxford: Oxford University Press.

Cornelissen, S. (2005). 'Tourism impact, distribution and development: The spatial structure of tourism in the Western Cape, South Africa', *Development Southern Africa*, 22, 2 (forthcoming).

Cornelissen, S. (2004a). 'Sport mega-events in Africa: processes, impacts and prospects', *Tourism Hospitality Planning and Development*, 1, 1: 39-55.

Cornelissen, S. (2004b). '"It's Africa's turn!" The narratives and legitimations surrounding the Moroccan and South African bids for the 2006 and 2010 FIFA finals', *Third World Quarterly*, 25, 7: 1293-1309.

Craik, J. (1997). 'The culture of tourism', in C. Rojek and J. Urry (eds.) *Touring Cultures: Transformations of Travel and Theory*. London: Routledge.

Crompton, J. L. (1995). 'Economic impact analysis of sports facilities and events: eleven sources of misapplication', *Journal of Sport Management*, 9:14-35.

Dann, G. (1996). 'The People of Tourist Brochures', in T. Selwyn (ed.) *The Tourist Image: Myths and Myth Making in Tourism*. London: Wiley, pp. 61-81.

Darby, P. (2000). 'Football, colonial doctrine and indigenous resistance: mapping the political persona of FIFA's African constituency', *Culture, Sport, Society*, 3, 1: 61-87.

De Kadt, E. (ed.) (1979). *Tourism – Passport to Development? Perspectives on the Social and Cultural Effects of Tourism in Developing Countries*. Oxford University Press. Published for Unesco and the World Bank.

De Knop, P. (1990). 'Sport for all and active tourism', *World Leisure and Recreation*, 32: 30-36.

Delaney-Smith, P. (1987). 'The tour operator: new and maturing business', in A. Hodgson (ed.). *The Travel and Tourism Industry: Strategies for the Future*. New York: Pergamon Press.

Department of Economic Affairs, Agriculture and Tourism (2001). *White Paper on Sustainable Tourism Development and Promotion in the Western Cape*. Cape Town: DEAAT.
Department of Economic Affairs, Agriculture and Tourism (2000). *Preparing the Western Cape for the knowledge economy of the 21st century*. Cape Town: DEAAT.
Department of Environmental Affairs and Development Planning (2004). *Rapid Review of Golf Course and Polo Field Developments – Draft Report*. Cape Town: DEADP.
Department of Environmental Affairs and Tourism (2004). 'Background: BEE in tourism', 24 September 2004, accessed at www.environment.gov.za.
Department of Environmental Affairs and Tourism (2003). Media release, 09 March 2003, accessed at www.environment.gov.za.
Department of Environmental Affairs and Tourism (2002a). *Responsible Tourism Manual*. Pretoria: DEAT.
Department of Environmental Affairs and Tourism (2002b). *Poverty Relief Programme 2000/2001*, accessed at ww.environment.gov.za.
Department of Environmental Affairs and Tourism (2000). *Transforming the South African Tourism Industry*. Pretoria: DEAT.
Department of Environmental Affairs and Tourism (1999/2000). *Annual Report*, Pretoria: DEAT.
Department of Environmental Affairs and Tourism (1996). *White Paper on the Development and Promotion of Tourism in South Africa*. Pretoria: DEAT.
Deutsche Reisebüro und Reiseveranstalter Verband (DRV) (2000). *Fakten und Zahlen zum deutschen Reisemarkt*. Frankfurt: DRV.
Diamond, J. (1977). 'Tourism's role in economic development: the case re-examined', *Economic Development and Cultural Change*, 25, 3: 539-53.
Die Burger. (2003). 'Bacher "was onder regeringsdruk oor Zim"', 17 February.
Die Burger. (2000). 'SA is logiese gasheer vir 2006 Sokkertoernooi', 2 February.
Dieke, P.U.C. (1995). 'Tourism and structural adjustment programmes in the African economy', *Tourism Economics*, 1, 1: 71-93.
Dieke, P.U.C. (1993). 'Tourism in the Gambia: Some issues in development policy', *World Development*, 21, 2: 277-289.
Done, K. (2005). 'Pressure is on for more air link-ups', *Financial Times*, 4 April 2005.
Dunning, J.H. and McQueen, M. (1982). *Transnational Corporations in International Tourism*. New York: United Nations Centre for Transnational Corporations.
Dwyer, L. and Forsyth, P. (1997). 'Impacts and benefits of MICE tourism: a framework for analysis', *Tourism Economics*, 3, 1:21-38.
Dwyer, L., Mellor, R., Mistilis, N., and Mules, T. (2000). 'A framework for assessing "tangible' and "intangible" impacts of events and conventions', *Convention Management*. 6, 3: 175-189.
Elkan, W. (1975). 'The relation between tourism and employment in Kenya and Tanzania', *Journal of Development Studies*, 11, 2: 123-130.
Eastern Province Herald (2000). 'The race card', 19 July.
Essex, S., Kent, M., and Newnham, R. (2004). 'Tourism development in Mallorca: Is water supply a constraint?' *Journal of Sustainable Tourism*, 12, 1: 4-28.

Euchner, C.C. (1999). 'Tourism and sports: The serious competition for play', in D.R. Judd and S.S. Fainstein (eds.) *The Tourist City*. London: Yale University Press, pp. 215-232.

Fainstein, S.S. and Gladstone, D. (1999). 'Evaluating urban tourism', in D.R. Judd and S.S. Fainstein (eds.) *The Tourist City*. London: Yale University Press, pp. 21-34.

Fainstein, S.S and Judd, D.R. 'Global forces, local strategies and urban tourism', in D.R. Judd and S.S. Fainstein (eds.) *The Tourist City*. London: Yale University Press, pp. 1-17.

Fayed, H. and Fletcher, J. (2002). 'Globalization of economic activity: issues for tourism', *Tourism Economics*, 8: 207-230.

Fayos-Solà, E. and Bueno, A.P. (2001). 'Globalization, national tourism policy and international organizations', in S. Wahab and C. Cooper (eds.) *Tourism in the Age of Globalisation*. London: Routledge, pp. 45-65.

Featherstone, M. (1991). *Consumer Culture and Postmodernism*. London: Sage.

Ferreira, S.L.A. and Harmse, A.C. (2000). 'Crime and tourism in South Africa: international tourists perceptions and risk', *South African Geographical Journal*, 82, 2: 80-85.

FIFA (2002). 'FIFA World Cup ratings success – results confirm event as a "24/7" viewing experience', *FIFA media release*, 24 June.

Fletcher, J.E. (1989). 'Input-output analysis and tourism impact studies', *Annals of Tourism Research*, 16: 514-529.

Fletcher, J.E. and Archer, B.H. (1991). 'The development and application of multiplier analysis', in C.P. Cooper (ed.). *Progress in Tourism, Recreation and Hospitality Management*, vol. 1. London: Belhaven., pp. 28-47.

Forschungsgemeinschaft Urlaub und Reisen (2000). *Reiseanalyse Aktuell 2000*. Hamburg: FUR.

Forsyth, T. (1997). 'Sustainable tourism and market interest', in W. Hein (ed.), *Tourism and Sustainable Development*. Hamburg: Schriften des Deutsches Übersee-Institut, pp. 251-270.

Foster, C. (2001). *Transformations: The construction of South African Landscapes in Tourist Brochures*. Unpublished Honours thesis. Glasgow School of Art.

France, L. (1997). (ed.) *The Earthscan Reader in Sustainable Tourism*. Earthscan: London.

Frank, A.G. (1967). *Capitalism and Underdevelopment in Latin America*. New York: Monthly Review Press.

Gajraj, A.M. (1981). 'Threats to the terrestrial resources of the Caribbean', *Ambio*, 10, 6: 307-311.

Geo Saison (1999). *Südafrika*. Vol. 10. Hamburg: Geo Saison.

Gibson, H.J. (2003). 'Sport tourism: an introduction to the special issue', *Journal of Sport Tourism Management*, 17: 205-213.

Gibson, H.J. (1998). 'Sport tourism: a critical analysis of research', *Sport Management Review*, 1:45-76.

Gilpin, R. (1987). *The Political Economy of International Relations*. Princeton University Press.

Go, F.M. and Pine, R. (1995). *Globalization Strategy and the Hotel Industry*. London: Routledge.

Goodall, B. and Bergsma, J. (1990). 'Destinations as marketed in tour operators' brochures', in G. Ashworth and B. Goodall (eds.) *Marketing Tourism Places*. London: Routledge, pp. 170-192.

Gottdiener, M. (2000). 'Approaches to consumption: classical and contemporary perspectives', in M. Gottdiener (ed.). *New Forms of Consumption: Consumers, Culture and Commodification*. Lanham, Maryland: Romand and Littlefield, pp. 3-32.

Gotham, K. (2002). 'Marketing Mardi Gras: Commodification, spectacle and the political economy of tourism in New Orleans', *Urban Studies*, 39, 3: 1735-1756.

Goudie, SC; Khan, F. and Kilian, D. (1999). 'Transforming tourism: black empowerment, heritage and identity beyond apartheid', *South African Geographical Journal*. 81, 1: 22-31.

Grant Thornton (2004). Southern Africa Tourism Update. www.gtkf.co.za.

Grundlingh, A. (1998). 'From redemption to recidivism? Rugby and change in South Africa during the 1995 Rugby World Cup and its aftermath', *Sporting Traditions*, 14, 2: 67-85.

Hall, C.M. (2001). 'Territorial integration and globalisation', in S. Wahab and C. Cooper (eds.) *Tourism in The Age of Globalisation*. London: Routledge, pp. 22-44.

Hall, C.M. (1994a). 'Gender and economic interest in tourism prostitution – the nature, development and implications of sex tourism in South-east Asia', in V. Kinnaird and D. Hall (eds.) *Tourism: A Gender Analysis*. New York: Wiley Publishers, pp. 265-280.

Hall, C.M. (1994b). *Tourism and Politics: Policy, Power and Place*. New York: John Wiley and Sons.

Hall, C.M (1992). *Hallmark Tourist Events*. London: Belhaven Press.

Hall, C.M. and Lew, A.A. (eds.) (1998). *Sustainable Tourism – A Geographical Perspective*. Essex: Longman.

Hall, C M and Page, S.J. (1999). *The Geography of Tourism and Recreation: Environment, Place and Space*. London: Routledge.

Hall, S. (1997). *Representation: Cultural representations and signifying practices*, London: Sage.

Harvey, D. (1989). 'From managerialism to entrepreneurialism: the transformation in urban governance in late capitalism', *Geografiska Annaler*, 71B: 3-16.

Hassan, A. (2003). 'Conference Report: Egypt's National Sustainable Tourism Conference on Golf Tourism Development, Sharm El Sheikh, October 28-30, 2002', *Journal of Sustainable Tourism*, 11, 1: 84-87.

Hein, W. (1997). 'Introduction', in W. Hein (ed.), *Tourism and Sustainable Development*. Hamburg: Schriften des Deutschen Übersee-Institut, pp. 7-20.

Heng, T.M. and Low, L. (1990). 'Economic impact of tourism in Singapore', *Annals of Tourism Research*, 17, 2: 246-69.

Hiller, H.H. (2000). 'Mega-events, urban boosterism and growth strategies: an analysis of the objectives and legitimations of the Cape Town 2004 Olympic Bid', *International Journal of Urban and Regional Research*, 24, 2: 439-458.

Hills, T.L. and Lundgren, J. (1977). 'The impact of tourism in the Caribbean: a methodological study', *Annals of Tourism Research*, 4, 3: 248-267.

Hirst, P. and Thomson, G. (1999). *Globalization in Question – The International Political Economy and the Possibilities of Governance* (2nd ed.). Cambridge: Polity Press.

Hoad, D. (2003). 'The General Agreement on Trade in Services and the impact of trade liberalisation on tourism and sustainability', *Tourism and Hospitality Research*, 4, 3: 213-227.

Hollinshead, K. (1999). 'Surveillance of the worlds of tourism: Foucault and the eye of power', *Tourism Management*, 20: 7-23.

Holcomb, B. (1999). 'Marketing cities for tourism', in D.R. Judd and S.S. Fainstein (eds.) *The Tourist City*. London: Yale University Press, pp. 54-70.

Holden, A. (2000). *Environment and Tourism*. London: Routledge.

Honey, M. (1999). *Ecotourism and Sustainable Development. Who Owns Paradise?* Washington DC: Island Press.

Horne, J. and Manzenreiter, W. (eds.) (2002). *Japan, Korea and the 2002 World Cup*. London and New York: Routledge.

Horton, P. A. (1996). '"Scapes" and "phases": an overview of two approaches to sport and globalisation', *Social Alternatives*. 15, 1: 53-62.

Horwath Tourism and Leisure Consulting (2001). *Federated Hospitality Association of South Africa Annual Conference*. www.horwath.co.za.

Horwath Tourism and Leisure Consulting (2000). *Focus on Aviation Policy*. December.

Houlihan, B. (1994). *Sport and International Politics*. New York: Harvester Wheatsheaf.

International Air Transport Association (IATA) (2002). *About IATA*. www.iata.org.

International Civil Aviation Organization (ICAO) (2002). *About ICAO*. www.icao.org.

International Marketing Council of South Africa (no date). *Brand South Africa – Alive with Possibilities*, Johannesburg: Brand Publishers.

Ioannides, D. (1998). 'Tour operators: the gatekeepers of tourism', in D. Ioannides and K.G. Debbage (eds.) *The Economic Geography of the Tourist Industry: A Supply-Side Analysis*. London: Routledge, pp. 139-158.

Ioannides, D. and Debbage, K.G. (eds.) (1998). 'Neo-Fordism and flexible specialization in the travel industry: dissecting the polyglot', in D. Ioannides and K.G. Debbage (eds.) *The Economic Geography of the Tourist Industry: A Supply-Side Analysis*. London: Routledge, pp.99-122.

Jarvie, G. (1993). 'Sport, nationalism and cultural identity', in L. Allison (ed.) *The Changing Politics of Sport*. Manchester: Manchester University Press, pp. 58-83.

Jessop, B. (1999). 'Reflections on globalisation and its (il)logic(s)', in K. Olds, P. Dicken, P.F. Kelly, L. Long and H. Yeung (eds.) *Globalisation and the Asia-Pacific: contested territories*. London: Routledge, pp. 19-38.

Jessop, B. (1997). 'The entrepreneurial city: re-imaging localities, redesigning economic governance, or restructuring capital?', in N. Jewson and S. MacGregor (eds). *Transforming Cities: Contested Governance and New Spatial Divisions*. London: Routledge, pp. 28-41.

Jessop, B. and Sum, N. (2000). 'An entrepreneurial city in action: Hong Kong's emerging strategies in and for (inter)urban competition', *Urban Studies*, 37(12): 2287-2313.

Judd, D.R. and Fainstein, S. (eds.) (1999). *The Tourist City*. London: Yale University Press.

Karns, M. and Mingst, K. (2004). *International Organizations: The Politics and Processes of Global Governance*. Boulder, Co: Lynne Rienner.

Keat, R. (1994). 'Scepticism, authority and the market', in R. Keat, N. Whiteley and N. Abercrombie (eds.) *The authority of the consumer.* London: Routledge.

Kearns, G. and Philo, C. (1993). *Selling Places: The City as Cultural Capital, Past and Present.* New York: Pergamon Press.

Keat, R. (1994). 'Scepticism, authority and the market', in R. Keat, N. Whiteley and N. Abercrombie (eds.) *The Authority of the Consumer.* London: Routledge, pp. 23-42.

Kellner, D. (2001). *Towards a Critical Theory of Society.* London: Routledge.

Kirstges, T. and Schusdziara, D. (1999). *Strukturanalyse des deutschen Reiseveranstaltermarktes – Konsequenzen der Marktkonzentration für den Mittelstand.* FBV Medien-Verlags/Wilhelmshavener Schriftenreihe Tourismuswirtschaft Band 6.

Khan, M.M. (1997). 'Tourism development and dependency theory: Mass tourism vs. Ecotourism', *Annals of Tourism Research*, 24, 4: 988-991.

Koch, E. (1994). *Reality or Rhetoric? Ecotourism and Rural Reconstruction in South Africa.* Johannesburg: United Nations Research Institute for Social Development.

Koch, E. and Massyn, P.J. (2001). 'South Africa's domestic tourism sector: promises and problems', in K.B. Ghimire (ed.) *The Native Tourist: Mass Tourism Within Developing Countries.* London: Earthscan Publications Ltd, pp. 142-169.

Krasner, S. (ed.) (1983). *International Regimes.* London: Cornell University Press.

Krippendorf, J. (1987). *The Holidaymakers – Understanding the Impact of Leisure and Travel.* London: Butterworth-Heinemann.

Krugman, P. (ed.) (1996). *Pop Internationalism.* Cambridge: MIT Press.

Kurtzman, J. and Zauhar, J. (1995). 'Research: sport as touristic endeavour', *Journal of Tourism Sport*, 3, 1: 30-54.

Lanfant, M.F. (1980). 'Tourism in the process of internationalization', *International Social Science Journal*, 32: 14-42.

Lea, J. (1988). *Tourism and Development in the Third World.* London: Routledge.

Ledbury, R. (1997). 'Sustainable tourism: A review and the research agenda', in W. Hein (ed.), *Tourism and Sustainable Development.* Hamburg: Schriften des Deutschen Übersee-Institut, pp. 211-224.

Leiper, N. (1990). 'Partial industrialization of tourism systems', *Annals of Tourism Research*, 17: 600-605.

Ley, D. and Olds, K. (1992). 'World's fairs and culture of consumption in the contemporary city', in K. Anderson and F. Gale (eds.) *Inventing places.* Melbourne: Longman Cheshire, pp. 178-183.

MacCannell, D. (1992). *Empty Meeting Grounds: The Tourist Papers.* London: Routledge.

MacCannell, D. (1976). *The Tourist: A New Theory of the Leisure Class.* New York: Schocken.

MacCannell, D. (1973). 'Staged authenticity: on arrangements of social space in tourist settings', *American Journal of Sociology*, 79: 589-603.

MacKay, K.J. and Fesenmaier, D.R. (1997). 'Pictorial element of destination in image formation', *Annals of Tourism Research*, 24, 3: 537-565.

Maguire, J. (1999). *Global Sport: Identities, Societies, Civilizations.* Cambridge: Polity Press.

Mail and Guardian. (2005). 'World Cup: "We started earlier than the Germans"', 25 April.

Mail and Guardian (2005). 'Allan Boesak: in golf we trust', 4 March.
Mail and Guardian (2003). 'Fifa slams Nigeria's 2010 plan', 18 March.
Mail and Guardian (2000). 'Morocco the fly in SA bid ointment', 6 July.
Malcolm, D. (2001). '"It's not cricket": colonial legacies and contemporary inequalities', *Journal of Historical Sociology*, 14, 3: 253-275.
Marcuse, H. (2001). *Towards a Critical Theory of Society – collected papers of Herbert Marcuse. Volume Two*. Edited by D. Kellner. London: Routledge.
Marks, R. and Bezzoli, M. (2001). 'Palaces of desire: Century City, Cape Town and the ambiguities of development', *Urban Forum*, 12, 1: 27-48.
Markwick, M. (2001). 'Postcards from Malta. Image, consumption, context', *Annals of Tourism Research*, 28, 2: 417-438.
Mathieson, A. and Wall, G. (1982). *Tourism: Economic, Physical and Social Impacts*. London: Longman.
May, T. (2001). *Social Research: Issues, methods and process* (3rd ed.). Buckingham: Open University.
Mecklenburg, R. (2000). 'The Facts and Figures File on the German Tourism market for Southern Africa', *Market Mirror*, no.2, February.
Medina-Muñoz, D. and García-Falcón, J. (2000). 'Successful relationships between hotels and agencies', *Annals of Tourism Research*, 27, 3: 737-762.
Meethan, K. (2001). *Tourism in Global Society: Place, Culture, Consumption*. Basingstoke: Palgrave.
Milne, S. and Ateljevic, I. (2001). 'Tourism, economic geography and the local-global nexus: theory embracing complexity', *Tourism Geographies*, 3, 4: 369-393.
Milne, S. and Pohlmann, C. (1998). 'Continuity and change in the hotel sector: some evidence from Montreal', in D. Ioannides and K.G. Debbage (eds.) *The Economic Geography of the Tourist Industry*, pp.180-196.
'Minister threatens tour operators', *Business Day*, 6 June 2003. Johannesburg: Business Day.
Mitchell, R.E. and Reid, D.G. (2001). 'Community integration – Island tourism in Peru', *Annals of Tourism Research*, 28, 1: 113-139.
Mittelman, J. (1995). 'Rethinking the international division of labour in the context of globalisation', *Third World Quarterly*, 16, 2: 273-293.
Mowforth, M. and Munt, I. (1998). *Tourism and Sustainability – New Tourism in the Third World*. London: Routledge.
Mules, T. and Faulkner, B. (1996). 'An economic perspective on special events', *Tourism Economics*, 2: 314-329.
Murphy, P.E. (1985). *Tourism: A Community Approach*. New York: Methuen.
Nedlac (1999). *South African Tourism Cluster Study*. Johannesburg: Nedlac.
Nel, P., Taylor, I. and Van der Westhuizen, J. (2001). *South Africa's Multilateral Diplomacy and Global Change: The Limits of Reformism*. Aldershot: Ashgate.
Norton, A. (1996). 'Experiencing nature: the reproduction of environmental discourse through safari tourism in East Africa', *Geoforum*, 27, 3: 355-373.
Ohmae, K. (1995). *The End of the Nation State: The Rise of Regional Economies*. New York: Harper Collins.

Ohmae, K. (1990). *The Borderless World: Power and Strategy in the Inter-linked Economy*. London: Collins.

Opperman, M. (1993). 'Tourism space in developing countries', *Annals of Tourism Research*, 20: 535-556.

Owen, K.A. (2002). 'The Sydney 2000 Olympics and urban entrepreneurialism: local variations in urban governance', *Australian Geographical Studies*, 40, 3, 323-336.

Page, S.J. (1999). *Transport and tourism*. Essex: Longman

Page, S.J. (1995). *Urban Tourism*. London: Routledge.

Paul, D. (2002). 'Re-scaling IPE: subnational states and the regulation of the global political economy', *Review of International Political Economy*, 9, 3: 465-489.

Palmer, A. and Bejou, D. (1995). 'Tourism destination marketing alliances', *Annals of Tourism Research*, 22, 3: 616-629.

Pearce, D.G. (1995). *Tourism Today: A Geographical Analysis* (2nd ed.). Essex: Longman.

Pearce, D.G. (1992). *Tourist Organizations*. Essex: Longman.

Perez, E.A. and Sampol, C.J. (2000). 'Tourist expenditure for mass tourism markets', *Annals of Tourism Research*, 27, 3: 624-637.

Phongpaichit, P. (1986). 'Prostitution in Bangkok', in *Klar, schön war's, aber.. Tourismus in die Dritte Welt*. Freiburg: Informationszentrum Dritte Welt.

Pieterse, J.N. (1992). *White on Black: Images of Africa and Blacks in Western Popular Culture*, Amsterdam: Koninklijk Institut voor de Tropen.

Poon, A. (1993). *Tourism, Technology and Competitive Strategies*. Wallingford: CAB International.

Pow, C.P. (2002). 'Urban entrepreneurialism, global business elites and urban mega-development: a case study of Sun-Tec City', *Asian Journal of Social Science*, 30, 1: 53-72.

Pritchard, A. and Morgan, N. (2001). 'Culture, identity and tourism representation: marketing Cymru or Wales?', *Tourism Management*, 22: 167-179.

Republic of South Africa (2003). *Broad Based Black Economic Empowerment Act no 53 of 2003*. Pretoria: Government Printers.

Republic of South Africa (1998a). *Skills Development Act no 97 of 1998*. Pretoria: Government Printers.

Republic of South Africa (1998b). *Employment Equity Act no 55 of 1998*. Pretoria: Government Printers.

Republic of South Africa (1994). *White Paper on Reconstruction and Development*. Pretoria: Government Printers.

Richter, L. (1989). *The politics of tourism in Asia*. University of Hawaii Press.

Ritzer, G. (1998). *The McDonaldization Thesis: Explorations and Extensions*. London: Sage.

Ritzer, G. and Liska, A. (1997). '"McDisneyization" and "Post-tourism"', in C. Rojek and J. Urry (eds.) *Touring Cultures: Transformations of Travel and Theory*. London: Routledge, pp. 96-109.

Roche, M. (2000). *Mega-events and Modernity*, London: Routledge.

Roche, M. (1992). 'Mega-events and micro-modernization: on the sociology of the new urban tourism', *British Journal of Sociology*, 43, 4: 563-600.

Rogerson, C. (2002). 'Driving developmental tourism in South Africa', *Africa Insight*, 32, 3: 33-42.

Rogerson, C. (2001). 'Spatial development initiatives in Southern Africa: The Maputo Development Corridor', *Tydschrift voor Economische en Sociale Geografie*, 92, 3: 324-346.

Rogerson, C. (1999). 'Place marketing for local economic development in South Africa', *South African Geographical Journal*, 81, 1: 32-43.

Rogerson, C. and Visser, G. (2004). 'Tourism and development in post-apartheid South Africa: a ten-year review', in C. Rogerson and G. Visser (eds.) *Tourism and Development: Issues in Contemporary South Africa*. Pretoria: Africa Institute of South Africa, pp. 2-25.

Rojek, C. and Urry, J. (1997). *Touring Cultures: Transformations of Travel and Theory*. London: Routledge.

Rooney, J. (1988). 'Mega-sports events as tourist attractions: a geographical analysis', in *Tourism Research – Expanding the Boundaries*. Montreal: Proceedings of the 19th TTRA Conference, pp. 93-99.

Rostow, W.W. (1960). *The Stages of Economic Growth: A Non-Communist Manifesto*. London: Cambridge University Press.

Sack, A.L. and Johnson, A.T. (1996). 'Politics, economic development, and the Volvo International Tennis Tournament', *Journal of Sport Management*, 10, 1: 1-14.

Sassen, S. and Roost, F. (1999). 'The city: strategic site for the global entertainment industry', in D.R. Judd and S.S. Fainstein (eds.) *The Tourist City*. London: Yale University Press, pp. 54-70.

Shaw, G. and Williams, A. (2004). *Tourism and Tourism Spaces*. London: Sage Publications.

Sheldon, P.J. (1986). 'The tour operator industry: an analysis', *Annals of Tourism Research*, 13: 349-365.

Sinclair, M.T. (1998). 'Tourism and economic development: A Survey', *The Journal of Development Studies*, 34, 5: 1-51.

Sinclair, M.T. (1991). 'The tourism industry and foreign exchange leakages in a developing country', in M.T. Sinclair and M.J. Stabler (eds.), *The Tourism Industry: An International Analysis*. Wallingford: CAB International, pp. 185-204.

Sinclair, M.T. and Bote Gòmez, V. (1996). 'Tourism, the Spanish economy and the Balance of Payments', in M. Barke, M. Newton, and J. Towner (eds.), *Tourism in Spain: Critical Perspectives*. Wallingford: C.A.B. International, pp. 89-117.

Sinclair, M.T. and Tsegaye, A. (1990). 'International tourism and export instability', *Journal of Development Studies*, 26, 3: 487-504.

Sklair, L. (1995) (2nd ed.). *Sociology of the Global System*. Baltimore: Johns Hopkins University Press.

Slater, D. (1998). 'Analysing cultural objects: content analysis and semiotics', in C. Seale (ed.) *Researching society and culture*, London: Sage.

Smith, S.L.J. (2000). 'Measurement of tourism's impact', *Annals of Tourism Research*, 27, 2: 530-531.

Smith, S.L.J. (1998). 'Tourism as an industry: debates and concepts', in D. Ioannides and K. Debbage, pp. 31-52.
Smith, S.L.J. (1989). *Tourism Analysis – A Handbook*. Essex: Longman.
Smith, S.L.J. (1988). 'Defining tourism: a supply-side view', *Annals of Tourism Research*, 15, 2: 179-90.
Smith, V.L. and Eadington, W.R. (1992). *Tourism Alternatives – Potentials and Problems in the Development of Tourism*. Philadelphia: University of Pennsylvania Press.
Smith, V.L. (ed.) (1989). *Hosts and Guests: The Anthropology of Tourism* (2nd ed.). Philadelphia: University of Pennsylvania Press.
Smithies, R. (2001). *Airline Views on the Proposed Tourism Annex to the GATS*. WTO/OMC Symposium on Tourism Services, Geneva, 22-23 February 2001. www.wto.org/english/tratop_e/serv_e/iata_omc_tourism.doc.
Sobel, M.E. (1981). *Lifestyle and Social Structure – Concepts, Definitions, Analyses*. New York: Academic Press.
South African National Parks (2000). *Transformation Mission*. Pretoria: SANP.
South African Tourism (2004). *2003 Domestic Report*. Pretoria: SA Tourism.
South African Tourism (2002a). *Tourism Growth Strategy*, Johannesburg: SA Tourism.
South African Tourism (2002b). *International Tourism Marketing Strategy Development Project: Phase I*. Johannesburg: South African Tourism.
South African Tourism (2002c). *Towards a National Events Strategy*. Johannesburg: SA Tourism.
South African Tourism (2000). *A Survey of South Africa's Foreign Visitor Market, January 2000*. Pretoria: SA Tourism.
Söderbaum, F. and Taylor, I. (2003). *Regionalism and Uneven Development in Southern Africa: the Case of the Maputo Development Corridor*. Aldershot: Ashgate.
Stabler, M.J. (ed.) (1997). *Tourism and sustainability – Principles to Practice*. Oxon: CAB International.
Standeven, J. and De Knop, P. (1999). *Sport Tourism*. Champaign, Illinois: Human Kinetics.
Standeven, J. and Tomlinson, A. (1994). *Sport and Tourism in South East England*. London: South East Council for Sport and Recreation.
Statistics South Africa (various years). *Tourism and Migration*. Pretoria: Statistics South Africa.
Stiles, K.W. and Akaha, T. (1991). *International Political Economy – A Reader*. New York: Harper Collins.
Stock, C. (ed.) (1997). *Trouble in Paradise – Tourismus in die Dritte Welt*. Freiburg: Verlag Informationszentrum Dritte Welt.
Strange, S. (1996). *The Retreat of the State – The Diffusion of Power in the World Economy*. Cambridge: Cambridge University Press.
Strange, S. (1988) (2nd ed.). *States and Markets*. London: Pinter Publishers.
Sugden, J. and Tomlinson, A. (2002). 'International power struggles in the governance of world football: the 2002 and 2006 World Cup bidding wars', in J. Horne and W. Manzenreiter (eds.), *Japan, Korea and the 2002 World Cup*. London and New York: Routledge, pp. 56-70.

Sugden, J. and Tomlinson, A. (1998). *Fifa and the Contest for World Football: Who rules the People's Game?* Cambridge: Polity Press.
Sunday Times (2003).'SA wins by hosting cricket', 23 March.
Sunday Times (2000). 'How a humiliated old man sold SA's World Cup hopes down the river', 9 July 2000.
Swanson, T.M. and Barbier, E.B. (1992). *Economics for the Wilds: Wildlife, Wildlands, Diversity and Development*. London: Earthscan Publications.
Swarbrooke, J. and Horner, S. (1998). *Consumer Behaviour in Tourism: An International Perspective*. Oxford: Butterworth-Heinemann.
Swart, K. and Bob, U. (2004). 'The seductive discourse of development: the Cape Town 2004 Olympic bid', *Third World Quarterly*, 25, 7: 1311-1324.
Teigland, J. (1999). 'Mega-events and impacts on tourism: the predictions and realities of the Lillehammer Olympics', *Impact Assessment and Project Appraisal*, 17, 4: 305-317.
Terpstra, V. and Simonin, B. (1993). 'Strategic alliances in the triad: an exploratory study', *Journal of International Marketing*, 1, 1.
The Economist (2000). 'The hopeless continent', 13 May.
The Citizen (2000). 'Boost for SA's World Cup bid', 20 October.
The Citizen (1999). 'Soccer boss urges single African bid', 20 August.
The Star (1995).'Pride of the nation', 26 June.
Theta (2001). *Business Plan 2001-2002*.
Thomas, W. (2005). '"Second economy" paths into South African tourism business', Centre for Tourism Research in Africa (CETRA), Research report 01/2005. Cape Town: CETRA, Cape Peninsula University of Technology.
Thomas, S. (1995). *Share and Share Alike? Equity in Campfire*. London: International Institute for Environment and Development.
Time Atlantic (2003). 'On a sticky wicket', 13 January.
Torres, R. (2002). 'Cancun's tourism development from a Fordist spectrum of analysis', *Tourist Studies*, 2, 1: 87-116.
Tremblay, P. (1998). 'The economic organization of tourism', *Annals of Tourism Research*, 25, 4: 837-859.
Turco, D., Riley, R., and Swart, K. (2002). *Sport Tourism*. Morgantown, WV: Fitness Information Technology Inc.
Turner, L. and Ash, J. (1975). *The Golden Hordes: International Tourism and the Pleasure Periphery*. London: Constable.
Urry, J. (1995). *Consuming Places*. London: Routledge.
Urry, J. (1990). *The Tourist Gaze: Leisure and Travel in Contemporary Societies*. London: Sage Publications.
Uysal, M. (1998). 'The determinants of tourism demand: a theoretical perspective', in D. Ioannides and K.G. Debbage (eds.) *The Economic Geography of the Tourist Industry: A Supply-Side Analysis*. London: Routledge, pp. 79-95.
Valenzuela, J. and Valuenzuela, A. (1978). 'Modernization and dependency: alternative perspectives in the study of Latin American underdevelopment', *Comparative Politics*, 10: 543-557.
Veblen, J. (1912). *The Theory of the Leisure Class*. New York: Macmillan.

Visser, G. (2004). 'South African Tourism and its role in the perpetuation of an uneven tourism space economy', in C. Rogerson and G. Visser (eds.) *Tourism and Development: Issues in Contemporary South Africa*. Pretoria: Africa Institute of South Africa, pp. 268-289.

Wahab, S. and Cooper, C. (eds.) (2001). *Tourism in the Age of Globalisation*. London: Routledge.

Waitt, G. (2002). 'Social impacts of the Sydney Olympics', *Annals of Tourism Research*, 30, 1: 194-215.

Waitt, G. (2001). 'The Olympic spirit and civic boosterism: the Sydney 2000 Olympics', *Tourism Geographies*, 3, 3: 249-278.

Waitt, G. and Head, L. (2002). 'Postcards and frontier mythologies: sustaining views of the Kimberley as timeless', *Environment and Planning D: Society and Space*, 20: 319-344.

Weber, K. and Chon, K. (eds.) (2002). *Convention Tourism: International Research and Industry Perspectives*. New York: The Haworth Hospitality Press.

Weed, M. (2003). 'Why the two won't tango! Explaining the lack of integrated policies for sport and tourism in the UK', *Journal of Sport Management*, 17: 258-283.

Weekend Post (2003). 'Fancourt teed-up for R120 million golf spectacular', 8 November.

Weiss, L. (1998). *The Myth of the Powerless State*. Ithaca, NY: Cornell University Press.

Wesgro and KPMG Leisure and Tourism (1998). *The Western Cape Tourism Sector – Background for Investors*. Cape Town: Wesgro.

Wheatcroft, S. (1998). 'The airline industry and tourism', in D. Ioannides and K.G. Debbage (eds.) *The Economic Geography of the Tourist Industry: A Supply-Side Analysis*. London: Routledge, pp. 159-179.

Wheatcroft, S. (1994). *Aviation and Tourism Policies: Balancing the Benefits*. London: Routledge.

Williams, A. and Shaw, G. (1998). 'Tourism and the environment: sustainability and economic restructuring', in C.M. Hall and A.A. Lew (eds.) *Sustainable Tourism – Geographical Perspectives*. Essex: Addison Wesley Longman Ltd.

Witt, S.F., Brooke, F., Michael, Z. and Buckley, P.J. (1995). *The Management of International Tourism* (2nd ed.). London: Routledge.

World Commission on Environment and Development (1987). *Our Common Future*. New York: Oxford University Press.

World Tourism Organisation (2003). *Tourism Highlights*. Madrid: WTO.

World Tourism Organisation (2001). *Tourism Highlights*. Madrid: WTO.

World Tourism Organisation (2002). *About the WTO*. www.world-tourism.org.

World Tourism Organisation. (2000). *Tourism Highlights 2000 – First Edition. (March)*.

World Tourism Organisation. *Basic References on Tourism Statistics*, www.world-tourism.org/statistics/basics_references/index-en.htm.

World Travel and Tourism Council (2002). *About WTTC*. www.wttc.org.

World Travel and Tourism Council (2000). *Year 2000 TSA Research Summary and Results – South Africa*. www.wttc.org/ecres/TSA.

World Travel and Tourism Council (1998). *South Africa's Travel and Tourism: Economic driver for the 21st Century*. London: WTTC.

Yamamoto, D. and Gill, A.M. (2002). 'Issues of globabilization and reflexivity in the Japanese tourism production system: The case of Whistler, British Columbia', *The Professional Geographer*, 54, 1: 83-93.

Zukin, S. (1995). *The Cultures of Cities*. Cambridge, MA: Blackwell.

Index

accommodation
  structure of sector 7, 77, 78, 79, 89-90, 95, 165
  usage patterns SA 58, 59, 60-61, 64, 68, 94-96, 109, 167
Accor Hotels 32
Adorno, T. 28
!Ais-!Ais/Richtersveld Transfrontier Park 54
Air France 33, 82, 87, 126
Air Mauritius 82
air transport 86, 117, 118
alliances *see strategic alliance networks*
alternative tourism, 18-20, 34, 40
American Airlines, 82
Amsterdam RAI 37
Appadurai, A. 28, 140-141
arts and crafts
  South Africa 109, 110, 111
aviation
  policy
    Africa, 52, 127
    European Union, 126
    South Africa 51-52, 95, 96, 127-133
    United States of America, 126-127
  regime (international) 82, 125-126, 133

Baudrillard, J. 29, 30
Best Western Hotels 32
Black Economic Empowerment 70
  in SA tourism 71-72
branding 32, 143, 165
  South Africa 102, 104, 112, 150, 160
British Airways 33, 83, 87, 92, 121, 126, 128, 131, 133
British Midland 82
Britton, S. 4, 5, 7, 8, 10, 13, 17, 18, 26, 27, 32, 34, 77, 90, 91, 92, 102, 118, 119
business tourism 5, 36, 90, 170

cabotage 126, 128
CAMPFIRE 25

Cape Town International Airport 87, 128, 131
car rental sector 34, 86, 90, 91, 92, 93
Chicago Convention 121, 125
Civil Aviation Authority of South Africa 131
cities
  sites of consumption 36, 27, 81, 166
  urban regeneration 36-37, 166
Cohen, E. 6
commodification 8, 13, 37
Community-based Natural Resource Management 22-25
community conservation *see Community-based Natural Resource Management*
community tourism 18, 21-26
competition
  among tourism producers 11, 34, 81-82, 93, 94, 164
  and GATS 117, 131-134
  globalisation and competition 81, 85
  impacts 76, 93-97, 100, 132, 171
  regulation by institutions 118, 122, 124, 126, 165
Computer Reservation Systems (CRS) 32, 81
Congress of South African Trade Unions 132
consolidation 11, 33-35, 76, 81, 83-84, 133, 165
consumer
  preferences 6, 9, 30, 79, 80, 85
  protection and standards, 35, 118, 124, 166
  society 8, 29-30
consumer over producer debate 9, 14, 30, 164
consumption
  visual 35
  place 101

cooperation
  among producers 4, 33, 82, 92-93, 94, 97, 103, 130, 164, 173, 174
crime 50-51, 61, 63, 72, 144, 150, 167
cultural tourism 19, 47, 61, 106, 112, 167
cultural turn in tourism 14, 28-30, 165
cultural village 106, 109, 111, 112

De Kadt, E. 10, 16, 17
dependency perspective in tourism 15, 17-18, 39-40
deregulation
  South African aviation 127, 131
destination
  imaging 100, 101, 103, 105, 165, 166, 173
  marketing 2, 9, 38, 82
  substitution effect 51, 53
domestic tourism in SA
  size 48
  policy 171

Earth Summit 20
Easyjet 34
economic geography 6, 15
ecotourism 19
empowerment
  in tourism 2, 14, 21, 23
  South Africa, 43, 45, 65, 69, 70-73, 112, 113
ethnic tourism 19
entrepreneurial cities 37, 140
environmental protection 19, 22-23, 118, 134
European Commission 127

FIFA 48, 140, 146, 147, 148, 159, 161, 168
flexible specialisation 31, 33, 81, 172
Fordism (neo or post-) 30, 31-33, 81, 89, 172
fortress conservation 23
Frankfurt School 28-30
free independent travellers (FIT) 83
freedoms of the air 125-126, 127
fynbos 44, 156

General Agreement on Trade in Services (GATS) 3, 12, 38, 116, 118-119, 132-134, 174
global cities 41
global commodity chains 80

Global Distribution Systems (GDS) 32, 81, 164
golf tourism 69, 151, 152-157
governance
  global institutions of governance 2-3, 38, 120-122
  self-regulation in production 2, 92-94, 97
Great Limpopo Transfrontier Conservation Area 54
Growth, Employment and Redistribution Programme 74

Hilton International 32, 121
horizontal integration 32
hospitality associations 79
host communities 21

industrial concentration in tourism 73, 81
information technology 31, 32, 81
International Air Transit Services Agreement 121, 125-126
International Air Transport Association 118, 120, 123
International Civil Aviation Organisation 120, 121-122, 127
intra-regional or –continental tourism 17, 40, 51, 170

Johannesburg International Airport 87, 127-129, 131

Kgalagadi Transfrontier Park 54
KLM 33, 82, 87
Krippendorf, J. 79

landscape 34, 42, 44, 55, 67, 100, 101, 104, 108, 110-111
Lanfant, M. 6
Lea, J. 6, 9, 15, 16, 18
leisure class 29
liberalisation of tourism 3, 12, 38, 115-116, 125-126, 132, 133, 134, 166
lifestyle 29, 30, 32
Limpopo Transfrontier Park 54
Local Economic Development 36
LTU 84, 87, 92, 97, 127, 128, 134
Lubombo Transfrontier Conservation Area 54, 74
Lufthansa 34, 51, 82, 87, 92, 120, 125, 126, 127, 128, 129

MacCannell, D. 6, 17, 30, 101
Makuleke community 25
Maldives 1
Maloti-Drakensberg Transfrontier Conservation Area 54
Mandela Syndrome 49, 62
Marcuse, H. 13, 28, 29
mass tourism 15, 19, 21, 31, 32, 34
media 102, 110, 139, 140, 148, 159, 168, 170
mega-events 36, 37, 48, 136, 166, 168-170
  significance 138-141
Meetings, Incentives, Conferences and Exhibitions 36, 37, 137, 138, 157
mergers 11, 28, 30, 33-34, 76, 132, 164, 173
modernisation perspective in tourism 15-17, 18, 39
Movement for Democratic Change 50

networks 31, 32, 33, 41, 51, 52, 76, 78, 81, 82, 91-92, 97, 121, 124, 128, 129, 131, 157, 164, 174
niche marketing 32, 84, 85

Olympic Games 36, 48, 136, 137, 138, 141, 142, 146
One World 82
outsourcing and subcontracting 2, 32, 81

pleasure periphery 37
political economy
  approach 3-4
  of destination marketing 100, 104, 113
post-modern 30, 34
Presidents Cup 143, 152-154
Preussag 33, 83, 121
price discounts 93
privatisation 120, 131
producer associations 78-79
producer-consumer nexus 2, 8-9, 30,

Qantas 82, 87

Reconstruction and Development Programme 46, 74
Regional Tourism Organisation of Southern Africa 53, 121
Richtersveld National Park 25, 40, 54
Ryanair 34

SA Alliance Air 51-52
SANParks 25, 54, 103
seasonality 10, 167
Severe Acute Respiratory Syndrome 1
Seychelles 1
Sheraton Hotels 32
Singapore Airlines 82, 87
Skyteam 82
small, medium and micro operators 85-86
South African Airways 51-52, 94, 126, 129, 131-132
Southern African Development Community 53-54, 120, 122
Spatial Development Initiatives 53
sport tourism 12, 137, 139, 158-160
Star Alliance 82
statistics 58, 46
strategic alliance networks 81-83
sustainable tourism 18-21, 26-27
Swiss International Airlines 82, 87, 96

Theta 72-73, 124-125
Tourism Grading Council of South Africa 124-125
Transboundary Natural Resource Management 53-54
transformation in tourism
  South Africa 45-46, 70-73
transfrontier conservation park or area 53
tour guides 70
tourism satellite accounts 63-64, 75
tourist gaze 101
township tourism 72, 167
trade commissions 2, 93-94, 95
TUI 33, 84, 98

United Airlines 82
Urry, J. 6, 28, 29, 31, 79, 80, 101, 102, 115

Veblen, J. 29
vertical integration 32
Virgin Atlantic Airways 87, 92, 110, 126, 128, 130, 133, 135
visiting friends and relatives 58, 59, 170

Waterfront 36, 56, 62, 109, 111
Winelands 56, 67, 107, 109
Western Cape 44, 55, 56, 61, 64-69, 96, 151-155

World Summit on Sustainable
    Development 47
World Trade Organisation 38, 116
World Travel and Tourism Council 120-121

ZANU-PF 50
Zimbabwe 24, 48, 50, 51, 52, 107, 108,
    148, 149, 150